IMAGES
of America

SAN MARCOS

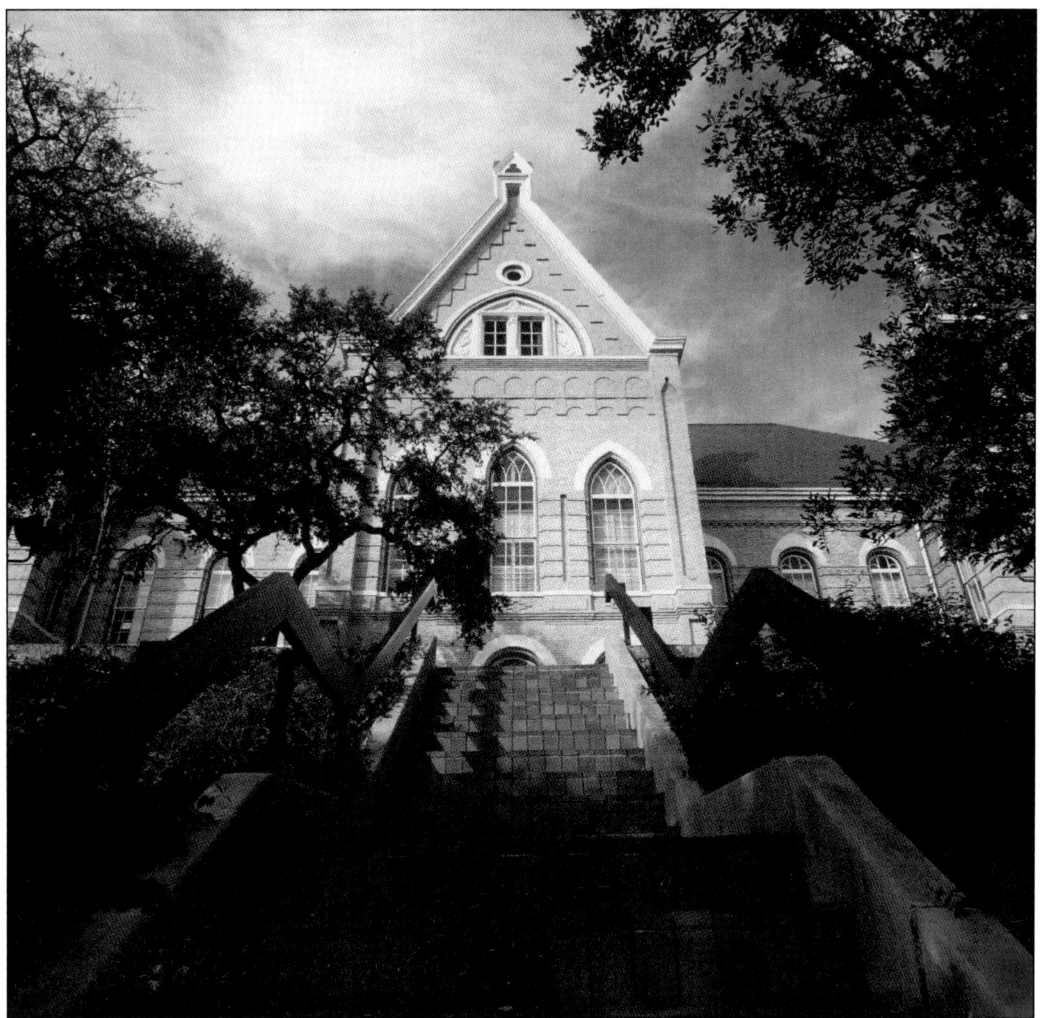

Old Main. The first building on the campus of what is now Texas State University in San Marcos, Old Main opened its doors to students for the first time in 1903. Its iconic profile is recognizable from many locations on campus and around town and serves as one of the most recognizable symbols of the university and the city of San Marcos. (Courtesy of Texas State University.)

On the Cover: Pictured here is a veterans' parade along East Hopkins Street across from the courthouse square in downtown San Marcos. Although the date of the photograph is unspecified, it has been dated between 1947 and 1951 by analysis of storefront business names along Hopkins Street. (Courtesy of San Marcos Public Library.)

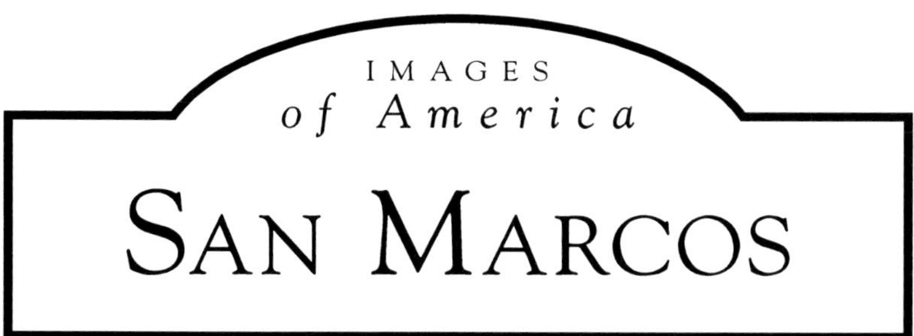

David R. Butler

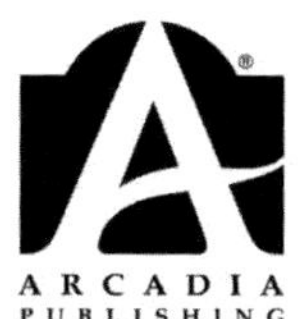

ISBN 978-1-4671-3350-0

Published by Arcadia Publishing
Charleston, South Carolina

Printed in the United States of America

Library of Congress Control Number: 2014959344

For all general information, please contact Arcadia Publishing:
Telephone 843-853-2070
Fax 843-853-0044
E-mail sales@arcadiapublishing.com
For customer service and orders:
Toll-Free 1-888-313-2665

Visit us on the Internet at www.arcadiapublishing.com

To Janet and Will Butler, who came to Texas with me.

Contents

Acknowledgments 6

Introduction 7

1. San Marcos: The Early Days 9
2. Downtown San Marcos: Change over the Years 17
3. Texas State: From Teachers' College to Emerging Research University 37
4. San Marcos's Most Famous Citizen: LBJ 59
5. The Town Lifeline: Spring Lake and the San Marcos River 73
6. Around Town: Icons and Landmarks 91
7. Modern Destinations: Town Growth and the Outlet Mall 111

Bibliography 127

ACKNOWLEDGMENTS

Assistance in locating historical photographs of San Marcos was provided by Michelle (Misha) Bussemey and Lauren M. Johnson. Janet and Will Butler provided moral support and love throughout the process of creating this book. My editor, Matt Todd, was extremely patient and wonderful to work with.

The abbreviated annotations used in courtesy lines for this book's images are as follows: San Marcos Public Library (SMPL), Texas State University (TxSt), Hays County Historical Commission (HCHC), Texas State Library and Archives Commission (TSLAC), City of San Marcos (CSM), City of San Marcos Main Street Program (CSMMSP), LBJ Museum of San Marcos (LBJSM), the LBJ Presidential Library in Austin, TX (LBJPL), and Texas Historical Commission (THC). Photographs from individuals are listed by photographer name. All unattributed photographs are from the author's personal collection.

Introduction

San Marcos, Texas, is located in an area locally referred to as Central Texas. The town is split between the western section that sits astride the eastern edge of the Hill Country, an area of rolling limestone hills, and the eastern section at the base and east of the Balcones Escarpment, on the fertile plains of the Blackland Prairie. San Marcos is roughly 30 miles southwest of the state capital, Austin, and about 45 miles northeast of San Antonio. Interstate 35 is the main highway running through town on a northeast-southwest trend.

San Marcos has been home to people for over 10,000 years. Archeological studies show that people associated with the Clovis culture settled adjacent to the San Marcos Springs, and Native Americans continued to live around the springs and along the San Marcos River for thousands of years. The San Marcos River, formed by the hundreds of springs collectively known as the San Marcos Springs that emerge from the Edwards Aquifer at the base of the Balcones Escarpment, provides a continuous source of water that has never ceased to flow in recorded history.

European contact in the San Marcos area began in 1689, when Alonso de Leon led an expedition from Spanish Mexico to explore Texas. The path taken by de Leon's party became El Camino Real de los Tejas, a trail that connected settlements from Mexico across central and eastern Texas. De Leon's party reached the banks of the San Marcos River on April 25, recognized in the Catholic Church as the feast day of St. Mark the Evangelist. The river was thus christened with the Spanish name for St. Mark, San Marcos. In the early 1800s, a short-lived community called Villa de San Marcos de Neve was established on the banks of the river about four miles east from the center of present-day San Marcos by a group of families from New Spain (modern-day Mexico). In existence only from 1808 to 1812, difficulties with floods and Indian raids led to the settlement's abandonment. Archeological studies in 1995 through 1998 found that the settlement had a central plaza typical of New Spain settlements but also that most of the residents lived outside the town's center, making it more difficult to defend.

Anglo settlement began in 1846, with settlers moving from the Bastrop area to land located along the San Marcos Springs and River. These settlers had been members of Jack C. Hays's company of Texas Rangers during the years of the Republic of Texas. In 1848, Hays County was created from the southern end of the adjacent Travis County to the north, and the nascent village of San Marcos was named as the county seat. An official plat of the town's layout was filed in 1851, and this year is recognized by the City of San Marcos as its official establishment date.

From its establishment until June 19, 1865, slavery was a part of early San Marcos. On that date, the abolition of slavery was announced throughout Texas. This date is annually celebrated in San Marcos and throughout Texas as the Juneteenth holiday.

Early San Marcos was primarily an agricultural community, with cotton and cattle ranching the primary economic activities. The arrival of the International–Great Northern Railroad in 1881 further solidified San Marcos as a center for transportation and commerce based around the cattle and cotton industries.

In the 1890s, the Chautauqua movement, associated with the Methodist Church and the young Coronal Institute in San Marcos, led to religious and educational activities held on a hilltop above Spring Lake, a lake that had been formed at the head of the San Marcos River by damming of the San Marcos Springs. This hilltop became known as Chautauqua Hill, and San Marcos became known in the region as a community with a strong educational focus. This local commitment to education ultimately led to the selection of San Marcos as the home of a new state normal school. The Southwest Texas State Normal School was authorized to be built in San Marcos by the Texas legislature in 1899, and opened to its first students in 1903. Since that first year of operation, the school has seen several name changes and expansive growth. Today, the school is an emerging research university known as Texas State University. The school has grown from the original 303 students in 1903 to a current enrollment of over 36,000 students, making it the fourth-largest university in the state of Texas. The school's most famous alumnus is Lyndon B. Johnson, 36th president of the United States, who graduated from the school when it was known as Southwest Texas State Teacher's College, in 1930.

Modern-day San Marcos is a rapidly growing community. In the three years between 2013 and 2015, it has been named each year by the US Census Bureau as the fastest-growing small city in the United States. The 2013 census population estimate for the city was 54,076 people. The 2010 census illustrated the demographics of the city as 53.7 percent white not Hispanic, 37.8 percent Hispanic or Latino, 5.5 percent black or African American, 1.6 Asian, .9 percent American Indian, Native American, or Alaskan, and .1 percent Native Hawaiian or Pacific Islander (values do not exactly equal 100 percent).

Texas State University is the largest employer in San Marcos, but many other organizations, industries, and retail establishments provide a broad economic base for the community. The San Marcos outlet malls, comprised of the San Marcos Premium Outlets and the Tanger Factory Outlets, are together the largest outlet shopping center in the United States.

The culture of San Marcos reflects the city's ethnic diversity and history, with a variety of annual celebrations as well as cultural and historic museums. Annual events that highlight the many cultures of the city include the annual VIVA! Cinco de Mayo Celebration, the Texas Natural and Western Swing Festival, Juneteenth celebrations, the Chilympiad Republic of Texas Chili Cookoff, and the Sights and Sounds of Christmas. Several city-recognized historic districts preserve elements of neighborhood history and architecture. The downtown courthouse square is also a historic district, with the 1908 Hays County Courthouse at its center.

Numerous city parks provide ample recreation for residents and university students along the San Marcos River. Tubing and kayaking are popular activities on the river, which maintains a constant 72-degree temperature in its upper reaches as a result of being fed from the springs that emerge beneath Spring Lake. Spring Lake itself is an educational and recreational center with a rich history as the former Aquarena Springs Resort, with glass-bottom boat tours operated by Texas State University's Meadows Center for Water and the Environment.

One

San Marcos
The Early Days

The presence of the permanently flowing San Marcos Springs has attracted settlers to what is now San Marcos for thousands of years. Mastodon bones and Clovis point arrowheads from the area date back to more than 12,000 years ago. Spanish attempts at colonizing the area began in 1755 but were short-lived and abandoned by 1812.

In 1846, the first Anglos settled in the vicinity of San Marcos Springs and along the San Marcos River. These settlers were former members of John "Jack" C. Hays's company of Texas Rangers and included Thomas G. McGehee and William W. Moon, identified as the first resident of the site that became San Marcos proper. In 1848, Edward Burleson (a former vice president of the Republic of Texas), together with Eli Merriman and William Lindsey, founded what would become the community of San Marcos. That same year, the Texas legislature organized Hays County, created from the southern end of Travis County to the north, and designated the young community of San Marcos as the county seat. The City of San Marcos recognizes 1851 as the official year the town was founded, with the filing of an official plat of the town's layout.

In the years leading up to the Civil War, San Marcos was primarily an agricultural community. In the 1850 census, San Marcos had 387 residents, of whom 128 were slaves owned by 19 families. By 1860, thirty-seven percent of the population of San Marcos was slaves. When the Civil War began, many men of San Marcos served in the Confederate army. Following the war, many displaced Southerners moved west and settled in San Marcos. San Marcos incorporated in 1877, and by the 20th century, it flourished as a cotton-producing center. This growth was assisted by the arrival of the railroad in 1881, linking San Marcos to San Antonio and Austin with more rapid transportation. In 1870, San Marcos's population was only 742, but it jumped to over 2,300 in the decade following the railroad's arrival. In the mid-1890s, the US Fish and Wildlife Service established the first warm-water hatchery west of the Mississippi River, near the headwaters of the San Marcos River. The hatchery was focused on production and development of efficient cultural techniques of warm-water sport fish.

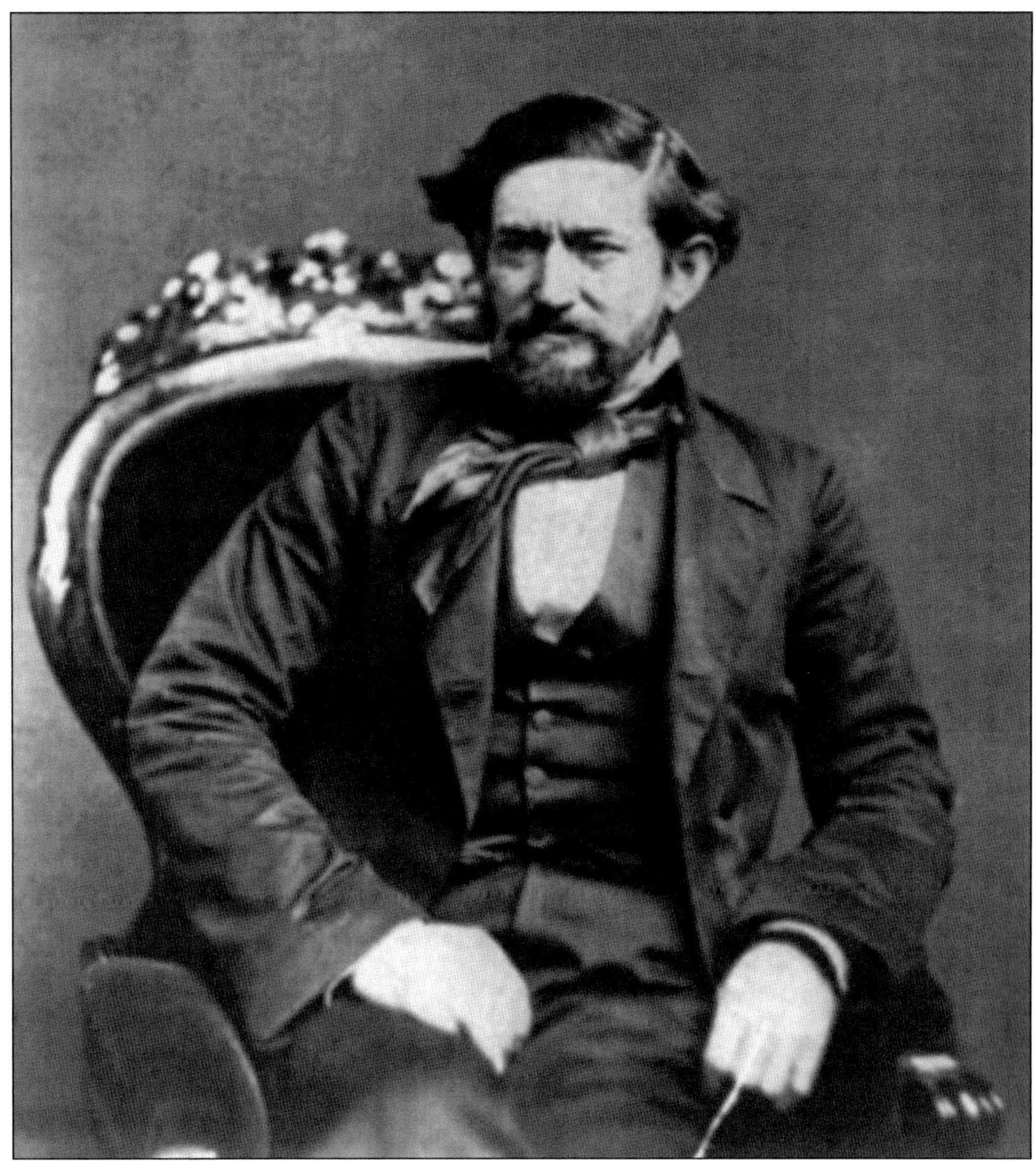

Jack Hays, Namesake for Hays County. Hays County, Texas, of which San Marcos is the county seat, is named after John Coffee "Jack" Hays (1817–1883). Born in Tennessee, Hays came to Texas in 1836. He only lived in Texas for 13 years, but during that time was a leader in the Texas Rangers during the Mexican-American War. He moved to California in 1849 during the Gold Rush. (HCHC.)

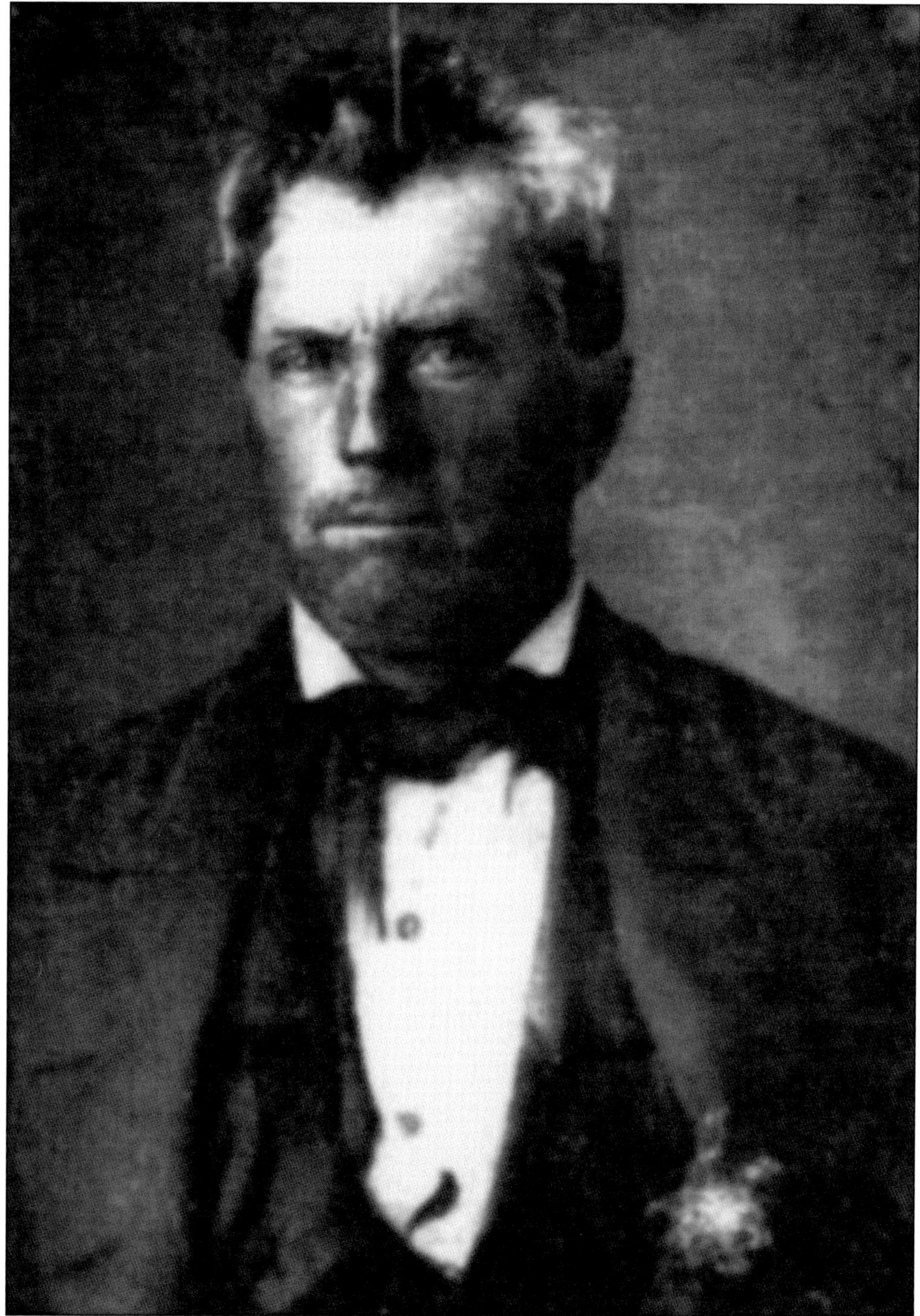

Edward Burleson, San Marcos Pioneer. Born in North Carolina, Edward Burleson (1798–1851) came to Texas in 1831 and settled near Bastrop, northeast of what would become San Marcos. This 1850 daguerreotype is the only known photographic image of Burleson. In 1848, Burleson introduced a resolution to establish Hays County and donated the land for the courthouse in what was to become San Marcos. (TSLAC.)

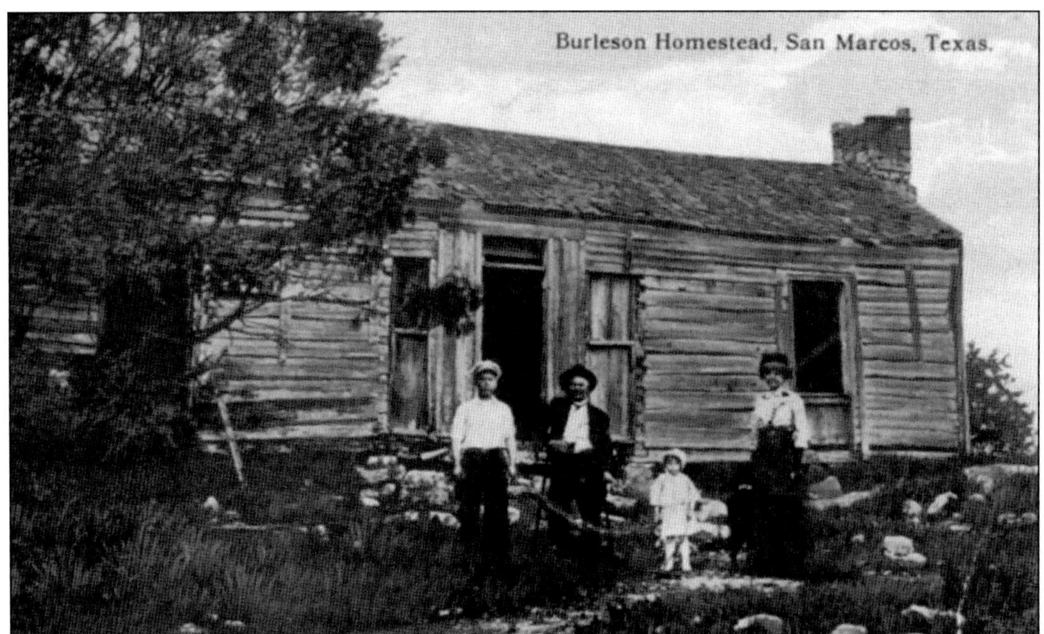

Burleson Homestead. This image of the Burleson Homestead in San Marcos is taken from an old postcard. It shows the cabin's east side. According to the Center for Archaeological Studies at Texas State University, it is thought that the postcard photograph was taken after the family had abandoned the cabin but prior to its collapse in a heavy rainstorm in 1917. (SMPL.)

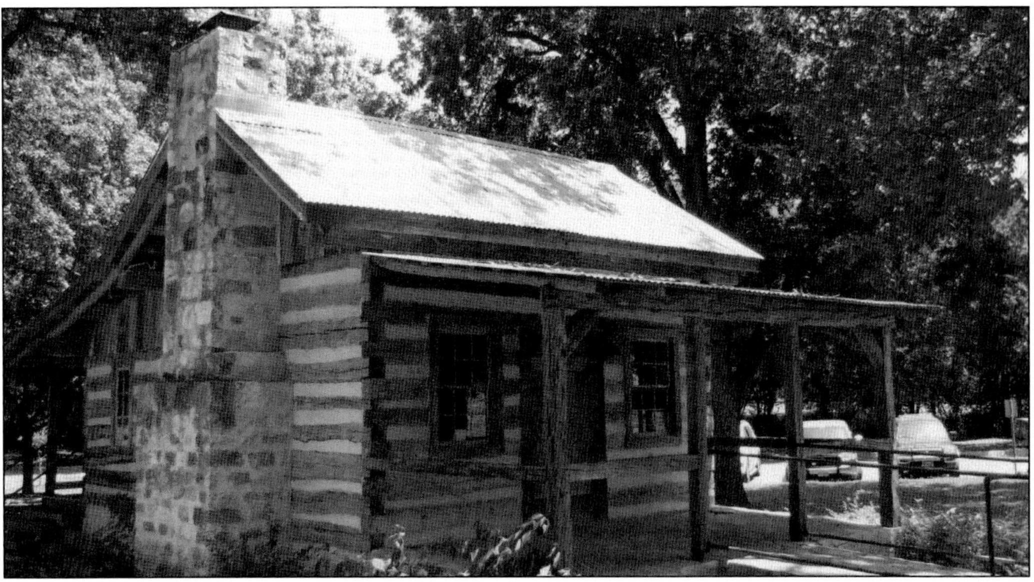

Historic Merriman Home in San Marcos. Eli Merriman, one of the original founders of San Marcos, established his homestead along the southern banks of the San Marcos River. His cabin has subsequently been moved twice and existed for several years as an attraction at the Aquarena Springs Resort. When Texas State University acquired that resort, the university gifted the cabin to the Heritage Association of San Marcos, and it was relocated to the Veramendi Plaza history park on C.M. Allen Parkway.

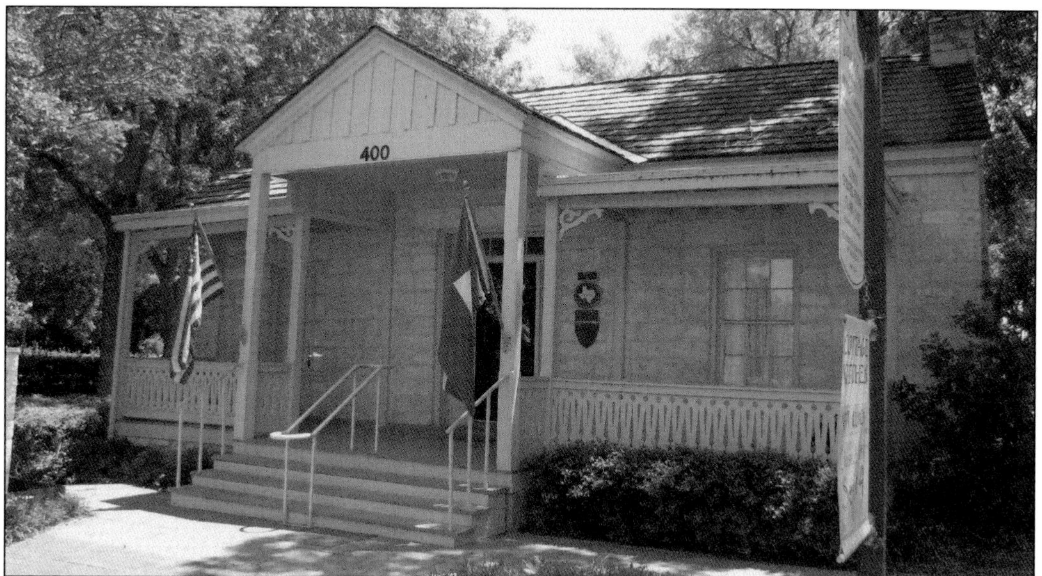

Charles S. Cock House. The Charles S. Cock House, erected in 1867, is the oldest remaining residential building in San Marcos. It is a modest Vernacular Greek Revival structure and today serves as a museum as well as the home of Cottage Kitchen, where volunteers prepare a home-cooked lunch on Fridays from 11:00 a.m. to 1:00 p.m.

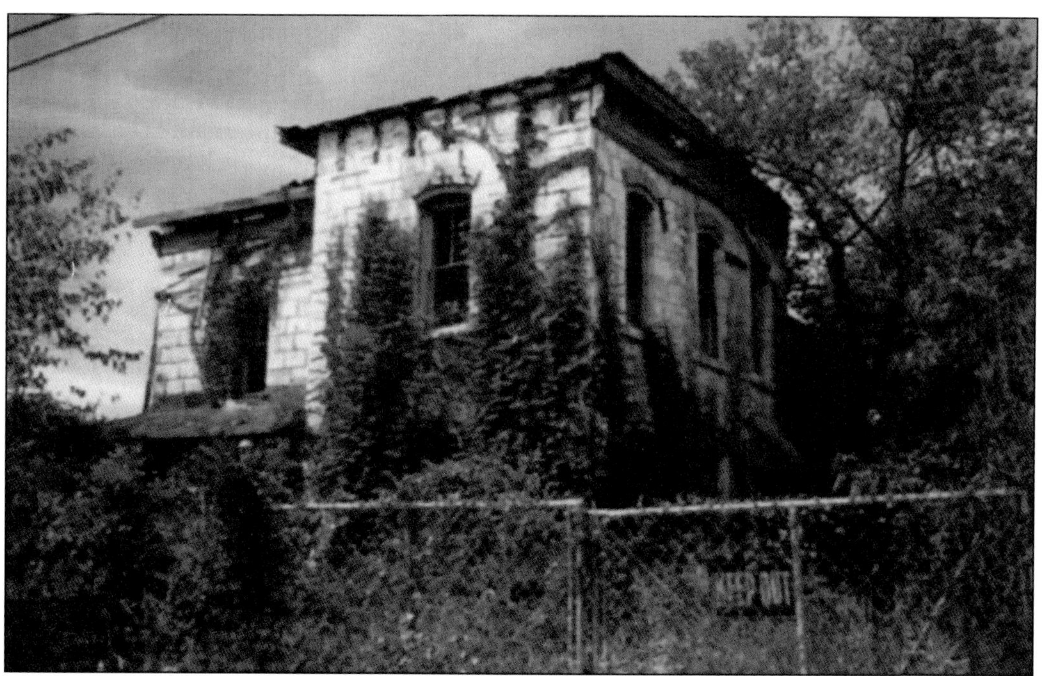

Old "Second" Hays County Jail. Pictured here in 1966, the old Hays County Jail is located on Fredericksburg Street not far from the courthouse square. The building, designed in the Italianate style, is a two-story limestone block structure. This jailhouse, designed by Edward Northcraft, was completed in 1885 and served as the county jail until 1936. (SMPL.)

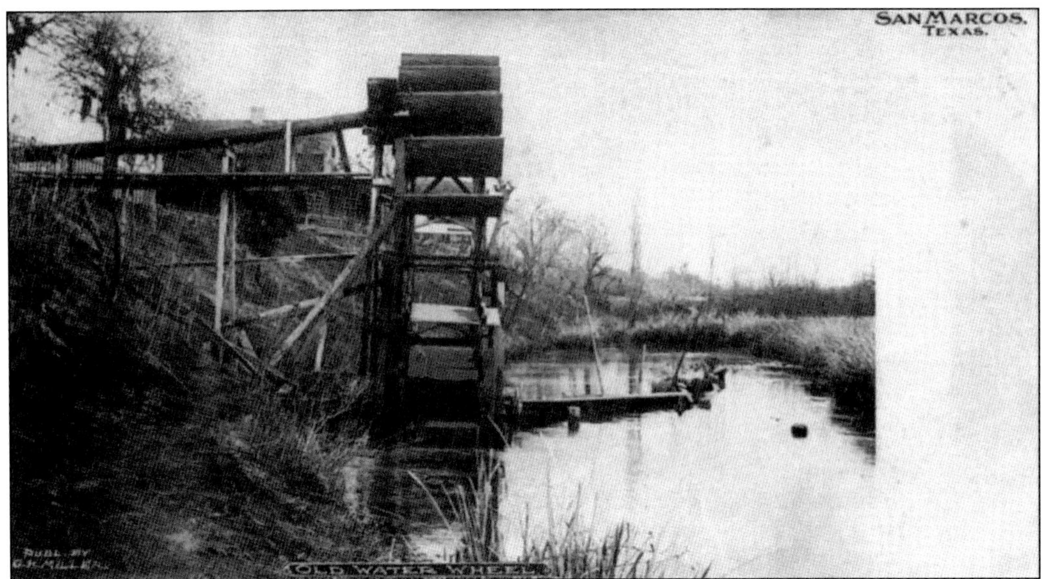

Gristmill at Spring Lake Dam. This 1906 real-photo postcard features an old waterwheel at the site where Edward Burleson dammed the San Marcos River and created Spring Lake in 1849. He built a gristmill at the site, for which this waterwheel presumably served as the power source. Today, a popular local restaurant sits at this site. (SMPL.)

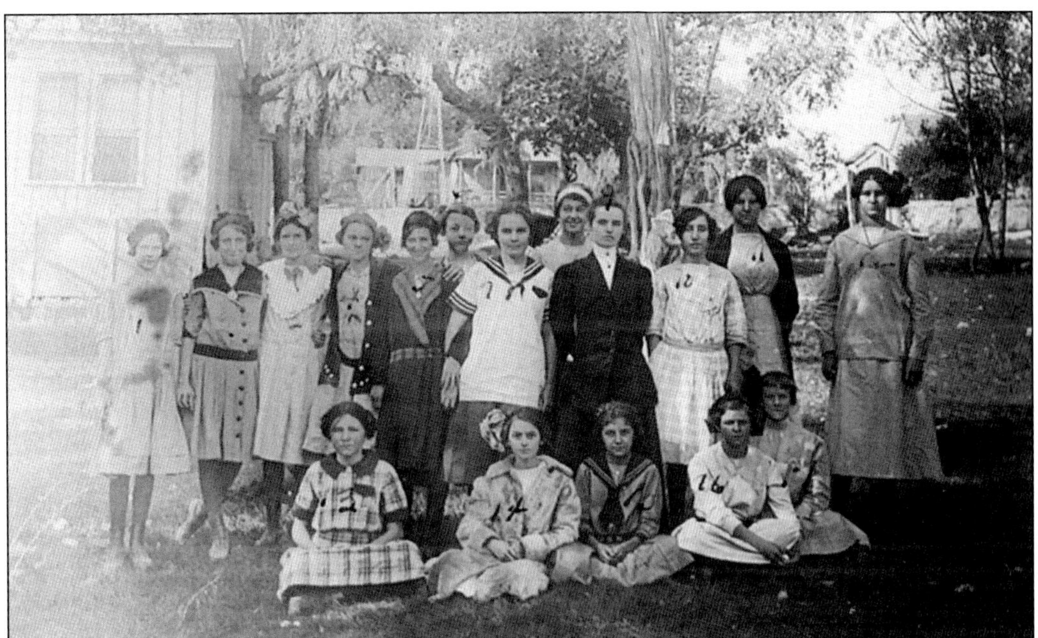

Old East End School Class. Pictured here is the class of 1912–1913 at the Old East End School on Wood Street. In 1912, the San Marcos School Board began a partnership with Southwest Texas State Normal School to allow students there to teach local children. The San Marcos East End Ward School (the first eight grades of the school district) was moved onto the normal school campus in 1917. (SMPL.)

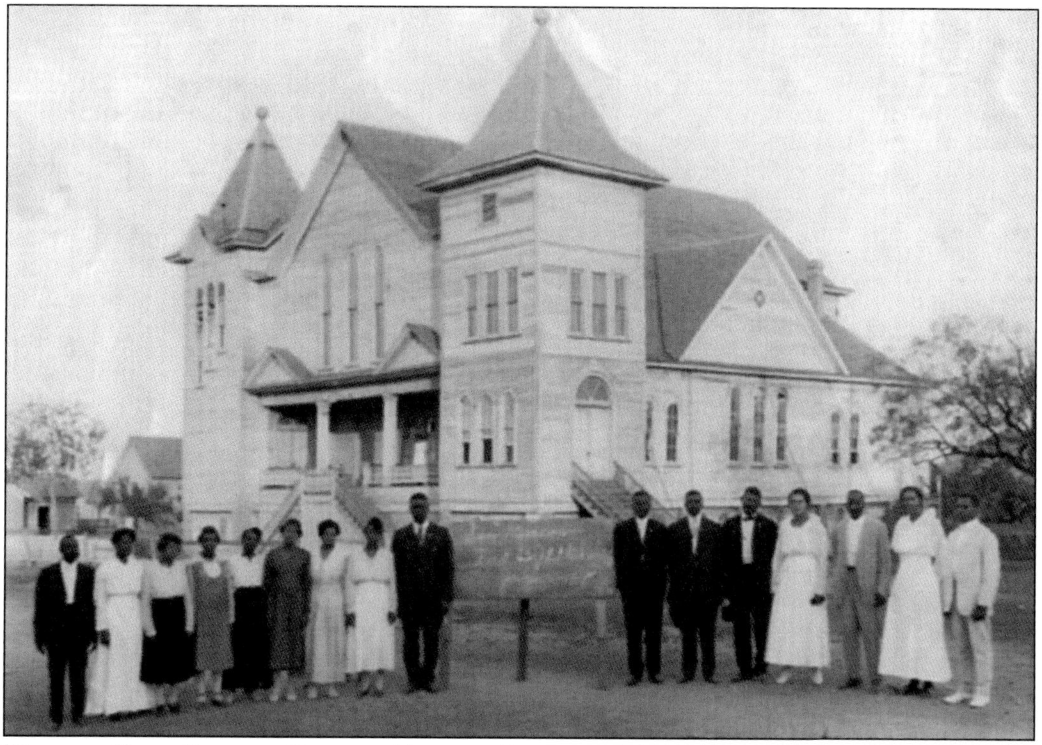

HISTORIC FIRST BAPTIST CHURCH, DUNBAR DISTRICT. The old First Baptist Church, built in 1908 on Comal (now M.L. King) Street, is shown here in the early 20th century with its original roofline and steeple. This roof and steeple were later destroyed by fire. The church was a vital component of the African American community in the Dunbar District (see chapter six) of San Marcos. (SMPL.)

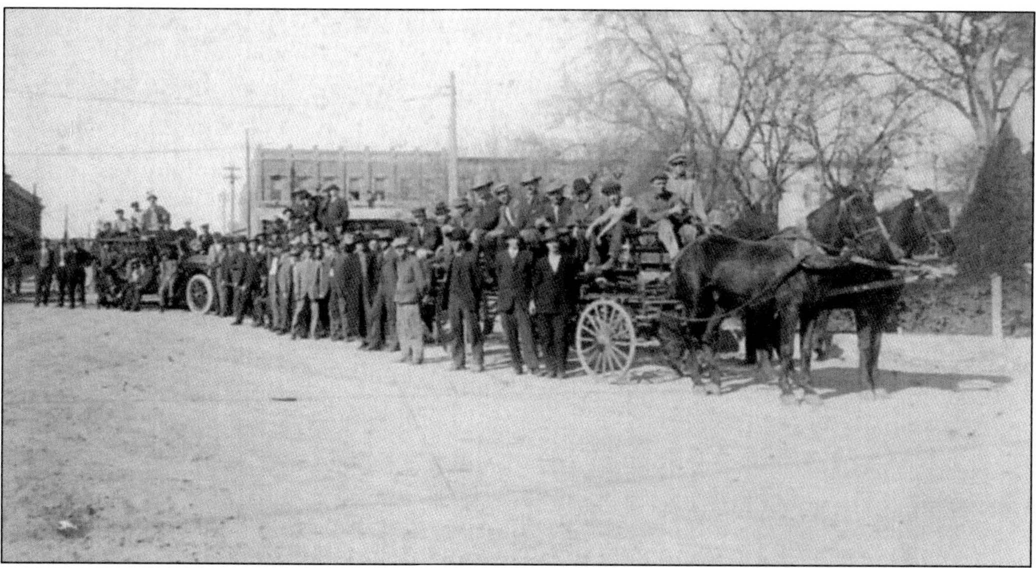

EARLY FIRE DEPARTMENT STAFF. The San Marcos Fire Department staff is pictured here in 1915, probably adjacent to the central courthouse square. The horse-drawn wagon on the right contrasts with the new fire truck on the rear left side of the group. (SMPL.)

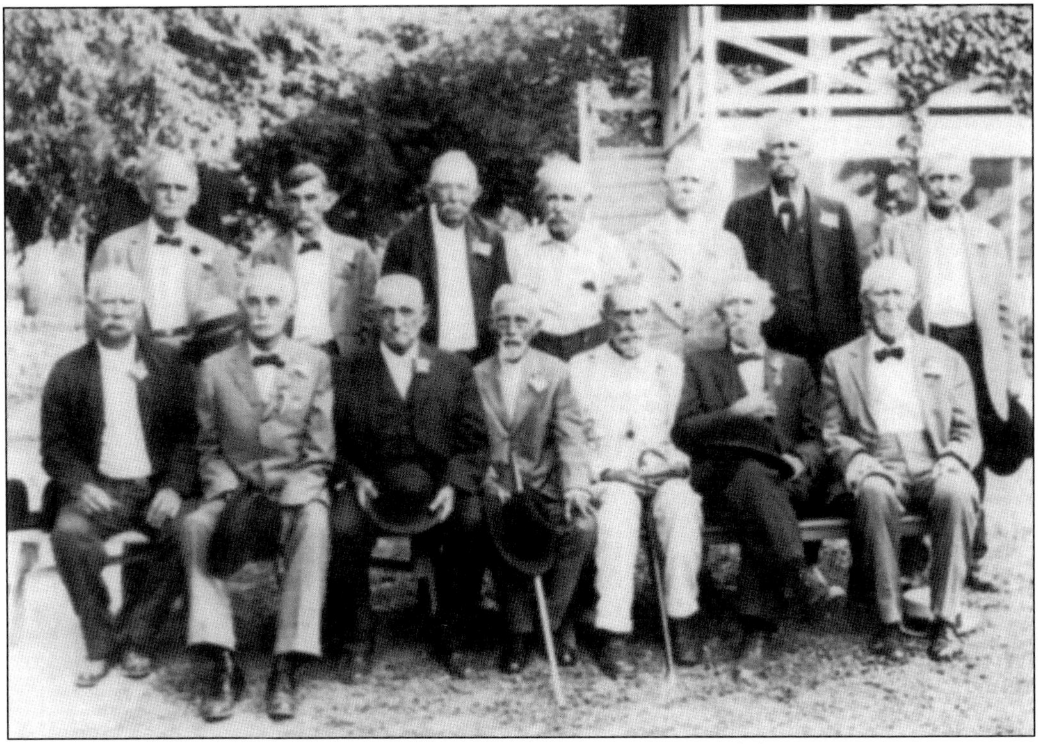

CONFEDERATE VETERANS REUNION, C. 1920. Pictured here is a Confederate veterans' reunion at Rio Vista Park in San Marcos. From left to right are (first row) ? Terrell, J.B. Rylander, Basil Dailey, ? Lester, Tom Dailey, George T. McGehee, and Dr. James Combs; (second row) P.J. Talbot, Calvert Watkins, George Petty, unidentified, John Montgomery, and two unidentified. (SMPL.)

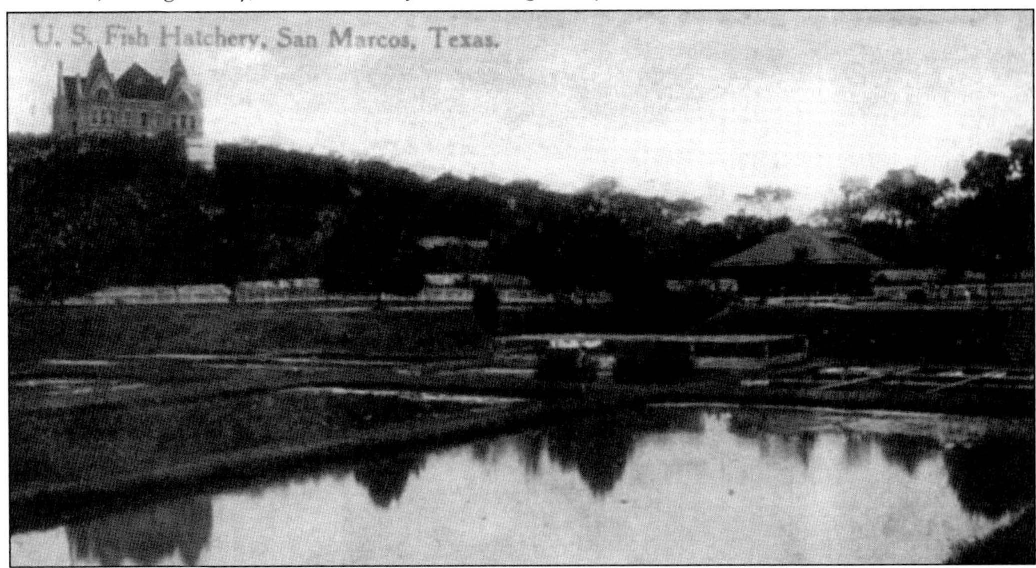

OLD FISH HATCHERY SITE, C. 1913. The US Fish Hatchery in San Marcos is the subject of this postcard. This location is now part of the Texas State University campus, and the ponds are an attractive landscape feature of the campus grounds between the J.C. Kellam Administration Building and the Theatre Center. (SMPL.)

Two

Downtown San Marcos
Change over the Years

San Marcos, like many Southern county seats, has a town square with the county courthouse at its center. The square dates back to the early days of the town—in 1850 the square had begun to take shape with two stores and several log homes. The first store was built by Caton Erhard, and served as a community meeting place, post office, and the county clerk's office in addition to its duties as a general store.

The first official courthouse for Hays County, at the center of the downtown square, was built in 1861. A two-story frame structure, it burned down in 1868. A new courthouse, built of local limestone, was completed in 1871. Unfortunately, this local limestone was quite soft and led to a shifting and unstable foundation. The second courthouse was therefore torn down in 1881. A third courthouse, built of much harder limestone, was completed in 1883. This courthouse was designed by F.E. Ruffini, a famous architect who had designed several buildings on the campus of the University of Texas in Austin as well as other courthouses in Texas. The Victorian-style Ruffini courthouse experienced a fire in 1908 that destroyed the upper portion of the building and destabilized the remaining structure. It, too, was subsequently torn down in 1908. The current and fourth Hays County Courthouse was completed in 1909. The courthouse has a large central copper dome similar to many other courthouse buildings.

The central courthouse square is bounded on the north by East Hopkins Street, on the south by East San Antonio Street, on the west by South Guadalupe Street, and on the east by South LBJ Drive (formerly South Austin Street). Like any other town, retail establishments surrounding the courthouse and on nearby streets have come and gone over the years. Historic downtown San Marcos is listed in the National Register of Historic Places. The centerpiece of the Courthouse National Register District is, of course, the 1909 Hays County Courthouse, listed in 1992. The surrounding square and its buildings are recognized for their rich and varied architectural styles.

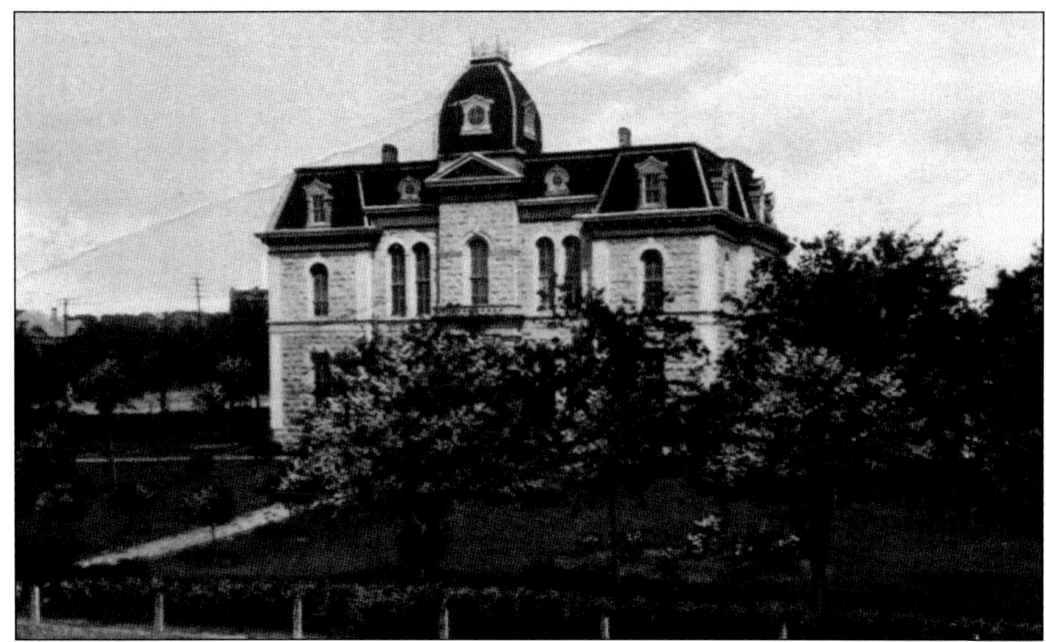

Third Hays County Courthouse. The third Hays County Courthouse, completed in 1883, is shown in this real-photo postcard from the very early 1900s. The Victorian-style structure was designed by F.E. Ruffini. Note the telephone lines and poles at center left. (SMPL.)

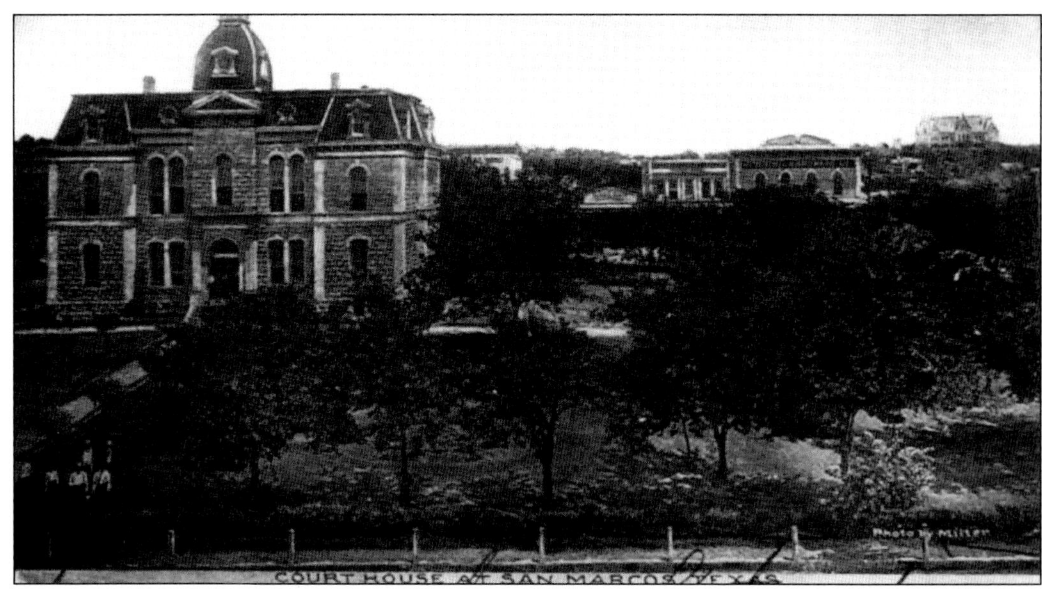

Hays County Courthouse and Old Main. This postcard view from the early 1900s shows the Hays County Courthouse relative to the location of Old Main on the normal school campus, in the distance. The presence of Old Main in this photograph dates it to between 1903, when the normal school opened, and 1908, when the third courthouse burned down. (SMPL.)

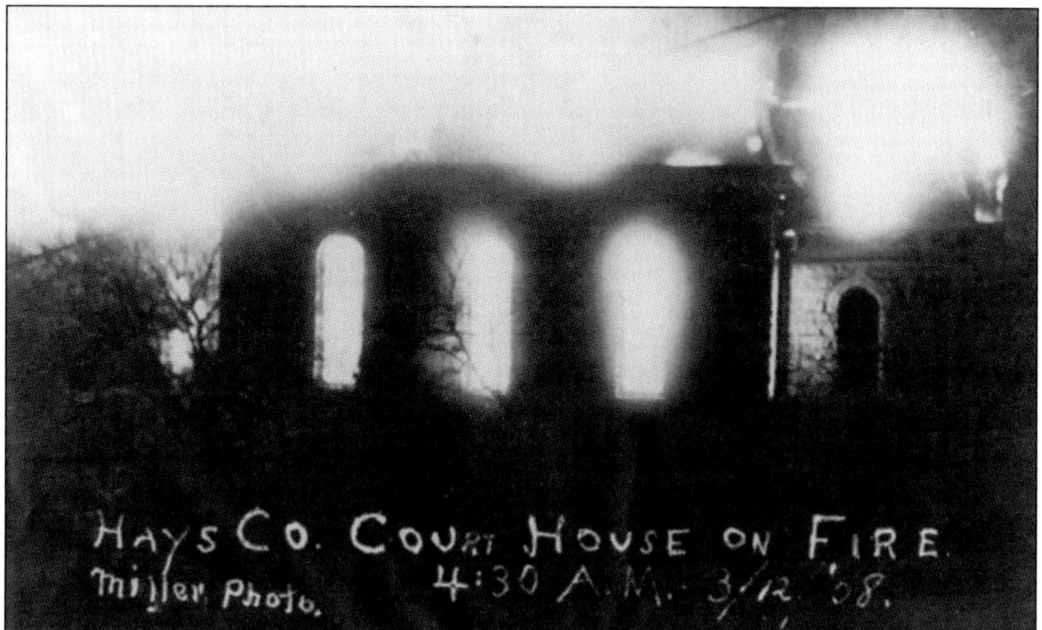

Fire Destroys Third Hays County Courthouse. Early in a morning in 1908, the third Hays County Courthouse burned and became structurally unstable. It was torn down later the same year, making way for the current fourth Hays County Courthouse. (SMPL.)

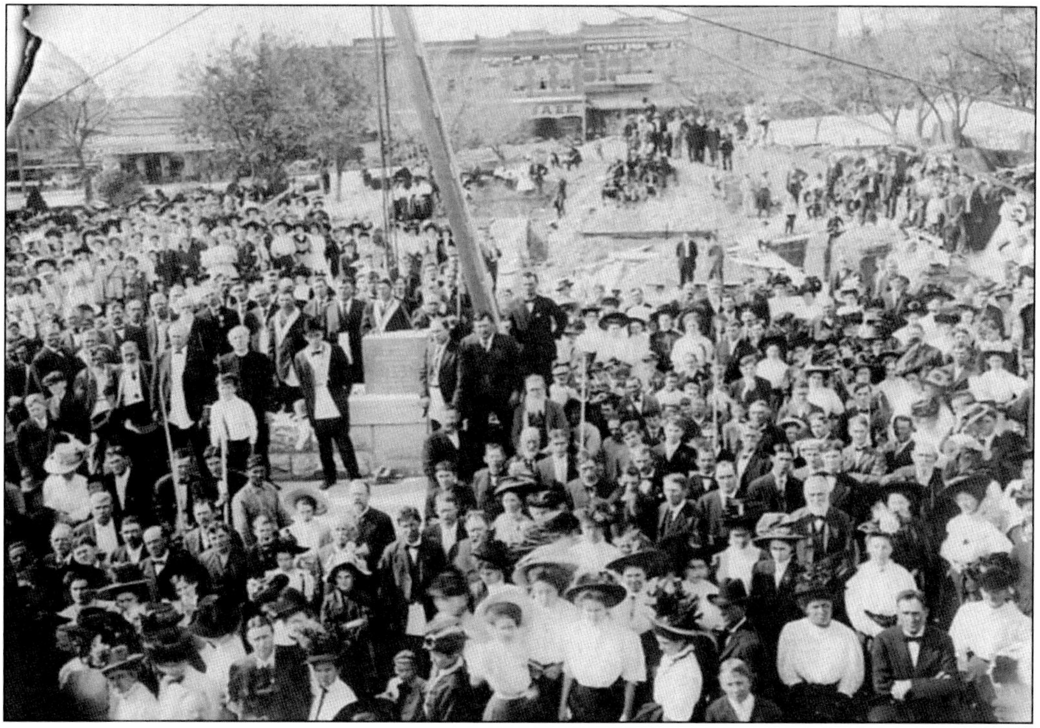

Cornerstone Ceremony for New Courthouse, 1909. The cornerstone for the current Hays County Courthouse building was laid on November 23, 1909. The ceremony for the laying of the cornerstone, pictured here, was attended by a crowd well in excess of 1,000 people. (SMPL.)

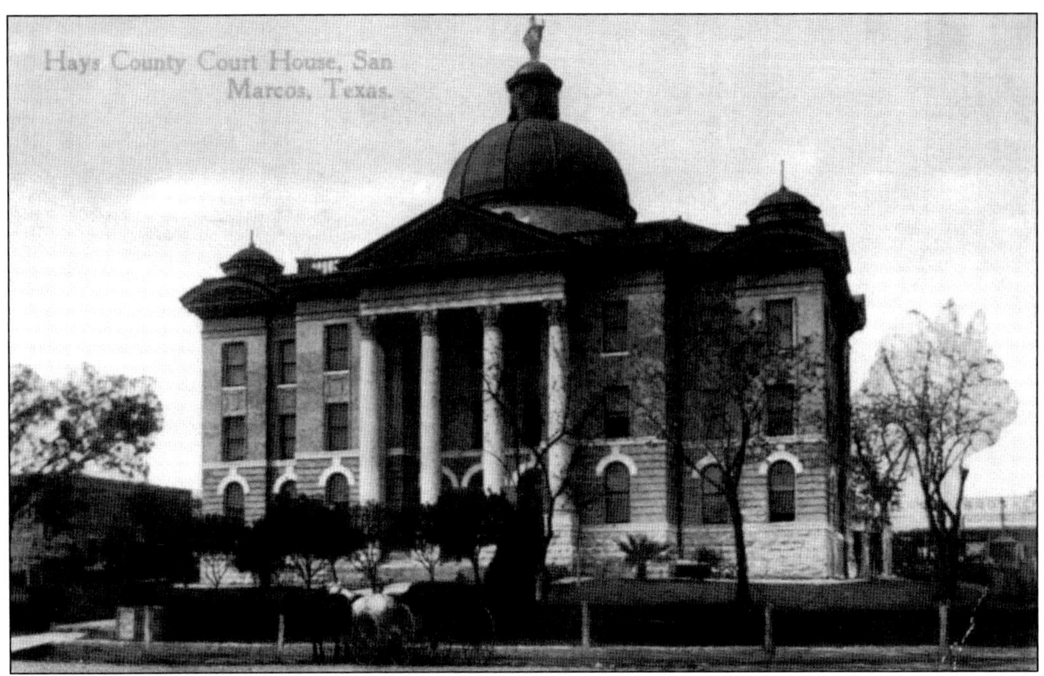

Hays County Courthouse, c. 1913. This real-photo postcard view of the fourth and current Hays County Courthouse is dated by the San Marcos Public Library to about 1913. The horse-drawn buggy in front of the courthouse attests to this date. (SMPL.)

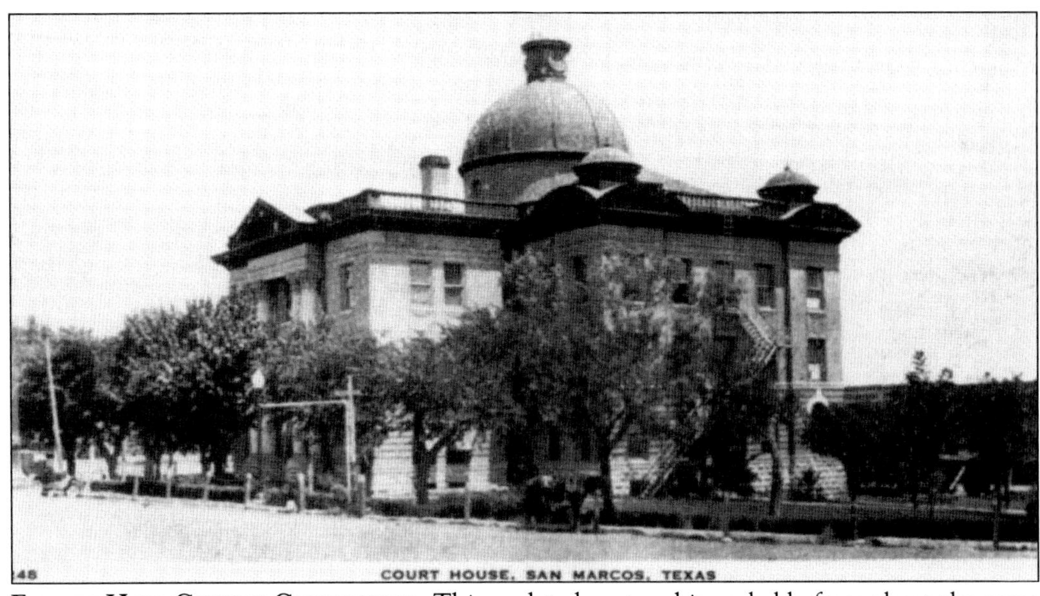

Fourth Hays County Courthouse. This undated postcard is probably from about the same time as the previous one, with a 1910s-era automobile on the far left contrasting with the horse on the right in front of the courthouse. (SMPL.)

Christmas at the Courthouse, 1948. The courthouse is decked out in lights for the Christmas holiday season in this 1948 view. The cars with running boards provide a real sense of the early postwar period. (SMPL.)

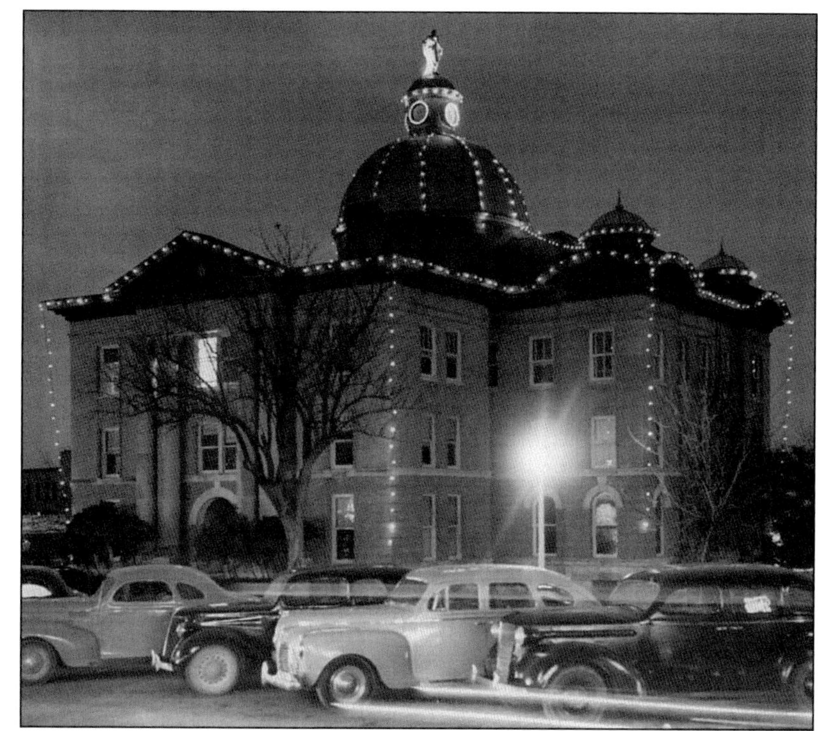

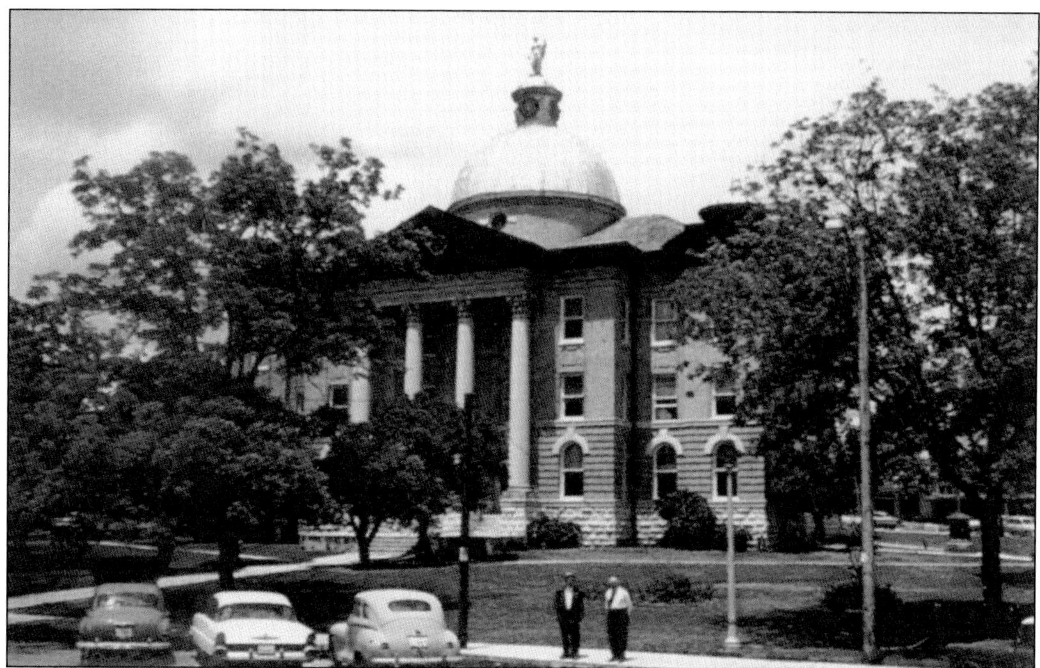

Hays County Courthouse, c. 1960. R.L. Bunting (left) and Bill Pappas are pictured standing in front of the courthouse. Although the photograph is labelled in the San Marcos Public Library collection as dating from February 27, 1969, the cars suggest that 1959 is a more likely year for the photograph to have been taken. (SMPL.)

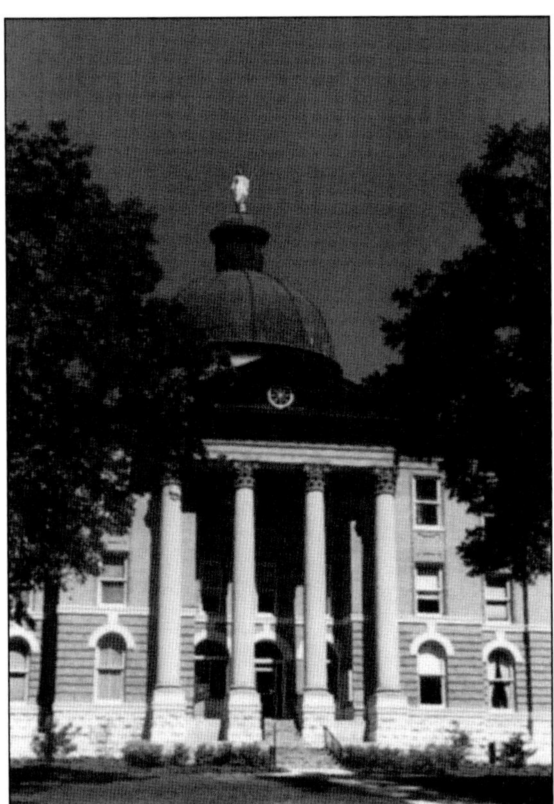

Hays County Courthouse, Early 1990s. The courthouse, pictured here around 1993, was designed in the Beaux-Arts style by C.H. Page and Brother. Four grand entrances provide access to the rotunda. Atop the courthouse dome, Lady Justice stands as a symbol of the county officials' responsibility. (SMPL.)

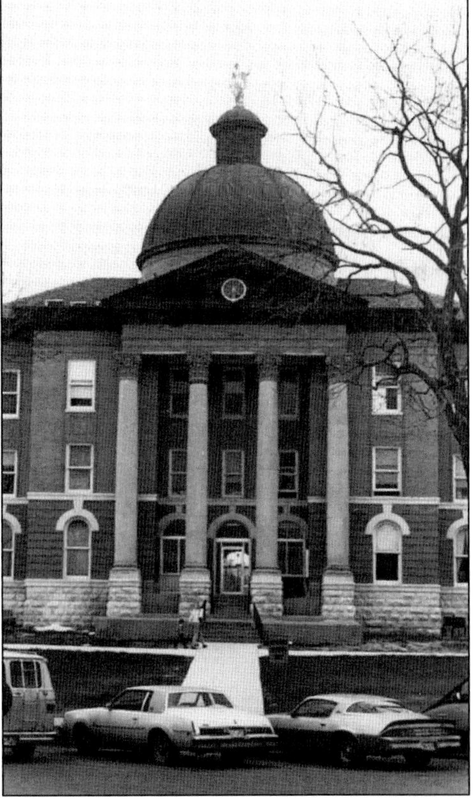

Hays County Courthouse Prior to Dome Restoration. Voters approved a nearly $2 million bond package in November 1993 for needed repairs for the courthouse, pictured here in 1996. An additional $2.2-million grant from the Texas Department of Transportation allowed the restoration of many features, including the reopening of all four entrances to the rotunda. (SMPL.)

Restored Copper Dome on Hays County Courthouse. By 1998, when this photograph was taken, the copper dome of the courthouse had also been restored. The 1990s repairs maintained the building's historic architecture and also brought it up to modern fire and disability-access codes. (SMPL.)

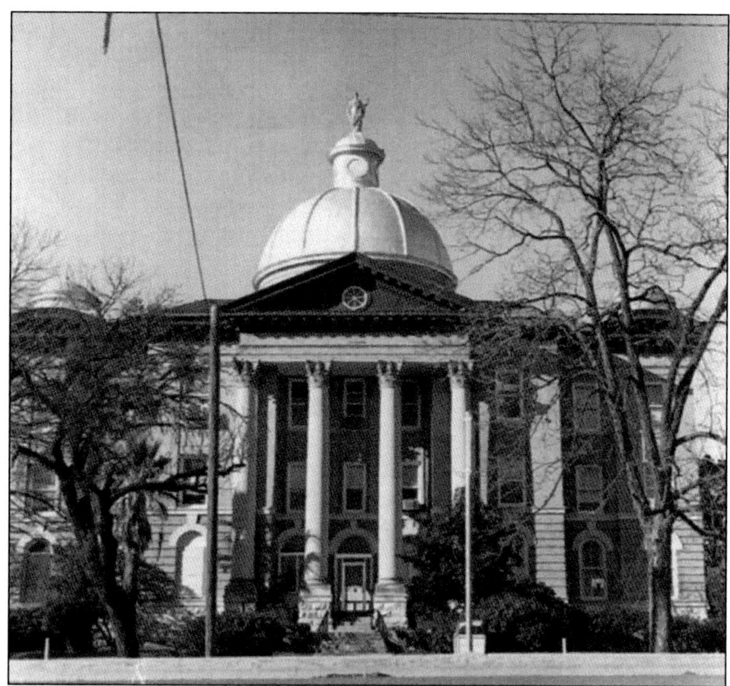

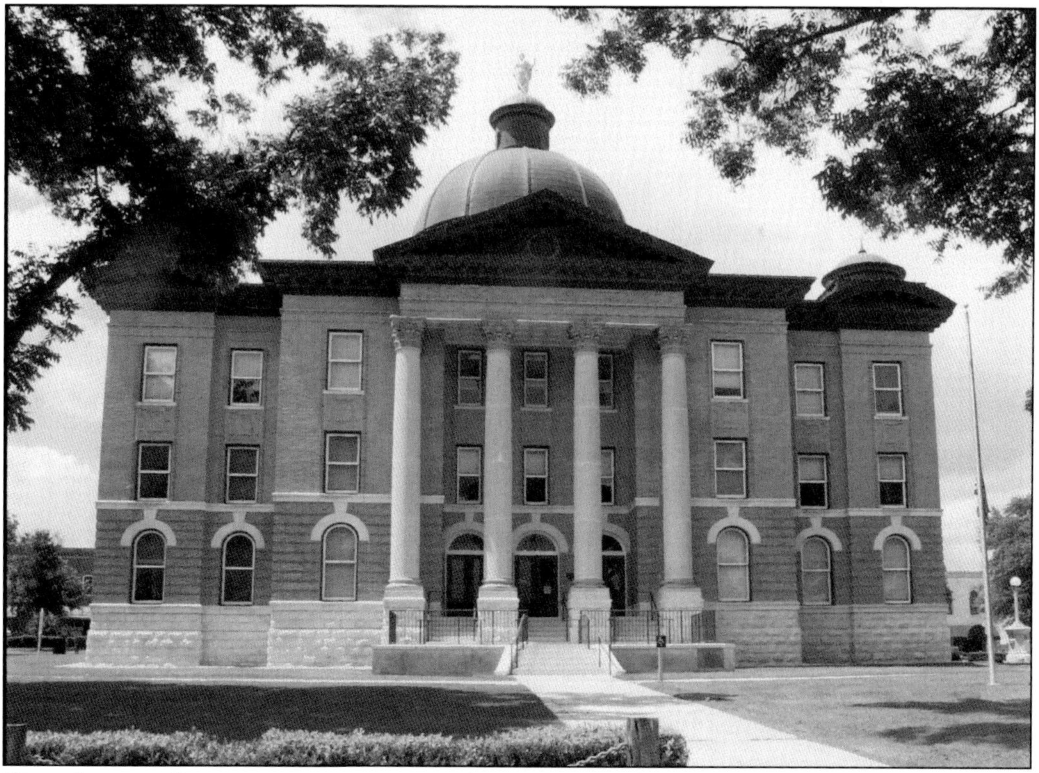

Hays County Courthouse in the 21st Century. Listed in the National Register of Historic Places in 1992, the restored Hays County Courthouse continues to attract visitors to downtown San Marcos and the surrounding courthouse square, which it anchors. (CSMMSP.)

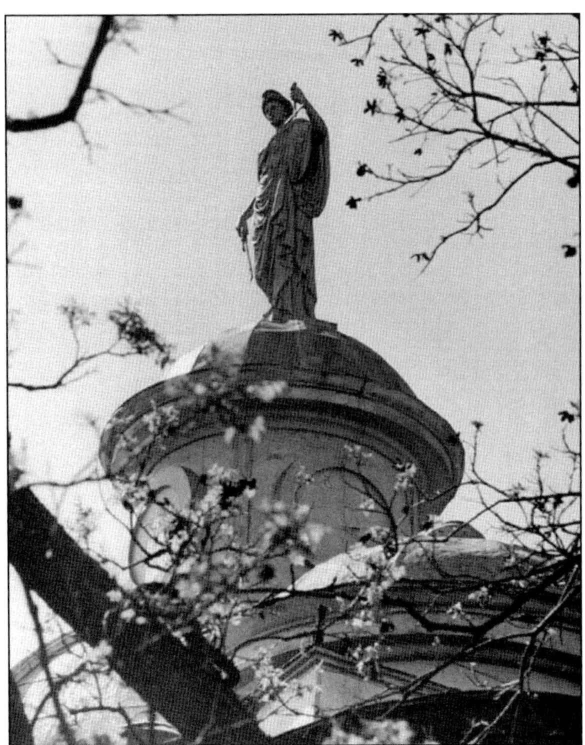

LADY JUSTICE ATOP THE COURTHOUSE. Pictured here, Lady Justice sits atop the central dome of the Hays County Courthouse. Unlike many other statues of Lady Justice, this one is not blindfolded. The scale Lady Justice holds measures the strengths of a case's support and opposition. The double-edged sword divides with the power of reason and justice in either direction. (SMPL.)

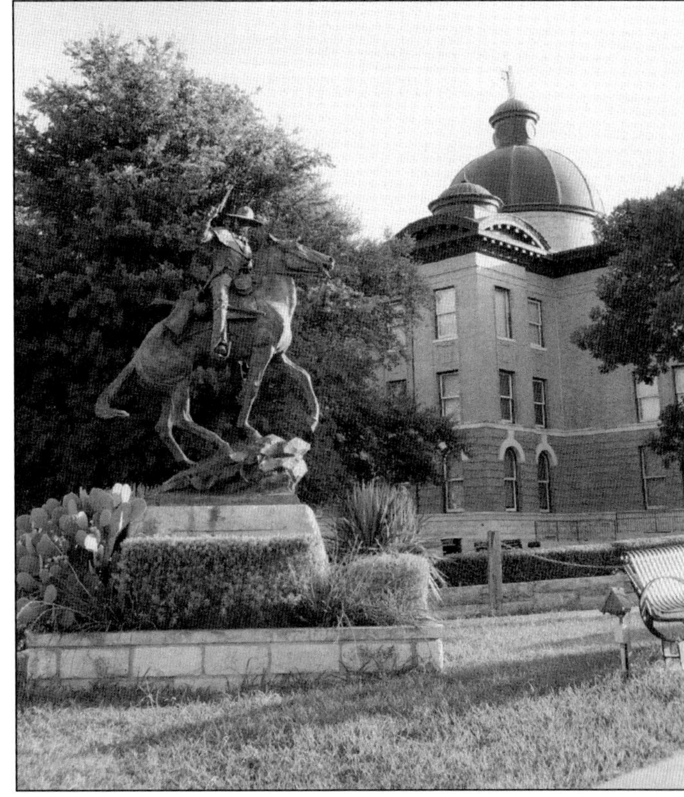

STATUE OF JACK HAYS ON COURTHOUSE LAWN. A statue of Hay County's namesake, John Coffee "Jack" Hays, stands on the courthouse square in downtown San Marcos. Depicting Hays in his days as a Texas Ranger, the statue was created by artist Jason Scull. (CSMMSP.)

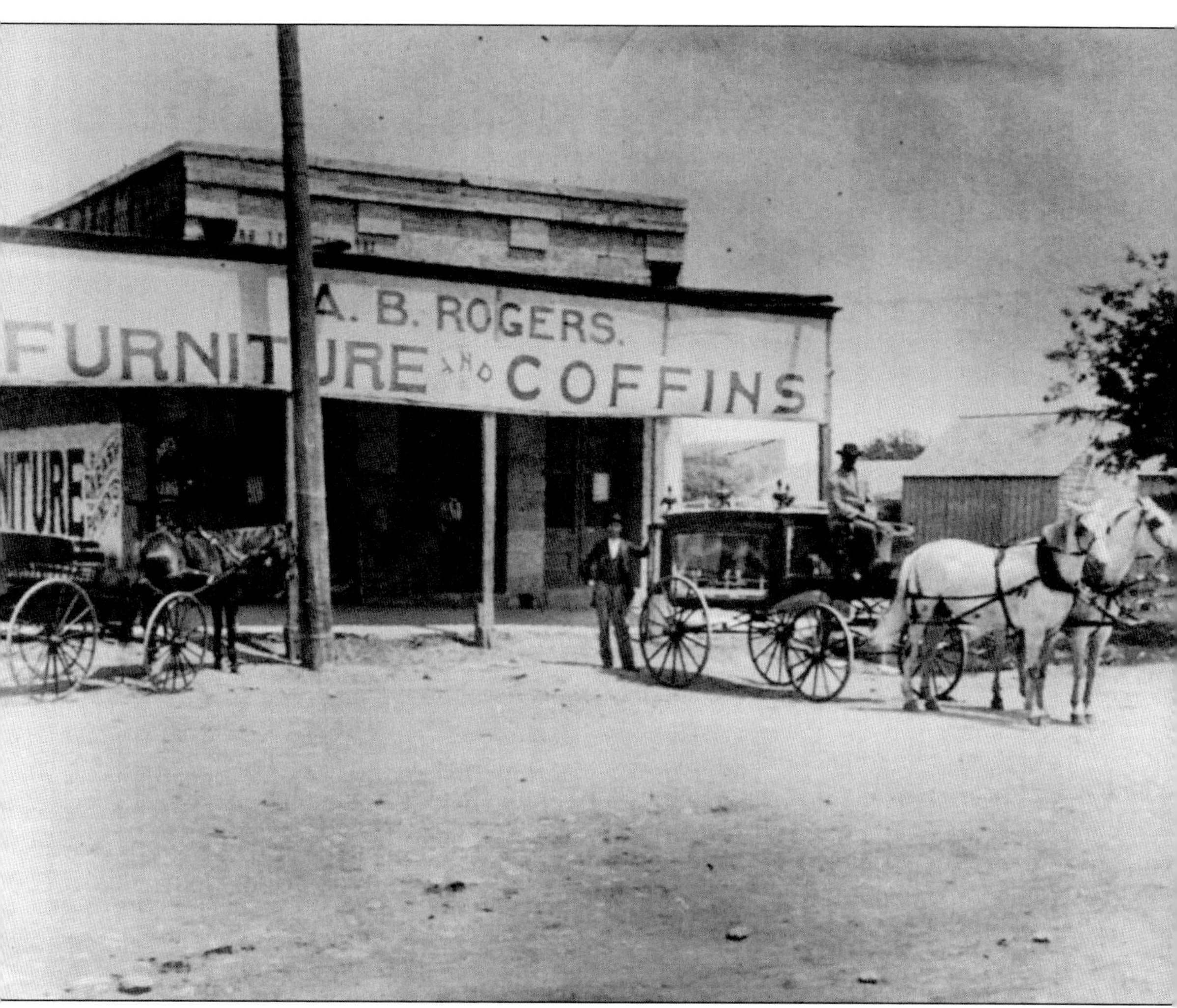

DOWNTOWN SAN MARCOS, C. 1897. A.B. Rogers, the founder of the Rio Vista Resort and later the Aquarena Springs Resort in San Marcos, had his furniture and coffin-making business at the corner of East San Antonio and Austin (now LBJ) Streets in downtown San Marcos. (SMPL.)

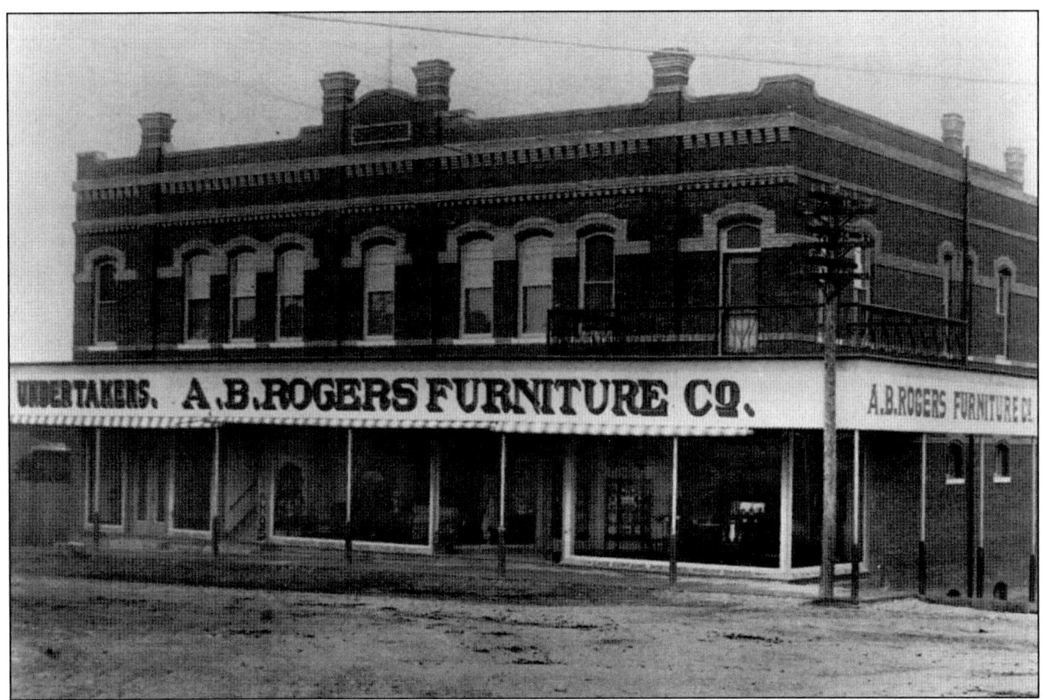

New Rogers Building, 1906. In 1906, when this photograph was taken, A.B. Rogers moved his business into a new building downtown on the northeast corner of the intersection of E. Hopkins and Austin (now LBJ) Streets. The Rogers furniture business remained in this store until 1944. Since that time, a number of changing businesses have occupied portions of the historic building. (SMPL.)

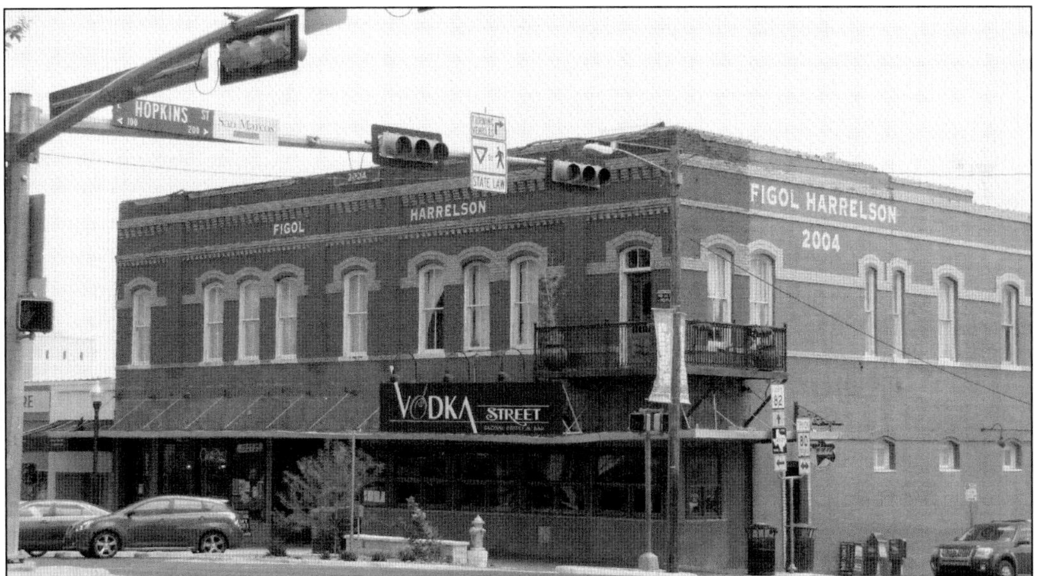

21st-Century View of A.B. Rogers Building. This 2015 view of the old A.B. Rogers building illustrates the changes to its external architecture that took place over more than 100 years. Nonetheless, the broad outline of the building and the number of windows remain the same as in the previous photograph.

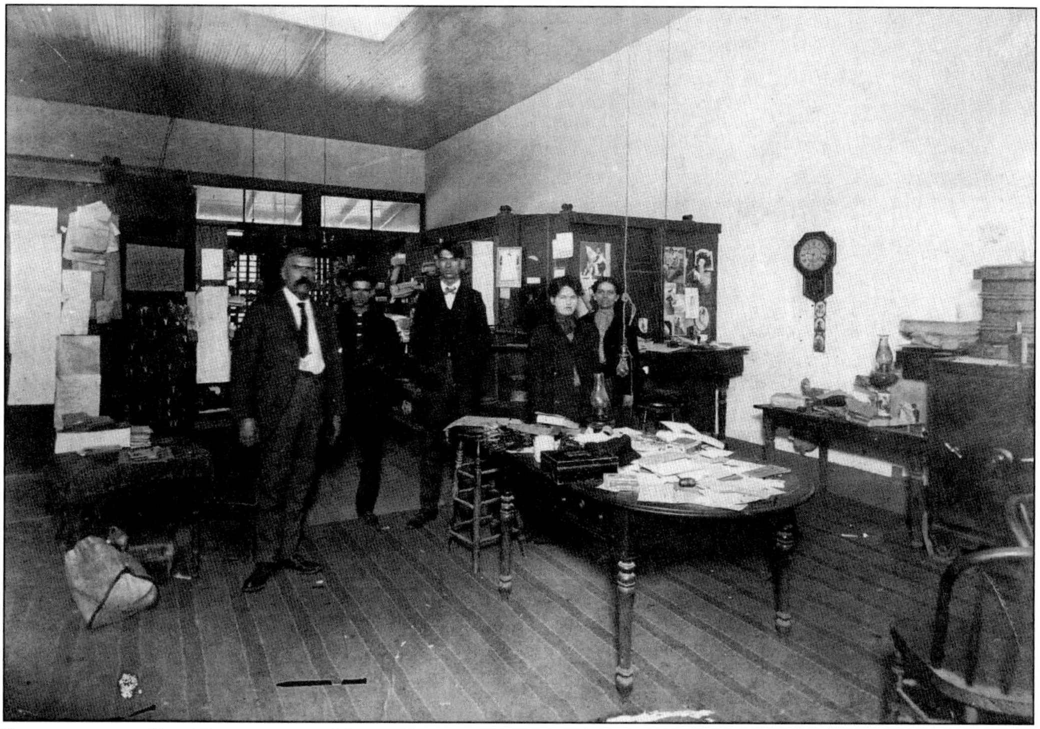

Interior of Old Downtown Post Office, 1905. These two photographs from 1905 show the interior of the old downtown San Marcos Post Office. The people are unidentified in each image, but above, the man on the left may be Owen Ford, San Marcos postmaster from 1898 to 1907. The same person is at far right below. (Both, SMPL.)

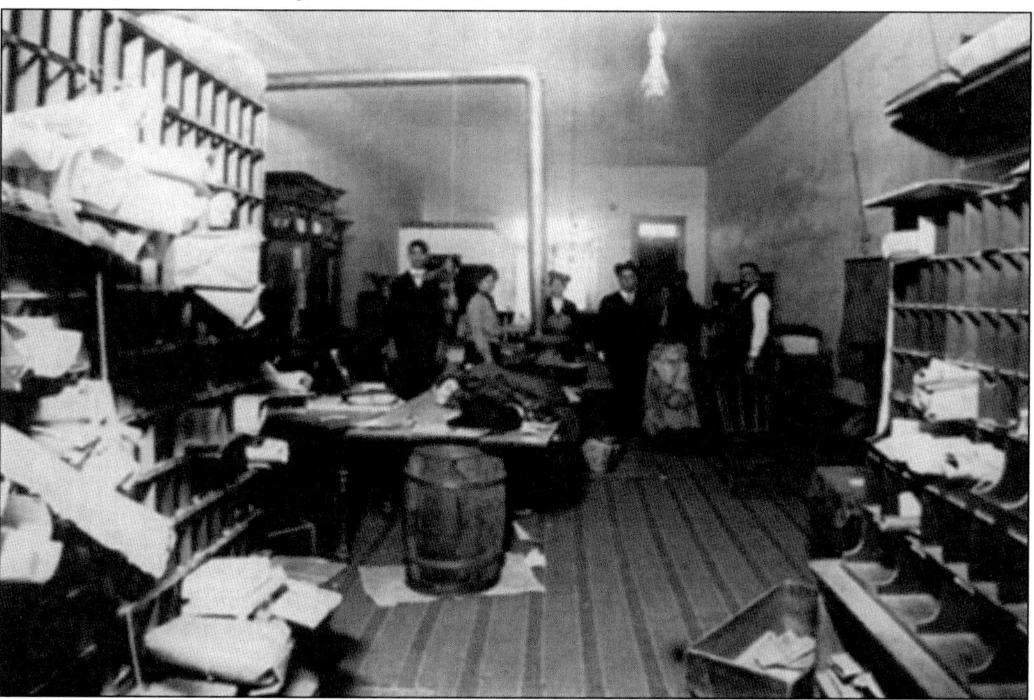

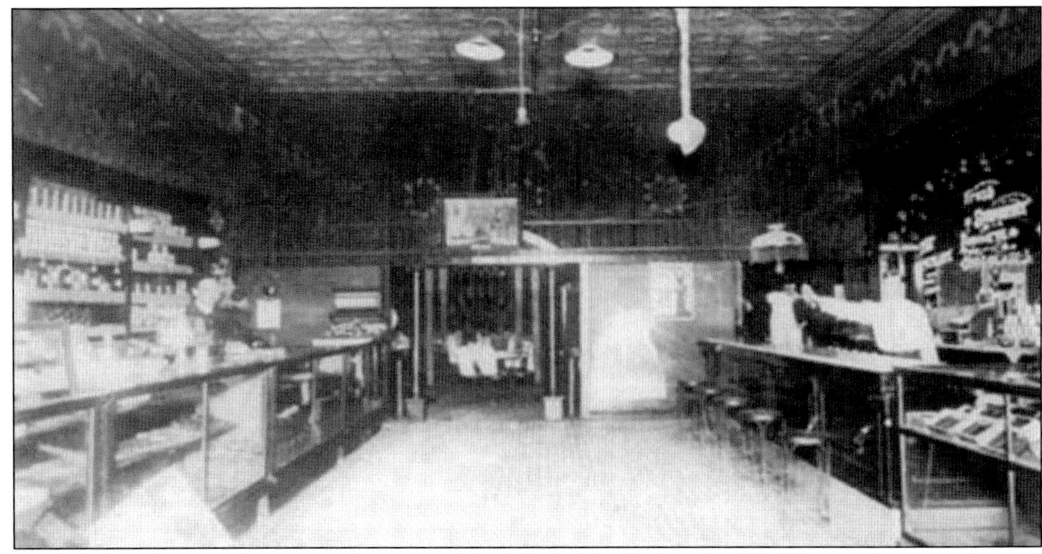

POPULAR DOWNTOWN SODA FOUNTAIN, 1916. The Café Royal Soda Fountain, once located at 116 West Hopkins Street, is pictured here in 1916. In the June 30, 1911, issue of the *Normal Star*, the weekly student newspaper from the normal school, the café advertised that "their soda fountain has everything good to drink. Delicious Cakes and Creams made daily. Royal Cream Bread, 3 Loaves for 25 cts." (SMPL.)

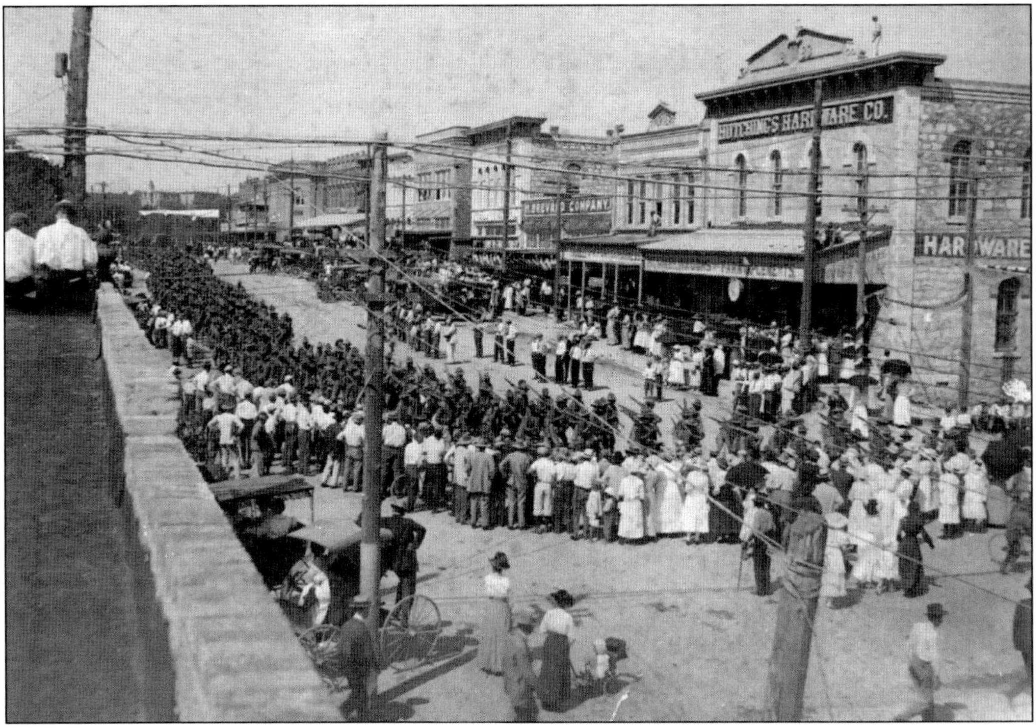

US TROOPS MARCH THROUGH DOWNTOWN. This photograph from September 20, 1916, shows US troops marching through downtown San Marcos on their way to Austin. The annotation on the photograph noted that this was the biggest crowd ever seen in town, except on circus day. The view is westward down Hopkins Street, with the Donalson building on the far right. (SMPL.)

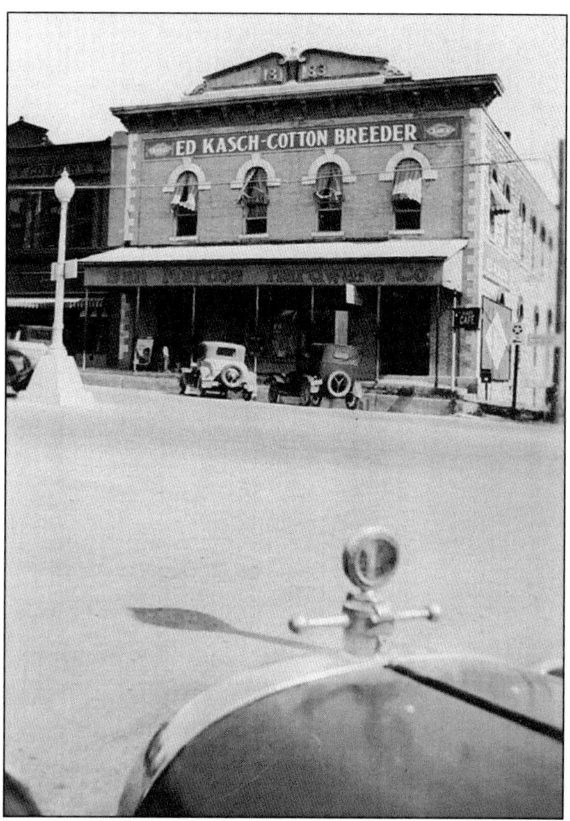

DONALSON BUILDING ON HOPKINS STREET. The Donalson building, on the northwest corner of Hopkins and LBJ Streets across from the courthouse square, is a stone and stucco structure built in 1883. The lower sign reads "San Marcos Hardware Co.," and that company occupied the building from 1925 to 1941, providing a range of dates for the photograph. (SMPL.)

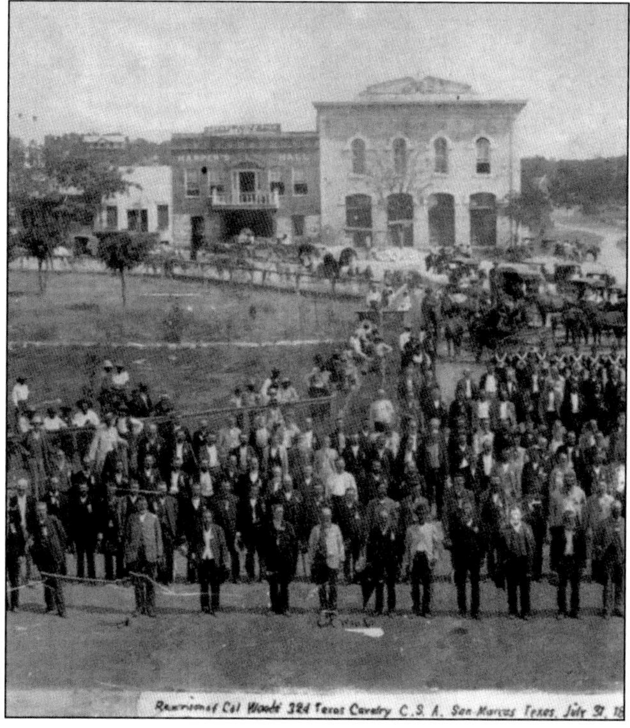

HARPER'S HALL AND CONFEDERATE CAVALRY REUNION. Harper's Hall is the oldest building on San Marcos's courthouse square, built in 1873. It is immediately adjacent to the Donalson building on East Hopkins Street, as seen here. Standing in the square in front of the two buildings is a reunion of Colonel Wood's 32nd Texas Cavalry (CSA), held on July 31 sometime after 1883. (CSMMSP.)

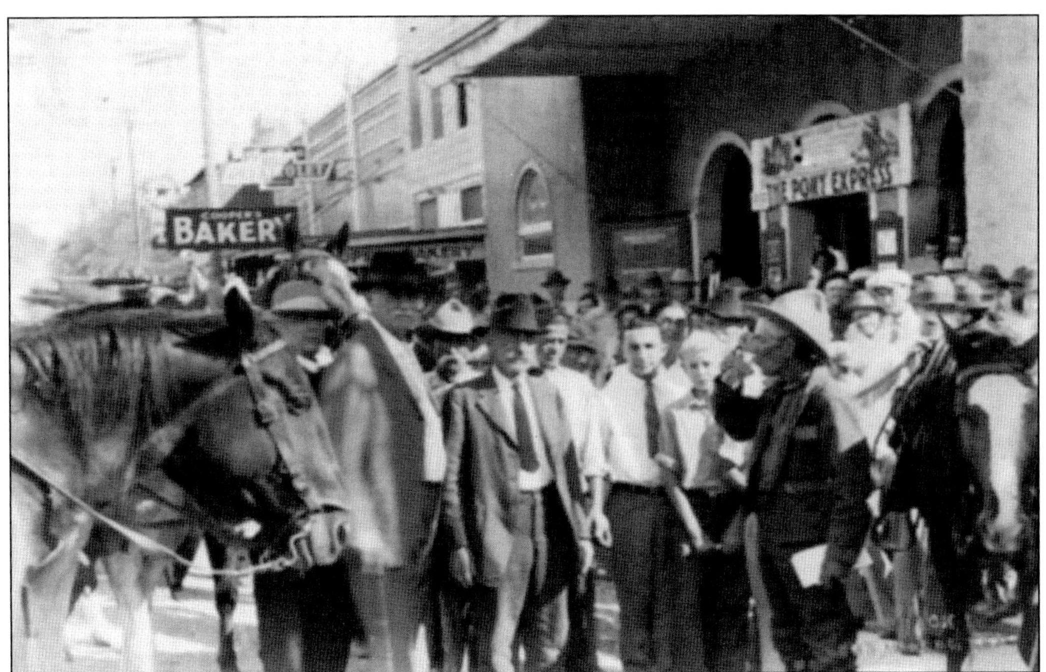

Pony Express Rider Celebration, Downtown. Taken on October 7, 1925, by A.A. Brack, this photograph captures a Pony Express rider passing through San Marcos on his way to San Antonio. The rider was carrying messages from mayors of cities he passed through on his way to meet George W. Saunders, president of the Old Trail Drivers Association. (SMPL.)

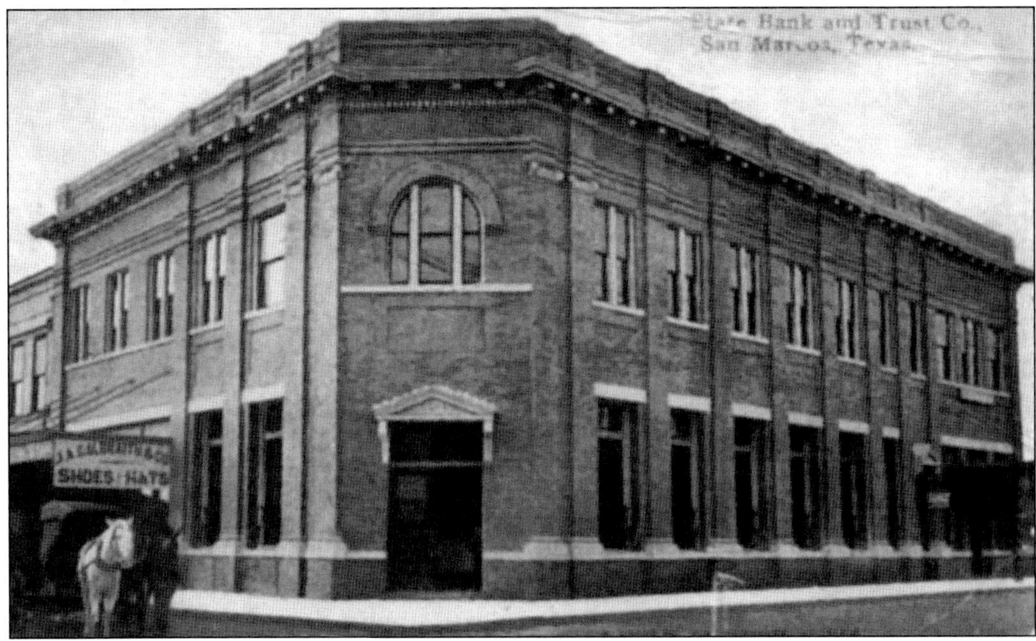

State Bank and Trust Building. This postcard photograph from the early 1900s shows the old State Bank and Trust building, located at the corner of Guadalupe and West Hopkins Streets on the corner of the courthouse square. Built in 1891, the bank was robbed by the infamous Newton Gang on January 4, 1924. (SMPL.)

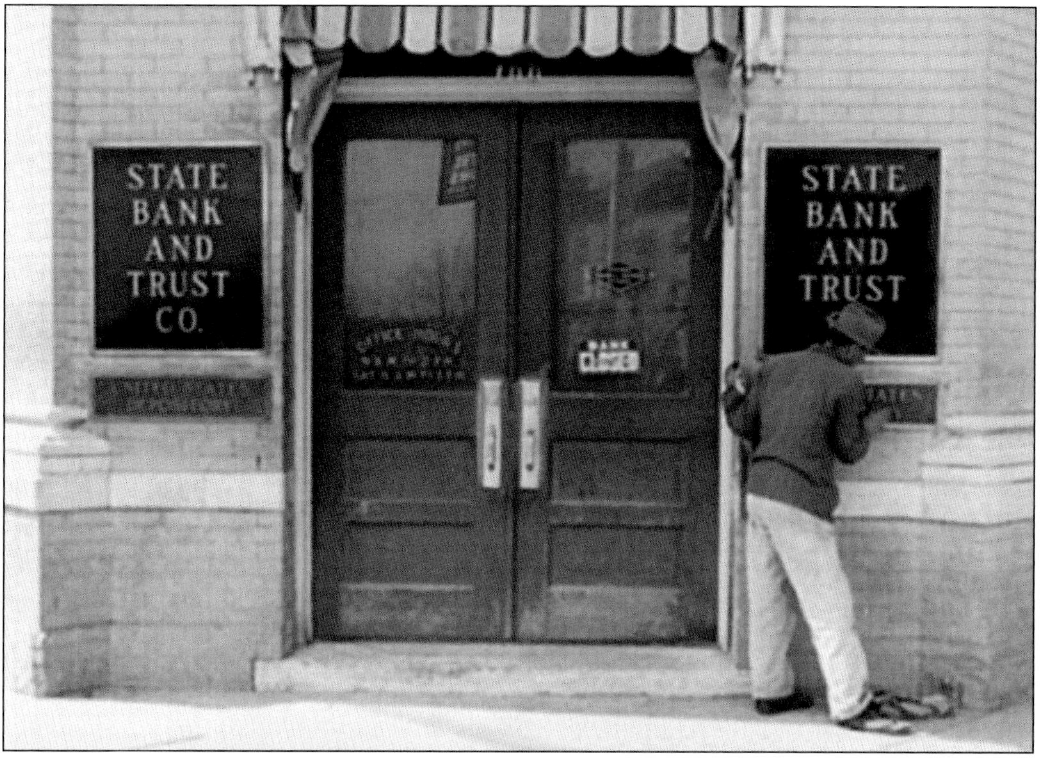

Entrance to Old State Bank and Trust Building. The State Bank and Trust building remained active as a bank until 1963. The entrance, seen here in an undated photograph, was diagonal to the intersection of Guadalupe and Hopkins Streets. (SMPL.)

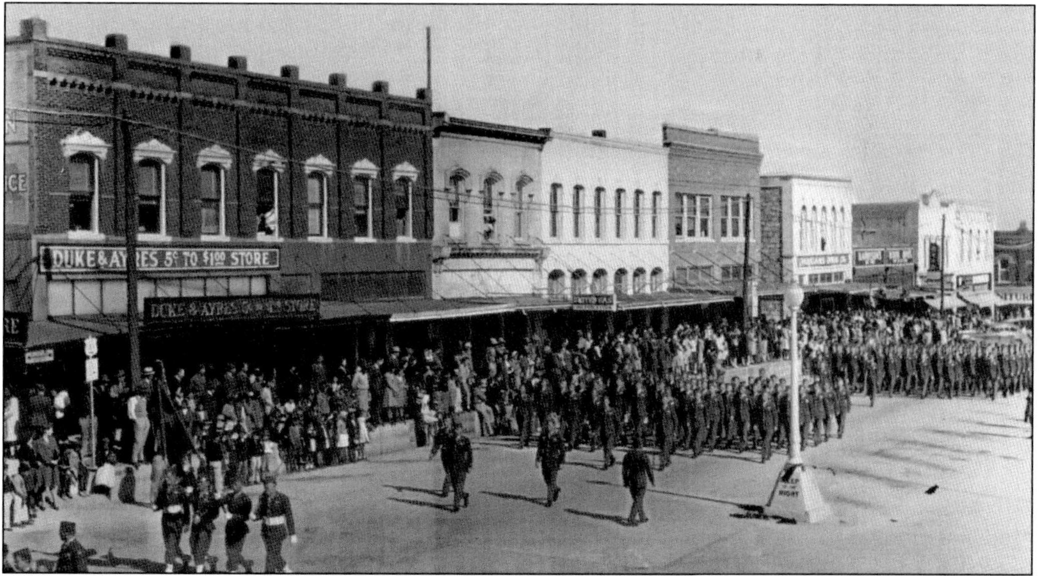

Post–World War II Veterans Parade on Hopkins Street. A veterans' parade takes place along East Hopkins Street across from the courthouse square. Although unspecified, the photograph has been dated to 1947–1951 by analyzing the storefront business names along Hopkins Street. (SMPL.)

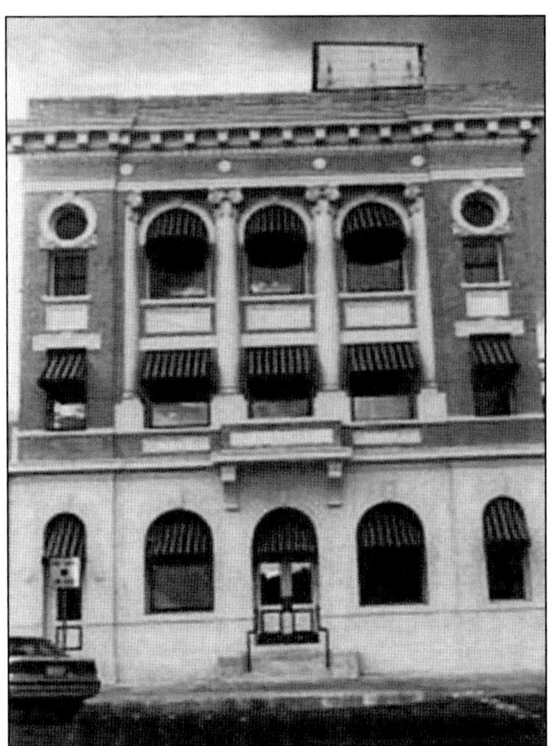

Hays County Courthouse Annex, 1989. This 1989 view shows the courthouse annex at the intersection of LBJ and San Antonio Streets across from the Hays County Courthouse. Built in 1909, the First National Bank building incorporated a portion of the historic Hofheinz Hotel when it was constructed. In 2012, the offices of the courthouse annex moved to a new facility on the south end of San Marcos. (SMPL.)

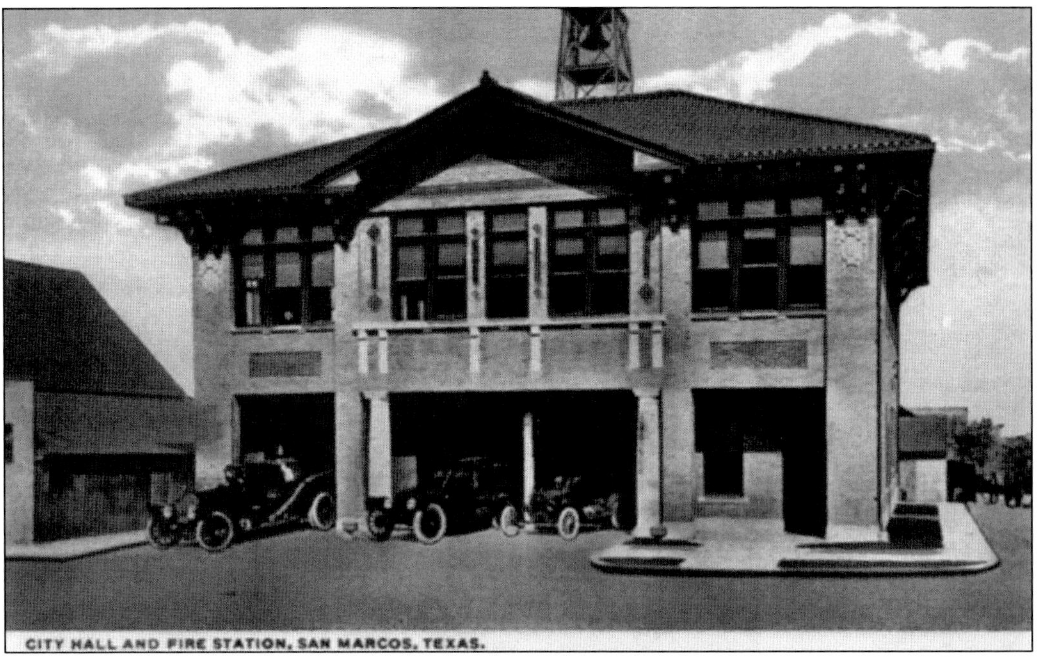
CITY HALL AND FIRE STATION, SAN MARCOS, TEXAS.

Old City Hall and Fire Station on Guadalupe Street. This linen postcard features the old city hall and fire station, built in 1915. The 1,000-pound cast-iron bell atop the roof was removed in 1973 because of concerns about the structural integrity of its tower. The bell was relocated in front of the present city hall at 630 East Hopkins Street in 2001 for the sesquicentennial celebration. (SMPL.)

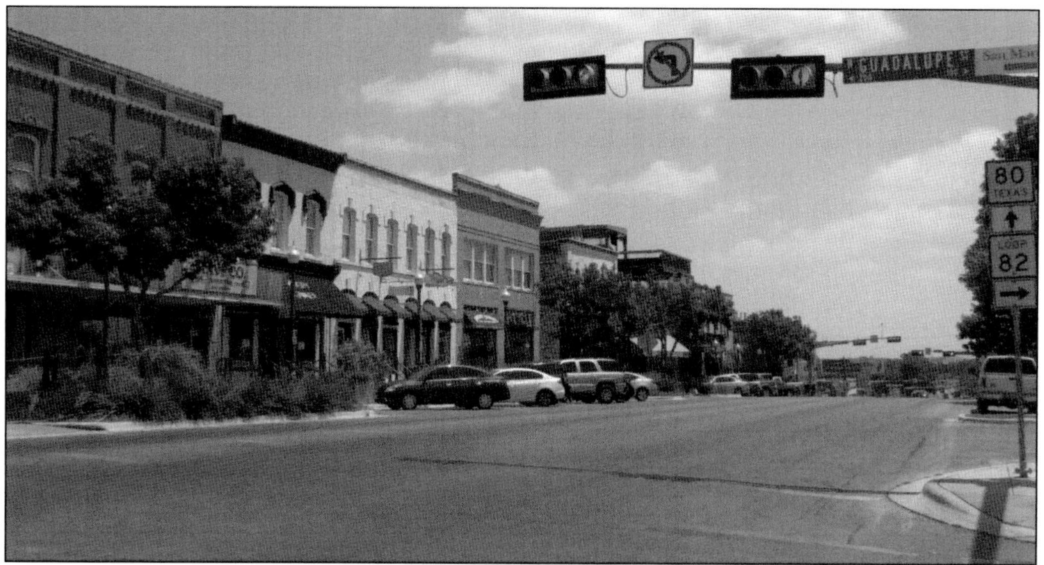

Modern Hopkins Street West of LBJ Drive. This modern view of Hopkins Street west of LBJ Drive can be compared with the parade photograph from the late 1940s on page 31 to see how the storefronts along the street have changed. Harper's Hall and the Donalson building are largely obscured by trees in the distance.

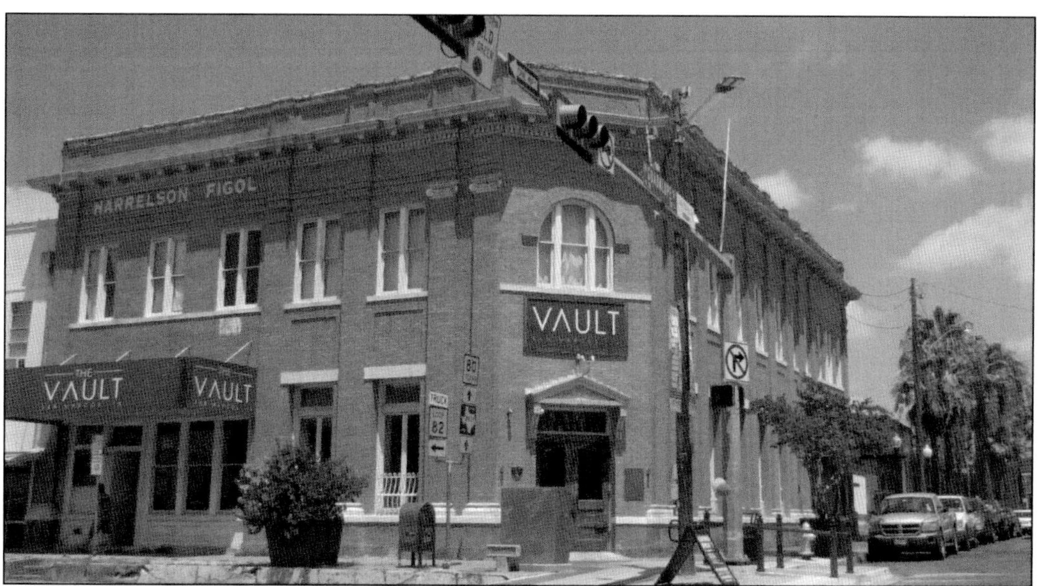

State Bank and Trust Building in the 21st Century. A modern view of the old State Bank and Trust building at the corner of Hopkins and Guadalupe Streets illustrates the changes that have taken place at that location since the closing of the bank in 1963. Compare with the view of the bank on page 30. A variety of restaurants have occupied the building in recent years.

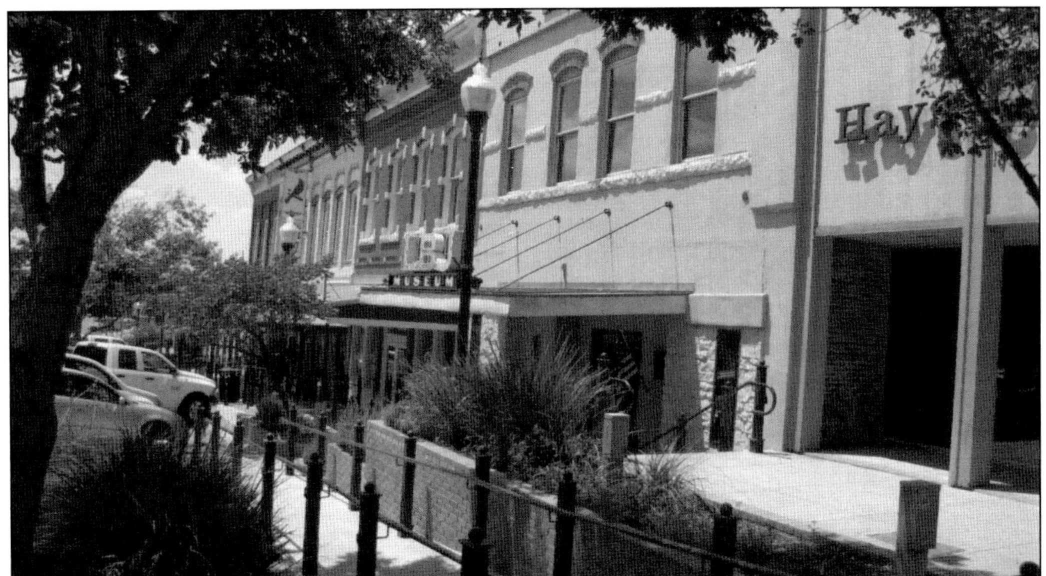

Modern Businesses along Guadalupe Street, Courthouse Square. In this modern view of Guadalupe Street on the west side of courthouse square, the LBJ Museum of San Marcos is visible along with a variety of storefronts. Several retail establishments as well as businesses such as law offices associated with the courthouse are located along the street and around the square.

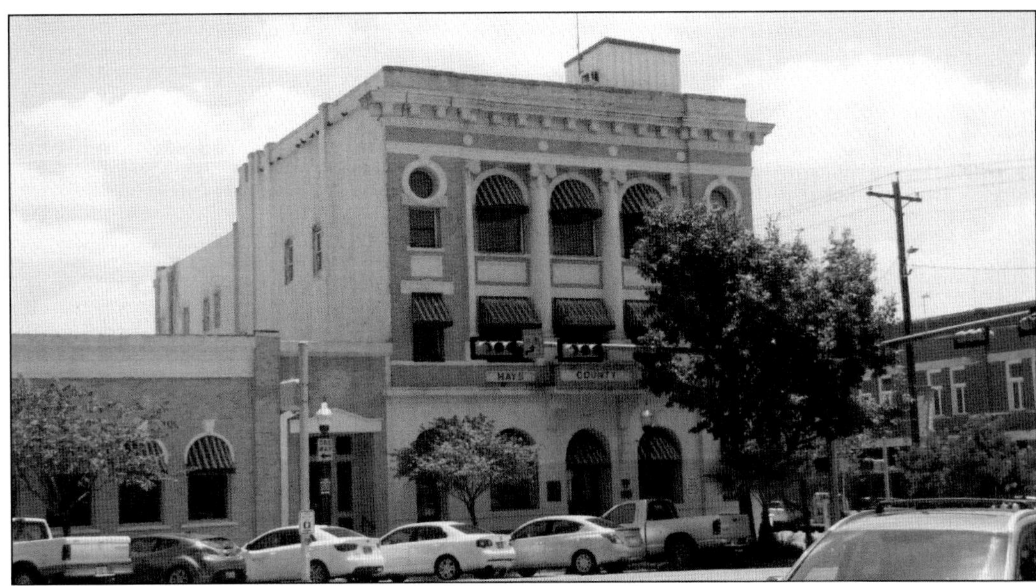

Old First National Bank Building. A present-day view of the intersection of South LBJ and San Antonio Streets shows the still-impressive architecture of the old First National Bank building that subsequently served as the Hays County Courthouse Annex. The bank occupied the building for 66 years, from 1909 to 1975, when it moved to a new building.

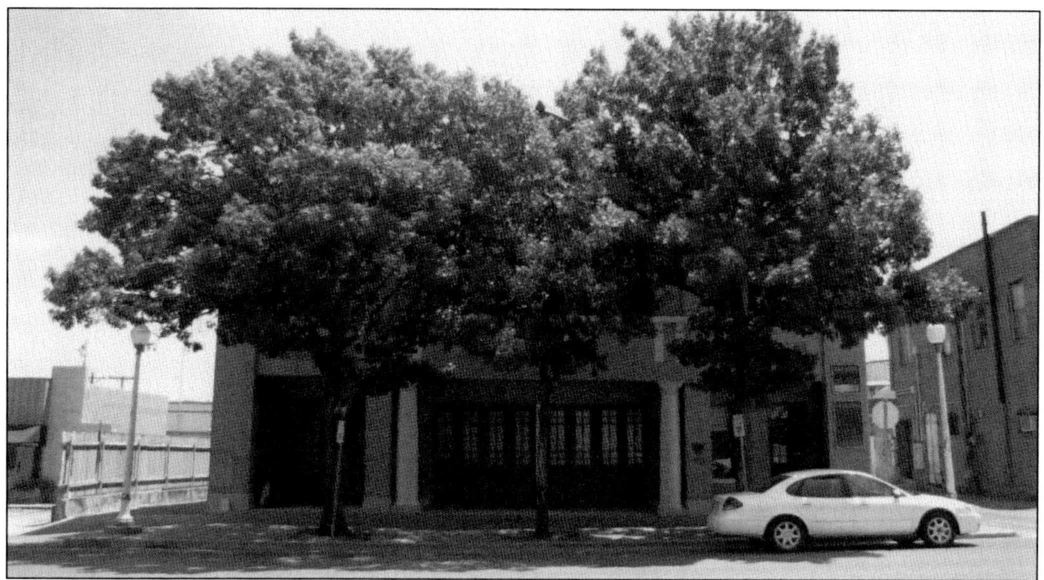

Texas State University Occupies Old City Hall and Fire Station. The old city hall and fire station on Guadalupe Street (page 32) now houses the Texas State University sound-recording technology program. Texas State is the only university in the Southwest to offer a bachelor's degree in sound-recording technology, and this historic building now houses a multipurpose recording facility with state-of-the-art equipment.

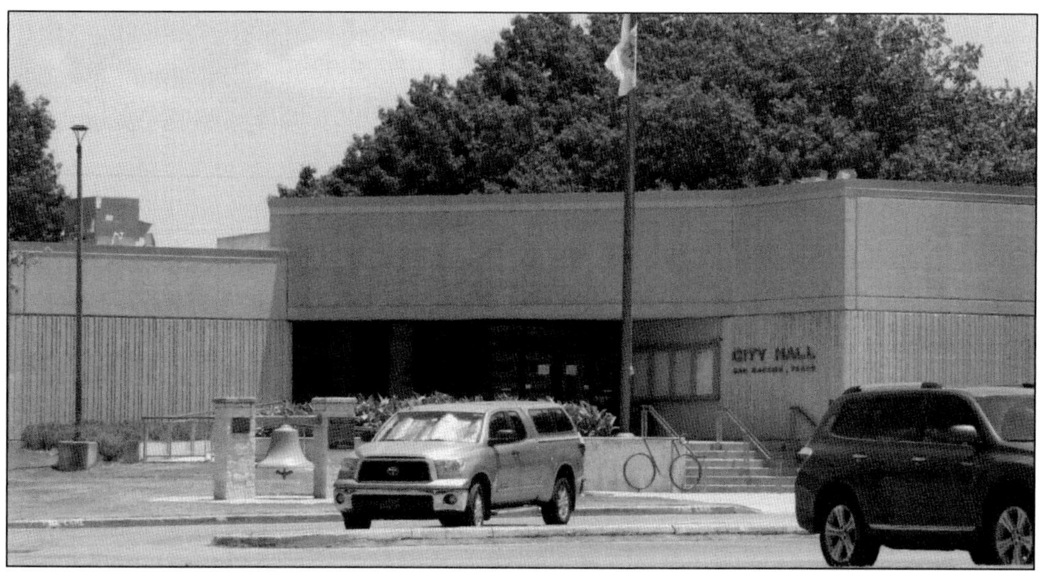

Modern San Marcos City Hall. The present-day San Marcos City Hall is located at 630 East Hopkins Street. The bell from the old fire station on Guadalupe Street now resides here, placed during celebrations of San Marcos's 150th anniversary.

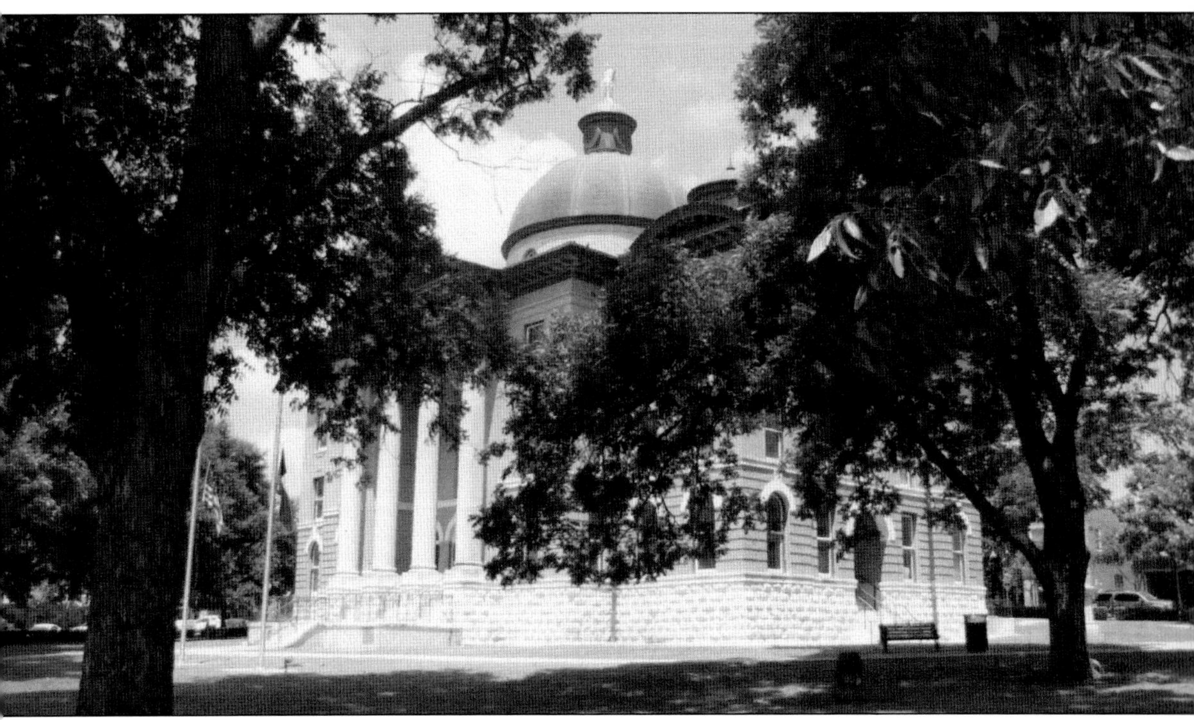

Modern-Day Courthouse Square. Courthouse square remains the heart of downtown San Marcos. This modern-day view illustrates the square on a typical summer day during the quiet time between the end of summer school and the beginning of fall classes at nearby Texas State University.

Three

Texas State

From Teachers' College to Emerging Research University

Southwest Texas State Normal School was authorized in 1899 by the Texas legislature. The school's original mission was to prepare Texas public school teachers, especially those in the south-central part of the state. The school opened its doors in San Marcos in 1903 with 303 students and 17 faculty members. The first building, Old Main, is a red-roofed castle-like landmark atop Chautauqua Hill, overlooking the adjacent Blackland Prairie.

Over the years, the Texas legislature has broadened the scope of the institution, and several name changes reflect these increases in the school's mission. The first name change occurred in 1918, when the school became Southwest Texas State Normal College. Five years later in 1923, the name was changed to Southwest Texas State Teachers College, reflecting a national trend away from the term normal school. The 1930s saw the addition of a master of arts degree in education, when in 1935 the school was authorized to form a graduate school. The first graduate courses were offered in 1936, and Margaret McClung Walker received the first master's degree conferred during the commencement ceremony held in May 1937.

The college continued to grow through the late 1930s into the 1950s and added many more master's programs, several beyond the scope of the original teacher's programs and degrees. In recognition of this increased breadth and depth of coursework available, the school's name was once again changed, this time in 1959 dropping the term teachers to become simply Southwest Texas State College. Continued growth and expansion of graduate programs in the 1960s led to yet another name change in 1969, to Southwest Texas State University. During the 1960s, the school also followed national trends and became desegregated, enrolling five African American women in February 1963.

Continued expansion of the role of research and graduate education at the university, combined with a broader statewide reach in enrollment, led the school to change its name to Texas State University–San Marcos in 2003. By this time, the university had created its first two doctoral programs, environmental geography and geographic education, in 1996, with the first two doctoral graduates, Lisa DeChano and Todd Votteler, receiving degrees in May 2000. With the achievement of "emerging research university" status within the Texas system of categorizing state-supported universities, the school dropped the San Marcos qualifier in 2013, becoming simply Texas State University, which it remains today. The university has grown to more than 36,000 students in 2014 and is now the fourth-largest university in the state. As the university's student population has grown, the campus also has expanded dramatically from the original single building at Old Main. Today, Texas State University has a 486-acre main campus and 5,038 additional acres in recreational, instructional, farm, and ranch land. The main campus is home to 268 buildings.

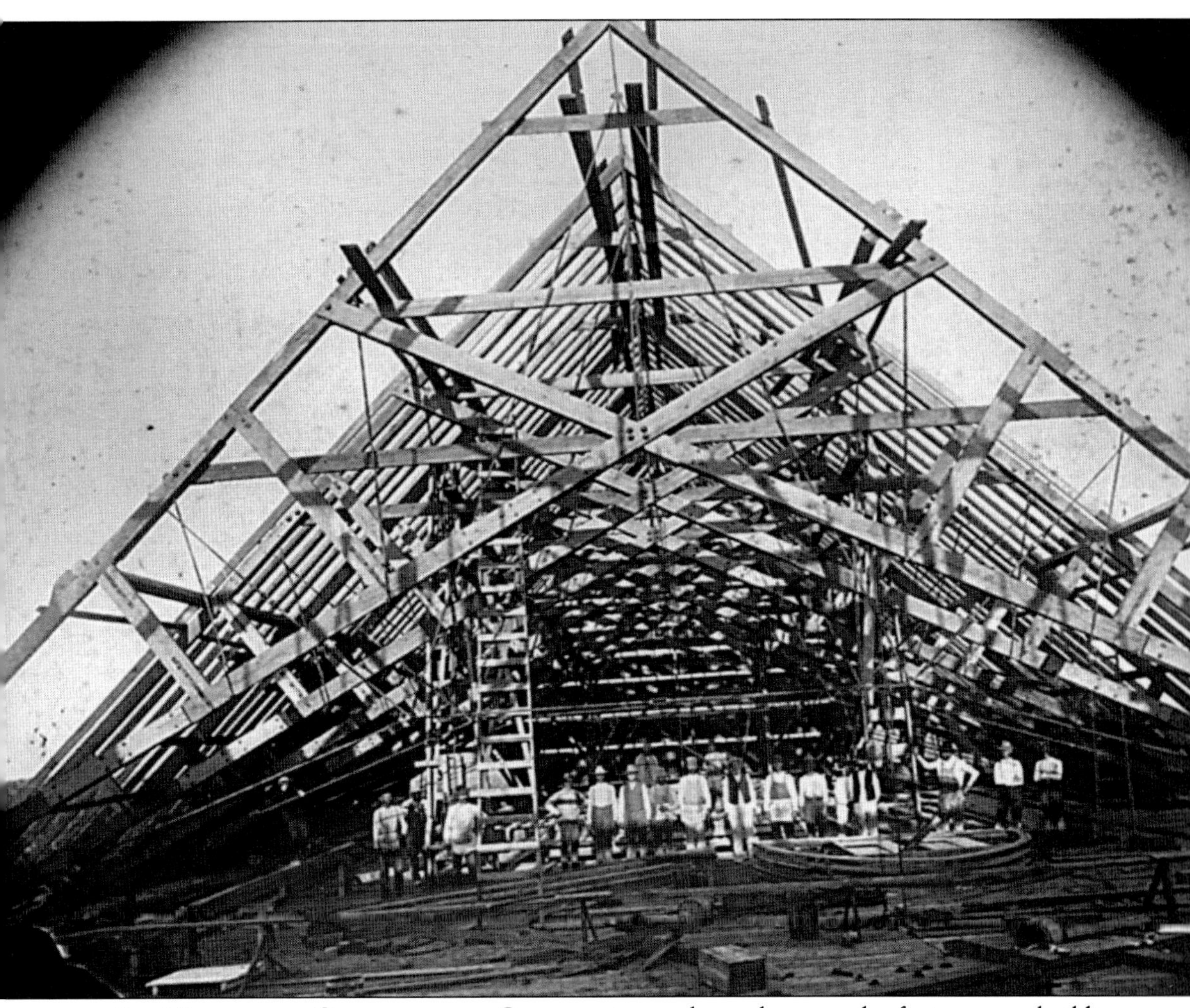

Old Main under Construction. Construction as shown here on the first campus building, Old Main, was authorized with the establishment of the school's charter in 1899. Old Main was designed by architect E. Northcraft and built in a style known as Victorian Gothic. Construction was completed in time for the first classes in the fall of 1903. (TxSt.)

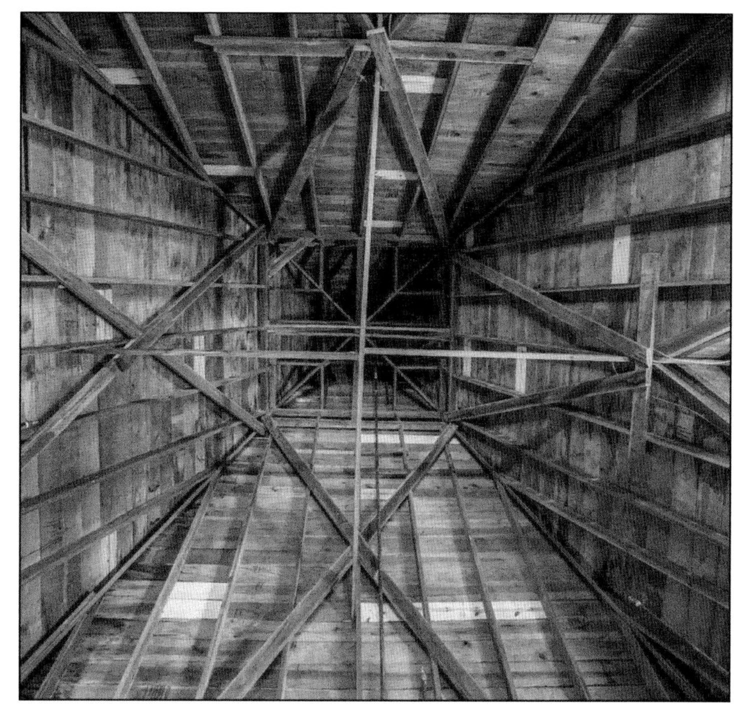

Interior Architecture of Old Main Steeple. This and the following view illustrate the complex architecture associated with the construction of Old Main's signature corner steeples and gables. These steeples and the central gables of the roof of the building are instantly recognizable to faculty, students, and visitors alike. (TxSt.)

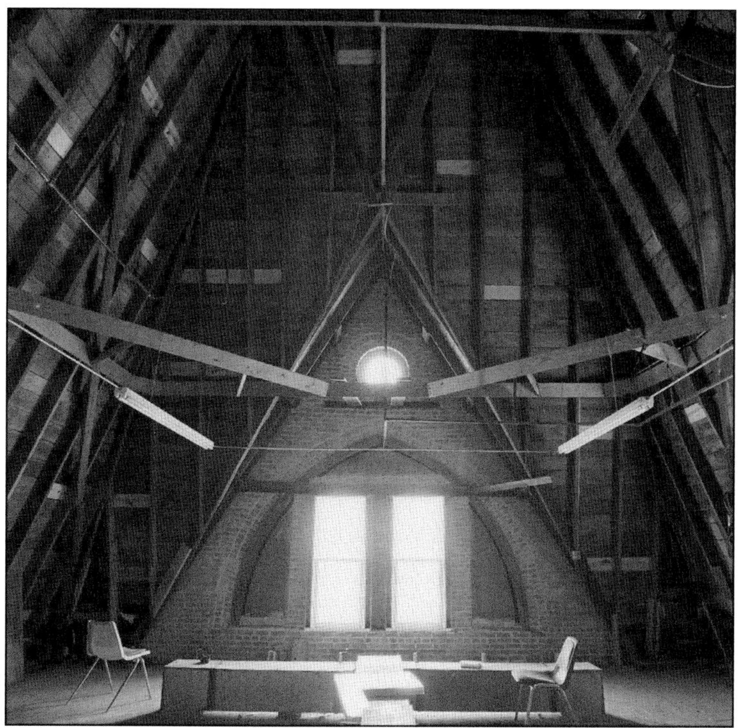

Interior Architecture of Old Main Window. As the modern chairs indicate, Old Main remains a central focal point on the university campus. The building has undergone many renovations since its completion in 1903, but the remnants of the ornate ceiling are still visible. Currently, Old Main houses the College of Fine Arts and Communication. The famous roof underwent a significant restoration in 1993–1994 to return it to its original style and color. (TxSt.)

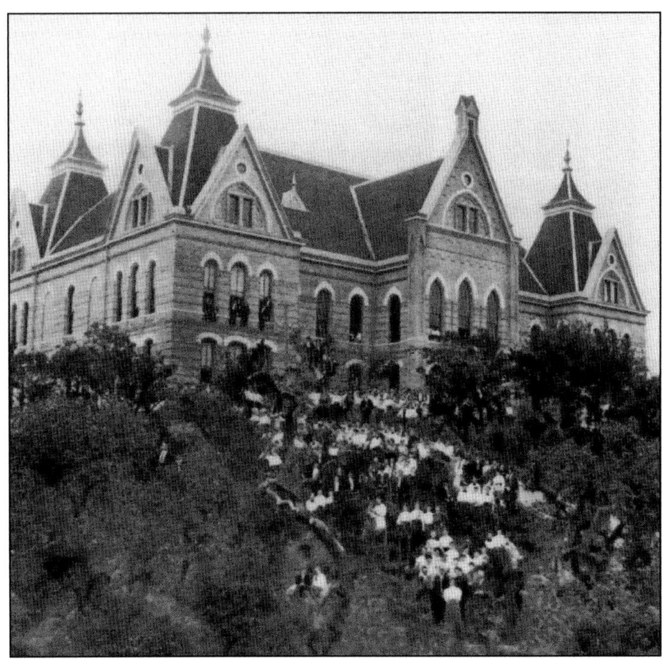

Faculty and Students, 1908. In this photograph, Old Main's prominent position atop Chautauqua Hill is emphasized. Faculty and students can be seen posing on the hillside, and several people are visible in the windows of the second floor. Old Main became the school's administration building as other buildings were added to the campus. (TxSt.)

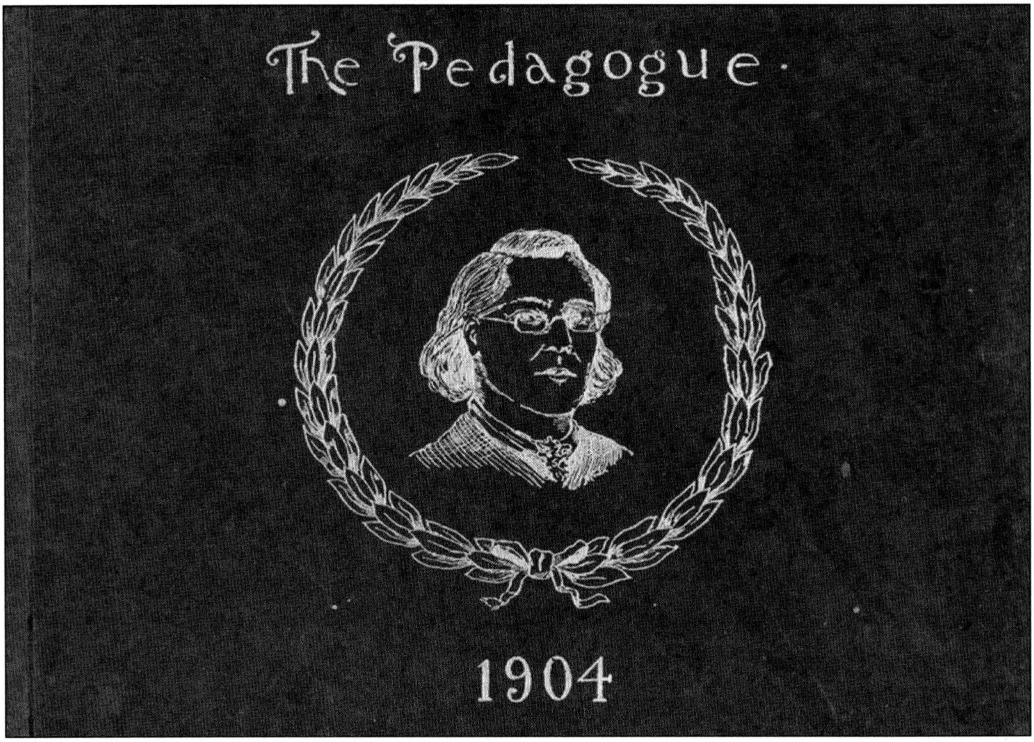

Cover of First Normal School Yearbook. In 1904, Southwest Texas State Normal School published its first yearbook, the *Pedagogue*. The cover of the yearbook, shown here, illustrates an unidentified academic-looking individual gazing thoughtfully into the future. The greetings in the yearbook noted that it was "an earnest effort to reflect the life of the students of the Southwest Texas State Normal—their environment and their achievements." (TxSt.)

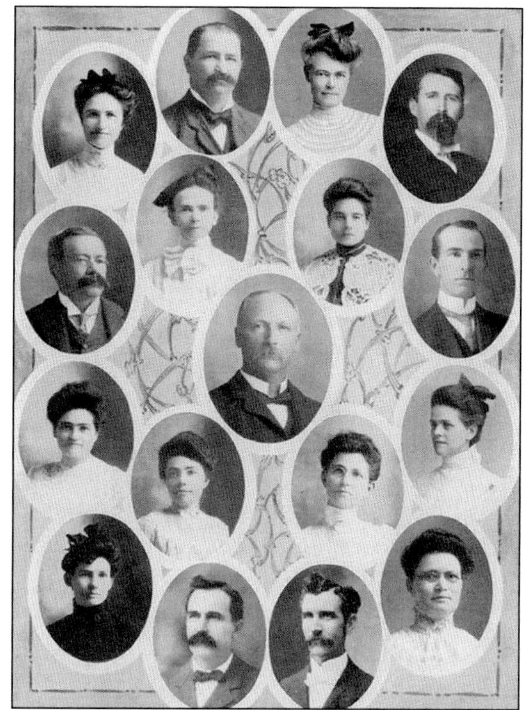

Normal School Faculty, 1904. From the 1904 *Pedagogue*, this photograph features the faculty at that time. At center is principal Thomas G. Harris. The other 16 faculty members are all named, but the names are not keyed to the individual photographs surrounding Principal Harris. Subjects taught are indicated as professional work, English, mathematics, history, physics, chemistry, primary work, reading, physical culture, German, civics, geography, drawing, Latin, vocal music, biological sciences, and penmanship. (TxSt.)

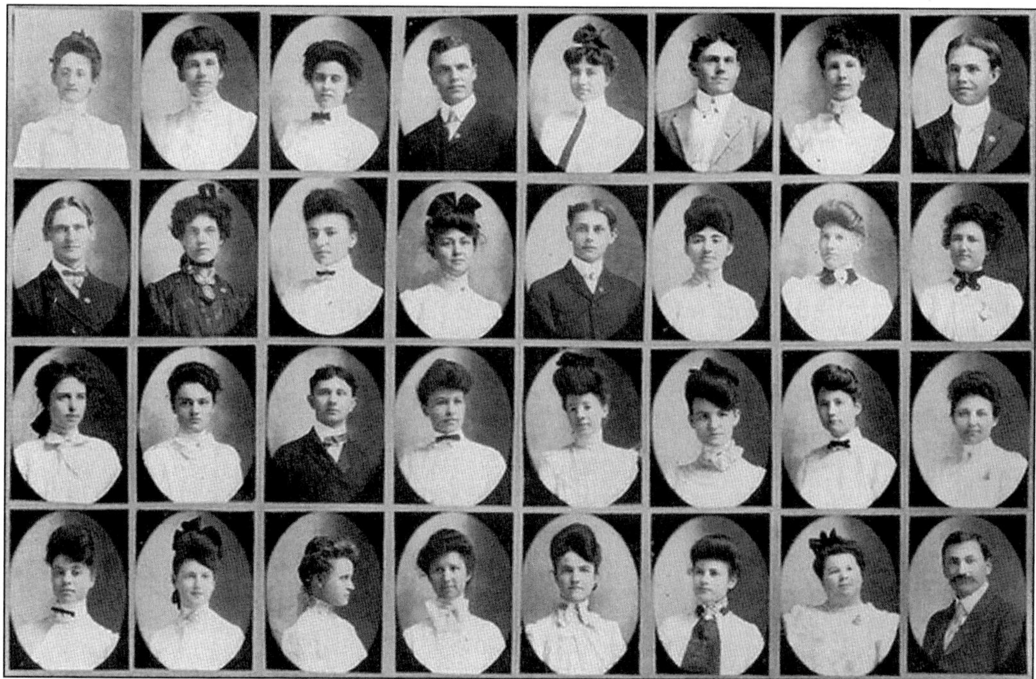

First Senior Class of Normal School, 1904. The first senior class of the normal school is shown in this photograph from the 1904 *Pedagogue*. Although all are named in the yearbook, the names are not keyed to the individual images. The yearbook notes that the class president was Charles Gault of Melburn, B.H. Glenn of Buffalo was vice president, and Hamah Smith of Port Lavaca was class secretary (all locations in Texas). (TxSt.)

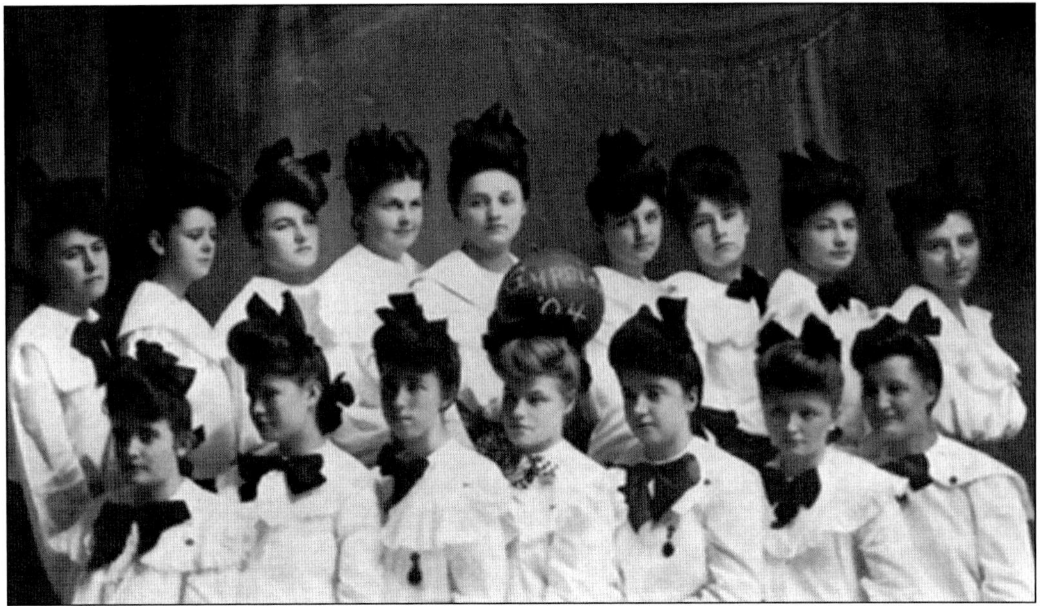

Normal School Women's Basketball Team, 1904. The normal school's women's basketball team from 1904 was named the Gypsies, as shown on the ball. The school mascot bobcat name was not adopted until 1921, when the school adopted the name on the recommendation of a committee formed to raise school spirit. (TxSt.)

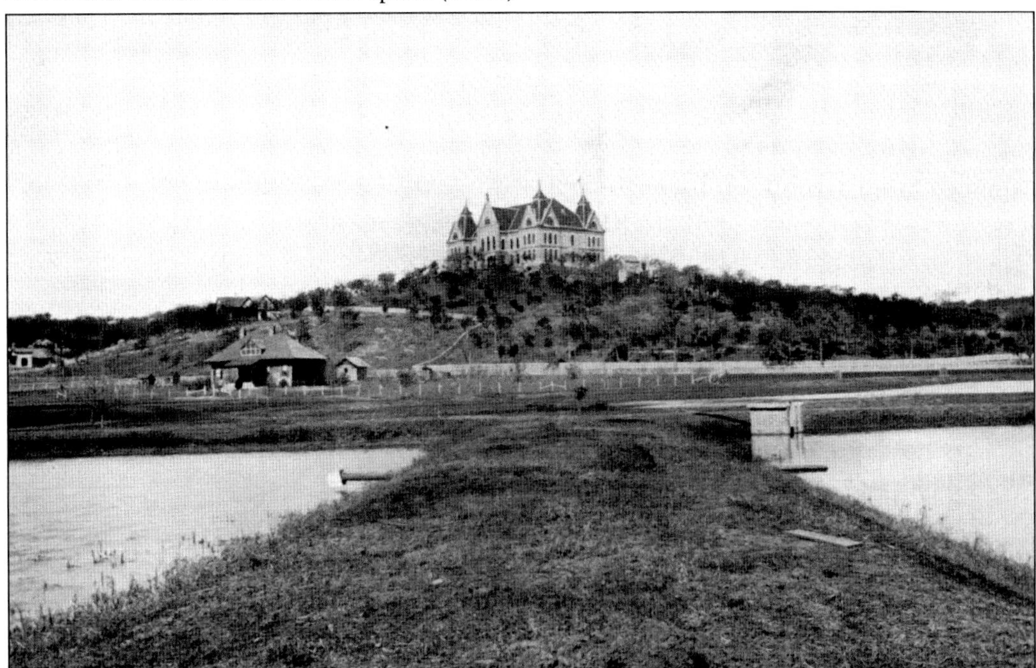

Old Main and Fish Hatchery Ponds. This view of Old Main atop Chautauqua Hill from around 1908–1910 illustrates how the building stands out as a prominent landmark in the San Marcos community. The ponds in the foreground were part of the US Fish and Wildlife Service's Fish Hatchery, long a part of the early San Marcos landscape. The ponds are now decorative portions of the university campus, and the fish hatchery has moved to the outskirts of town. (TxSt.)

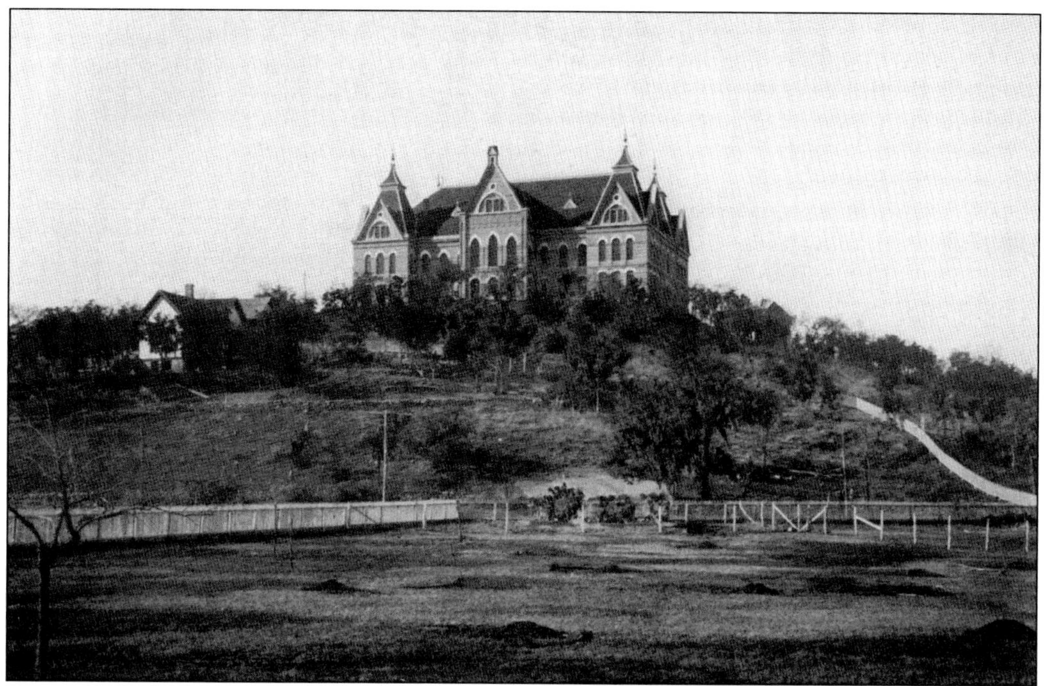

Old Main atop Chautauqua Hill, 1904. This photograph, published in the *Pedagogue*, provides a closer view of Old Main than the previous image. The house at center left is long gone, as are the fences and fields. These areas now support active parts of the university campus. The trees on the slope beneath the building have grown much larger and denser over the past 100 years. (TxSt.)

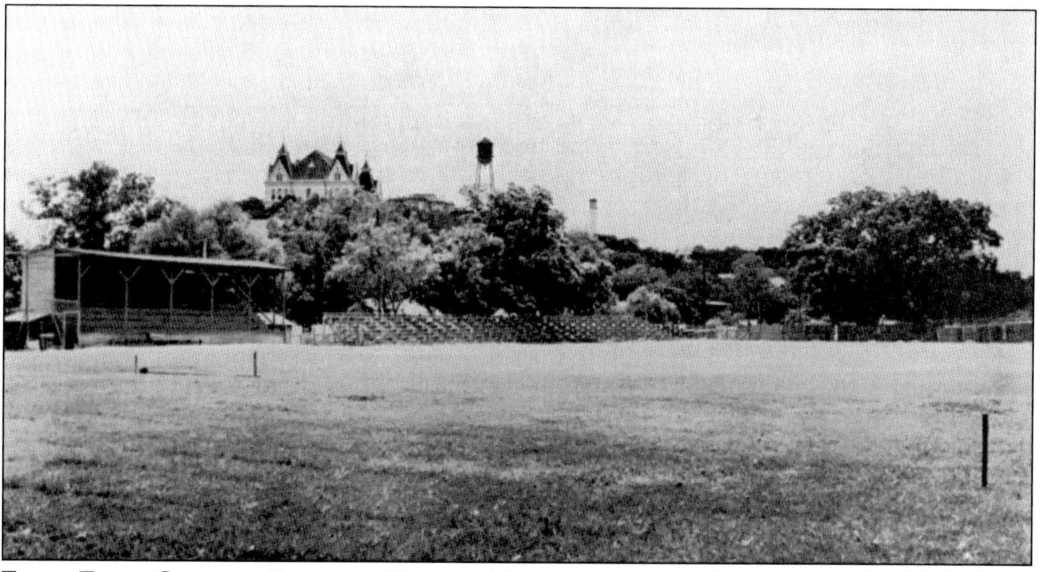

Evans Field, Original Football Field of Normal School. This view of Evans Field shows Old Main in the distance on Chautauqua Hill. Evans Field was the original football field for the school. In 1919, the school's marching band was formed after the board of regents provided 11 instruments. The band first performed on Evans Field on Thanksgiving Day 1919, when Southwest Texas Normal School played the San Marcos Academy in a football game. Evans Field serves today as the Bobcat Band's practice field. (TxSt.)

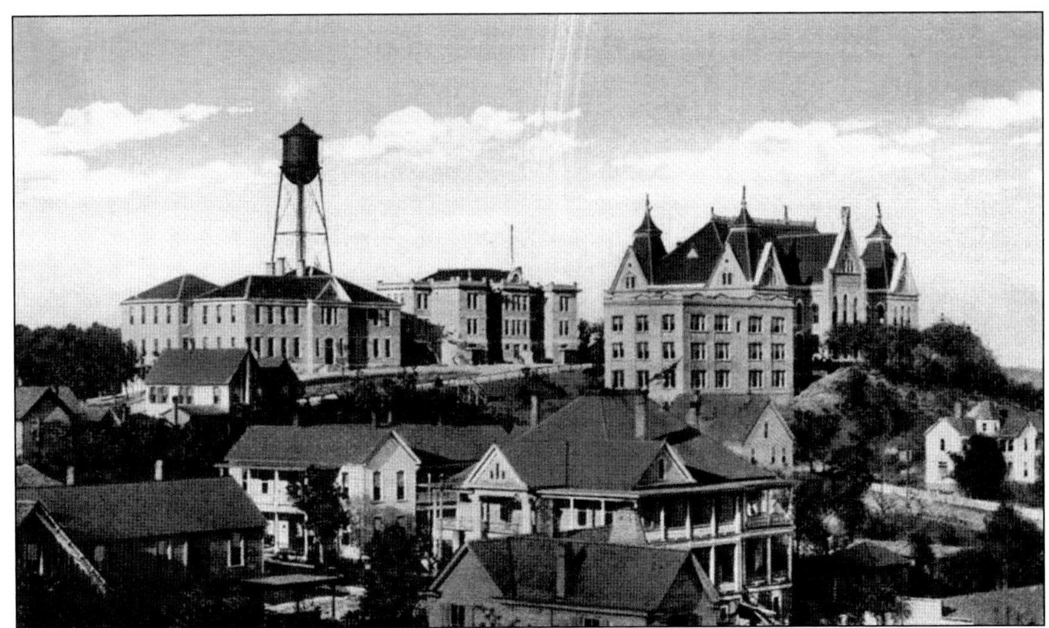

Normal School Expansion, c. 1918. This postcard view depicts how the school was expanding across the top of Chautauqua Hill. The label on the postcard refers to the Southwest Texas Normal School, which was renamed Southwest Texas State Normal College in 1918, indicating the postcard may predate 1918; however, postcard texts are not always accurate. (SMPL.)

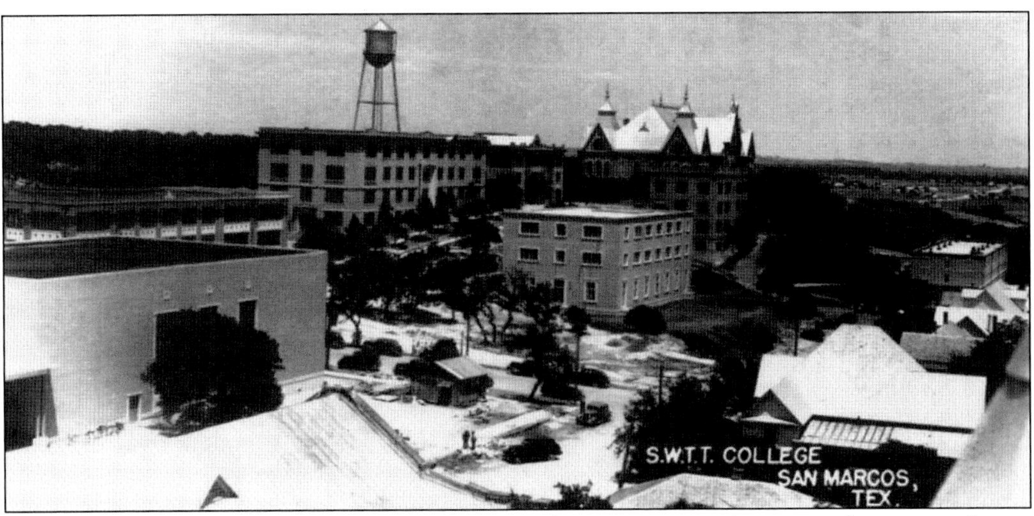

Continued Expansion of Teacher's College. The notation on this view of campus refers to Southwest Texas Teacher's College, a shortened version of the name Southwest Texas State Teacher's College, which was adopted in 1923. Pictured here is an expanding campus with numerous new buildings. The notation in the San Marcos Public Library collection attributes the photograph to the 1940s (with a question mark). (SMPL.)

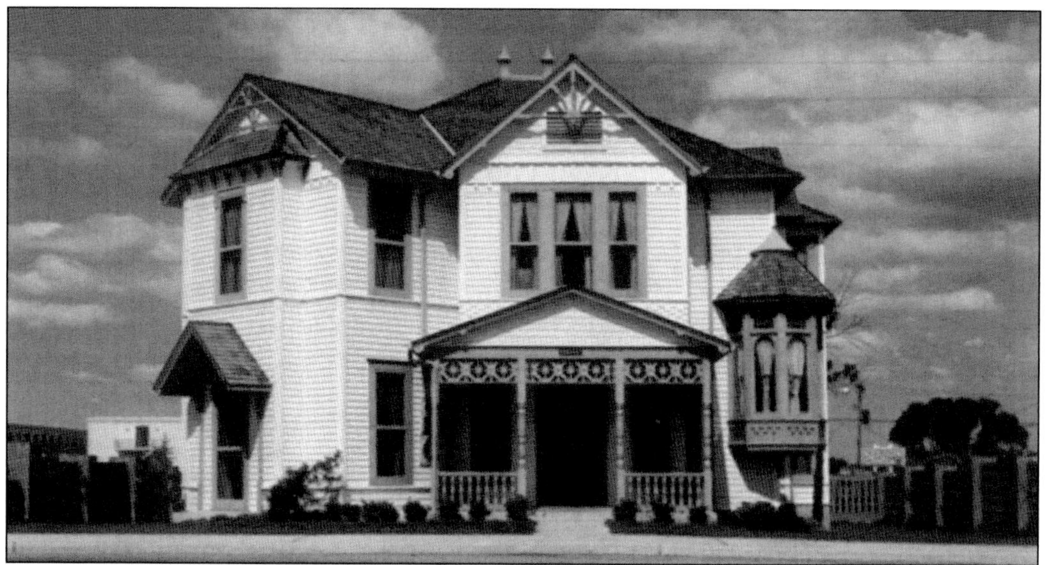

ALUMNI HOUSE ON SOUTH EDGE OF CAMPUS. Alumni House is located on the corner of LBJ and University Drive on the southern edge of campus, where the school gives way to downtown San Marcos. The Victorian-style home was built in 1896 by German craftsman Charles Sinz for the Beverly Hutchison family. The home was relocated from its original location to the Texas State campus sometime in the 1940s–1950s. (SMPL.)

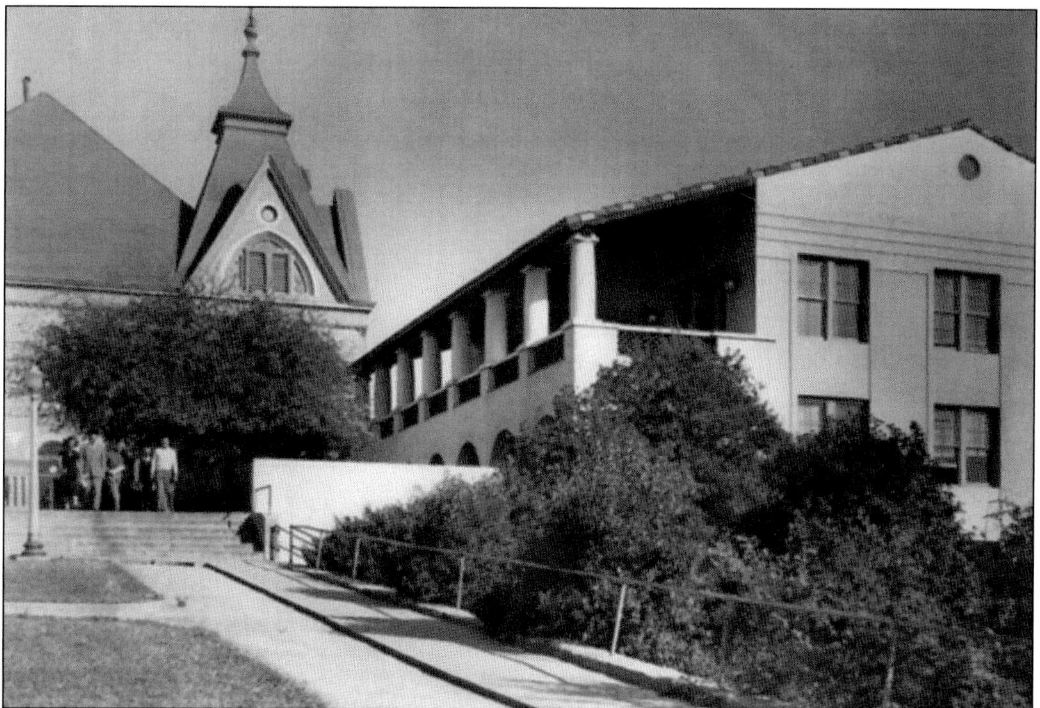

WALKWAY TO OLD MAIN, 1959. This view of Old Main and the adjacent art building features the attractive walkway that leads up to Old Main from the central campus quad. It was in 1959 that the name of the school changed from Southwest Texas State Teachers College to simply Southwest Texas State College, indicating the growth and expansion of its academic missions. (SMPL.)

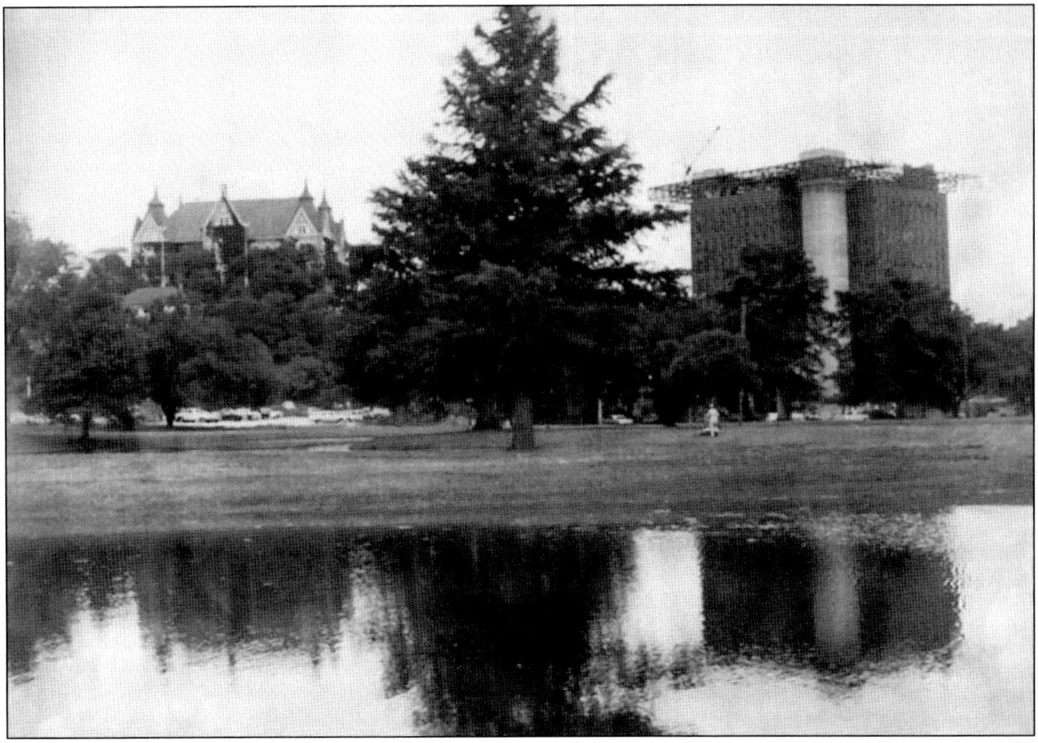

Construction of New Administration Building. Continued growth at the college required the construction of a new administration building and library, the J.C. Kellam Administration Building, shown under construction in this view from 1968. Situated below Chautauqua Hill and Old Main, the J.C. Kellam building (known across campus simply as JCK) opened in 1969 and continues to serve today as the primary administrative headquarters of the school. (SMPL.)

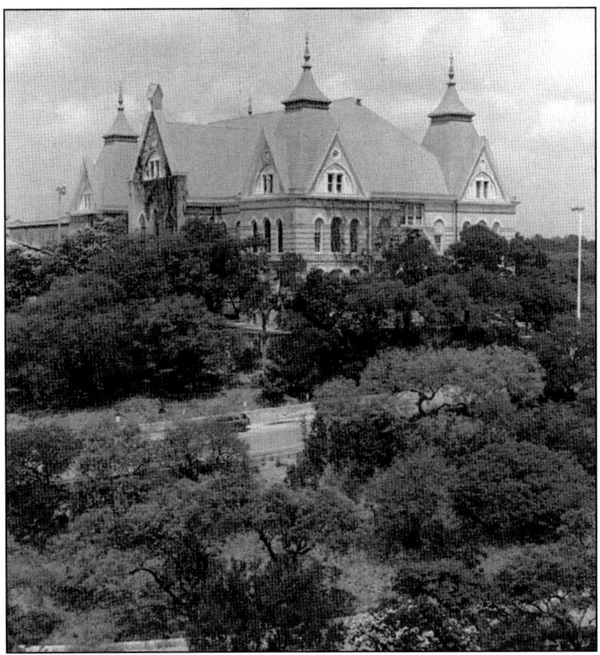

Old Main, 1983. This view of Old Main illustrates the maturing trees across Chautauqua Hill. By this time, the college had become a university, renamed Southwest Texas State University in 1969. Many new master's degree programs and additional undergraduate programs were created during this period of growth. (SMPL.)

J.C. Kellam Administration Building. The completed J.C. Kellam Administration Building, comprising 11 floors, is illustrated in this undated view from the hilltop above, near Old Main. The building houses the offices of the registrar and admission, the graduate college, the offices of the president and the provost, and other high-ranking academic officers of the university. (TxSt.)

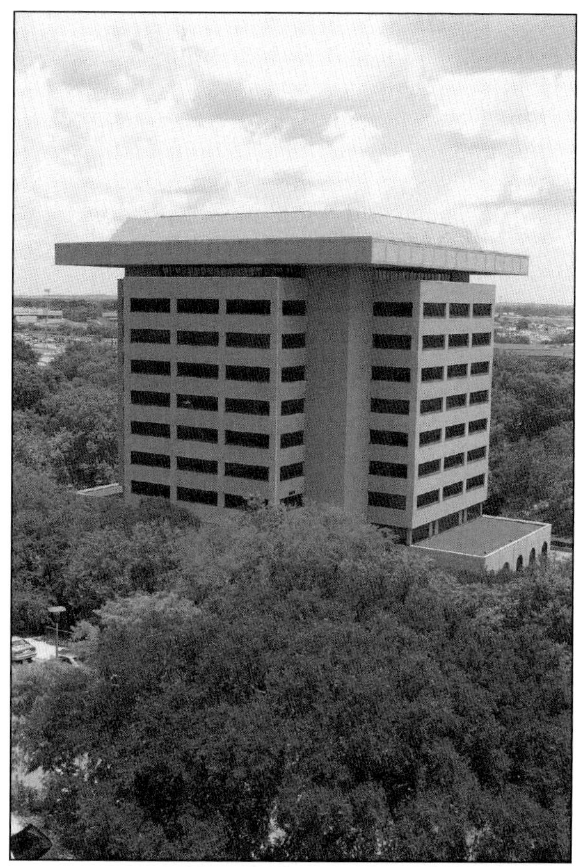

J.C. Kellam Building and Old Fish Hatchery Ponds. Taken from near C.M. Allen Parkway near Sewell Park, this view of the J.C. Kellam Administration Building shows its location relative to the old fish hatchery ponds. JCK is located at the foot of the Balcones Escarpment, which separates the hilly parts of campus (including Old Main, central campus, and west campus) from the flat-lying parts on the Blackland Prairie east side of campus. (TxSt.)

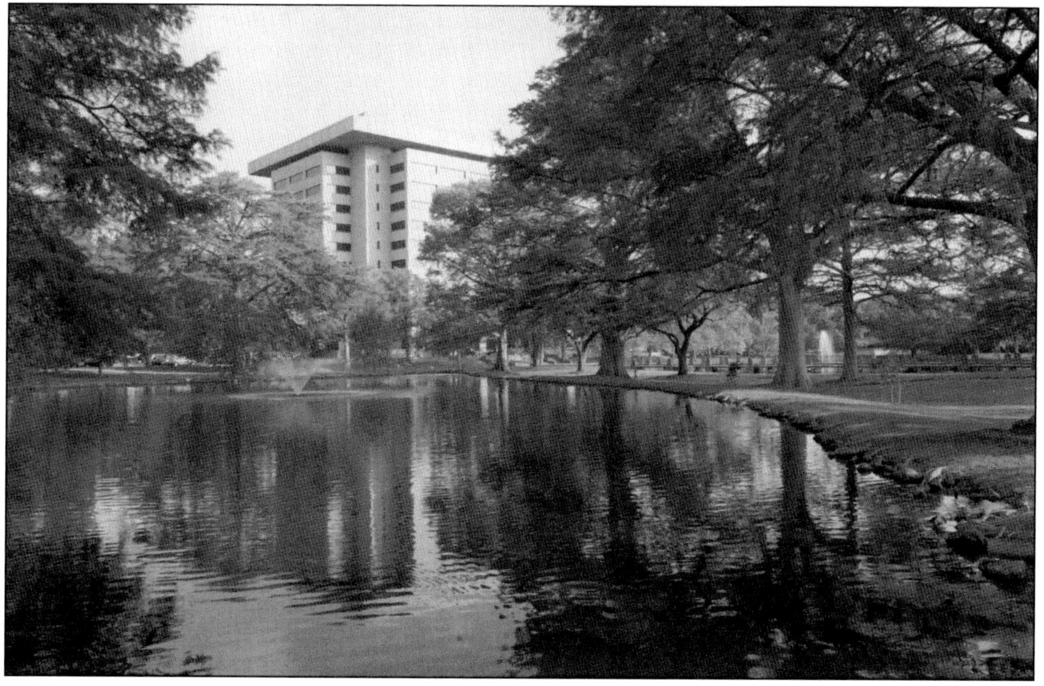

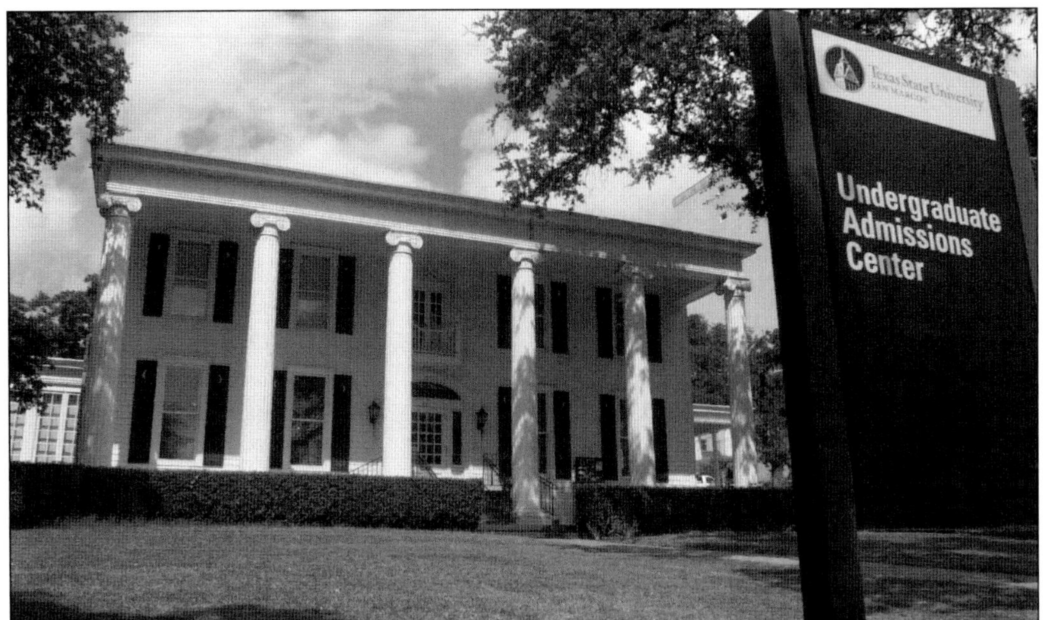

UNDERGRADUATE ADMISSIONS CENTER. The undergraduate admissions center, located on North Guadalupe Street immediately north of downtown San Marcos, was established in 1928. It is a classic building that serves as a landmark for visitors to the central part of campus. It is only a short walk from the admissions center to the student center, library, and new undergraduate academic center. (TxSt.)

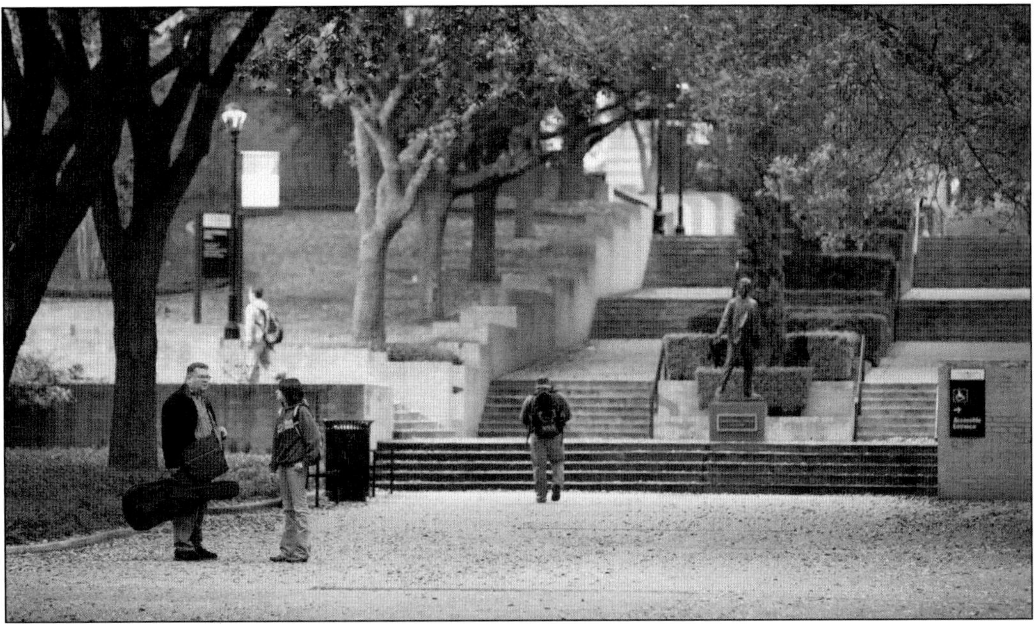

PORTION OF CENTRAL CAMPUS QUAD. The central campus quad, in front of Flowers Hall (home of the College of Liberal Arts, out of sight to the right), is often much busier than in this view looking uphill toward Old Main. The steps in the background lead to one of Old Main's primary entrances. The statue of Lyndon Johnson (see chapter four) is visible at right-center, directly above the lowest set of stairs. (TxSt.)

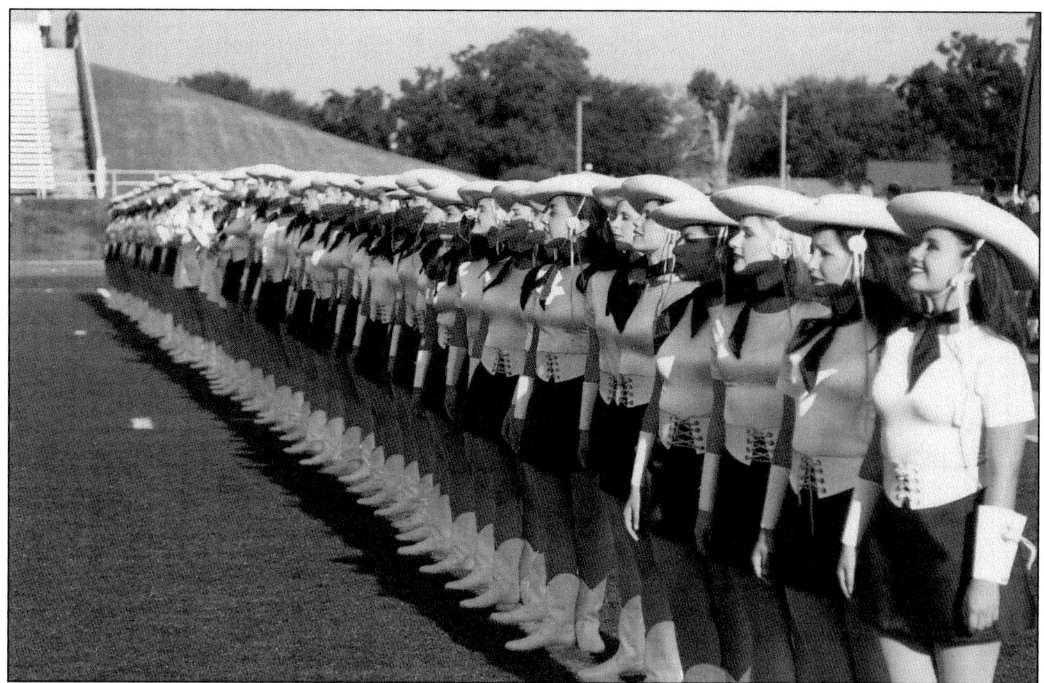

Strutters Dance Team. A tradition for over 50 years, the Texas State Strutters is a dance team founded in 1960 by Barbara Guinn Tidwell. The Strutters perform at home football games and in venues across the country and around the world. They were the first dance team in Texas to be organized on a major university campus. (TxSt.)

Strutters Dance Team with Batons. Since its inception in 1960, the Strutters have performed at numerous NBA and NFL games, on television, in parades such as the Macy's Thanksgiving Day Parade, and in presidential inaugural parades. They have performed in 24 countries around the world and were the first dance team from the United States to perform in the People's Republic of China. There are now over 3,000 Strutters alumnae. (TxSt.)

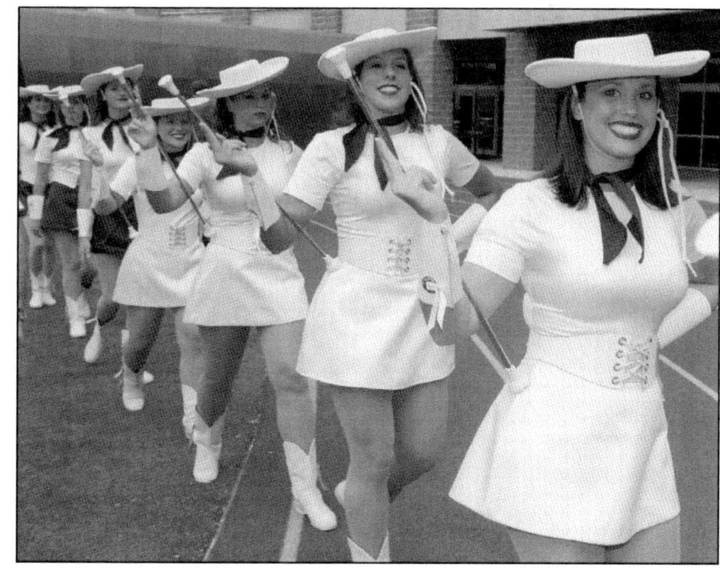

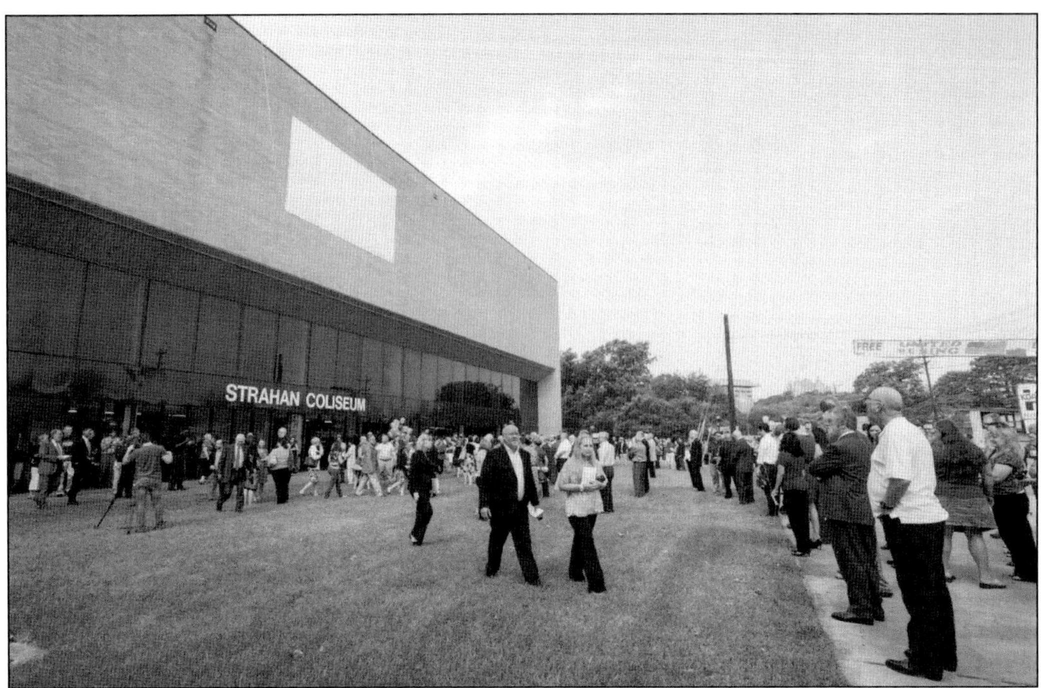

STRAHAN COLISEUM. Strahan Coliseum, the university's home for men and women's basketball and women's volleyball, is a 7,200-seat facility completed in 1982. It is named in honor of Oscar W. Strahan, who coached the first official university basketball team from 1920 to 1924 and again from 1944 to 1946. Strahan Coliseum is also home to the university's graduation ceremonies, held every May, August, and December. (TxSt.)

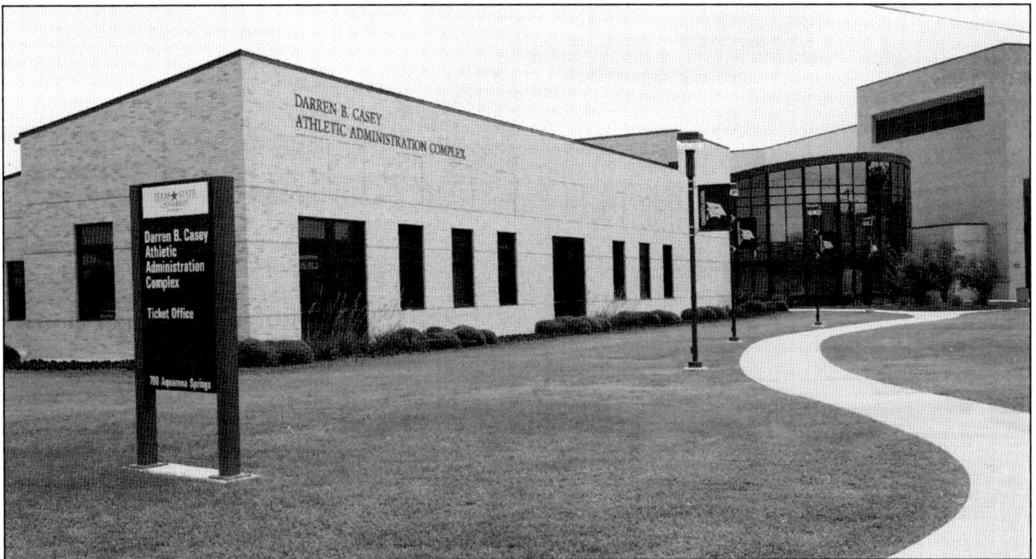

ATHLETIC ADMINISTRATION COMPLEX. The Darren B. Casey Athletic Administration Complex is located immediately adjacent and connected to Strahan Coliseum. The complex, completed in 2002, is home to the athletic department's administrative offices. It is named for Texas State alumnus Darren B. Casey, who made the single largest gift to the athletics department in the university's history. (TxSt.)

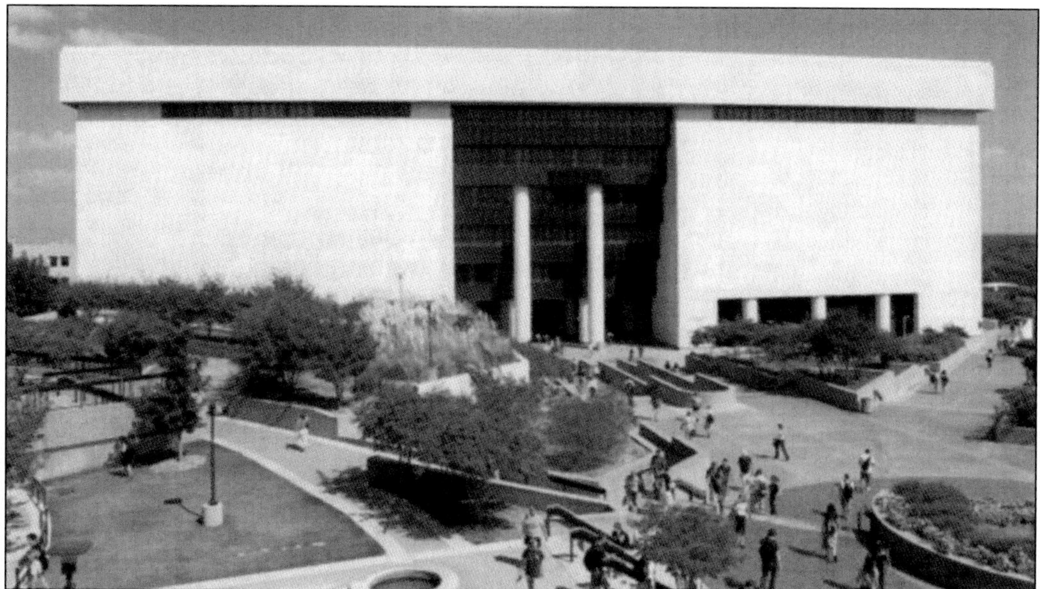

West Face of Alkek Library. The Albert B. Alkek Library opened to students on June 4, 1990. It replaced the old library housed in the J.C. Kellam building and provided twice the shelf space and study area. The library is almost directly in the center of campus. Shown here is the west face of the library, as viewed from the student center. (TxSt.)

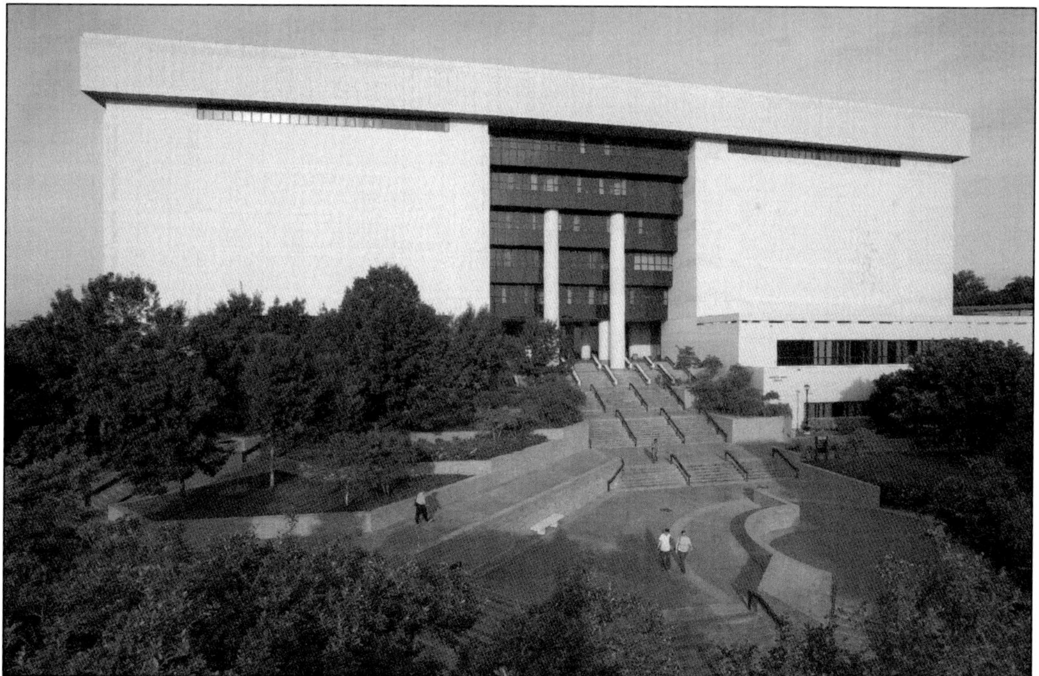

East Face of Alkek Library. The east face of Alkek Library, shown here, is reached via an extensive set of steps sometimes referred to by students, tongue-in-cheek, as the Mayan temple steps. The library currently has over 1.5 million printed volumes, access to more than 110,000 electronic journals, more than half a million e-books, 471 databases, and over two million microform and audio-visual materials. (TxSt.)

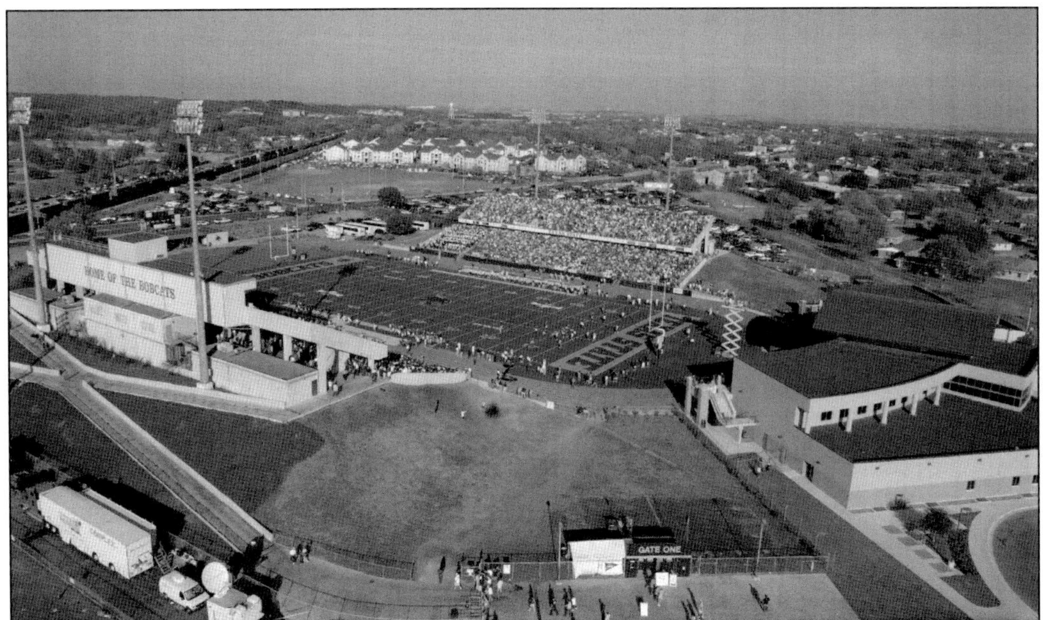

BOBCAT STADIUM, HOME OF THE BOBCATS. Bobcat Stadium was built in 1981 and is home to the Texas State Bobcats football team. Its capacity when constructed was approximately 16,000 seats, in a configuration similar to what is shown here, but without the end zone complex on the south (right, as seen here) side of the stadium that was completed and dedicated in 2002. The football operations of the university athletics program are housed in the end zone complex. (TxSt.)

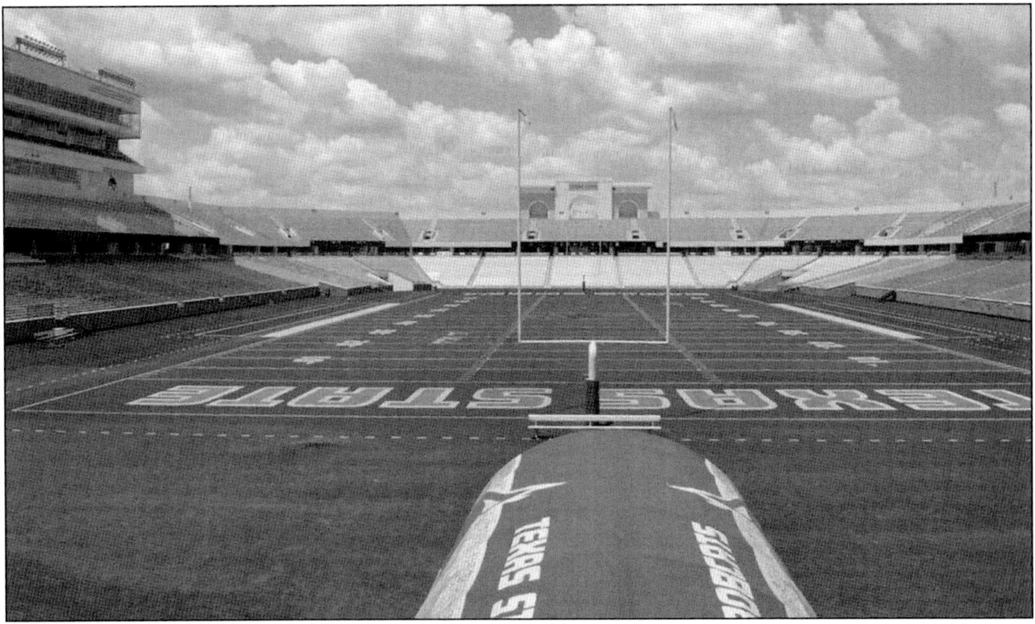

EXPANDED BOBCAT STADIUM SEATS 30,000. Texas State University made the transition from Division 1-AA (FCS) to Division 1-A (FBS) football in 2011. As part of the step up into the highest level of university football, Bobcat Stadium was expanded to a seating capacity of 30,000 with the addition of the Jerry D. and Linda Gregg Fields West Side Complex and the North Side Complex, both of which are shown in this view of the stadium from ground level looking north. (TxSt.)

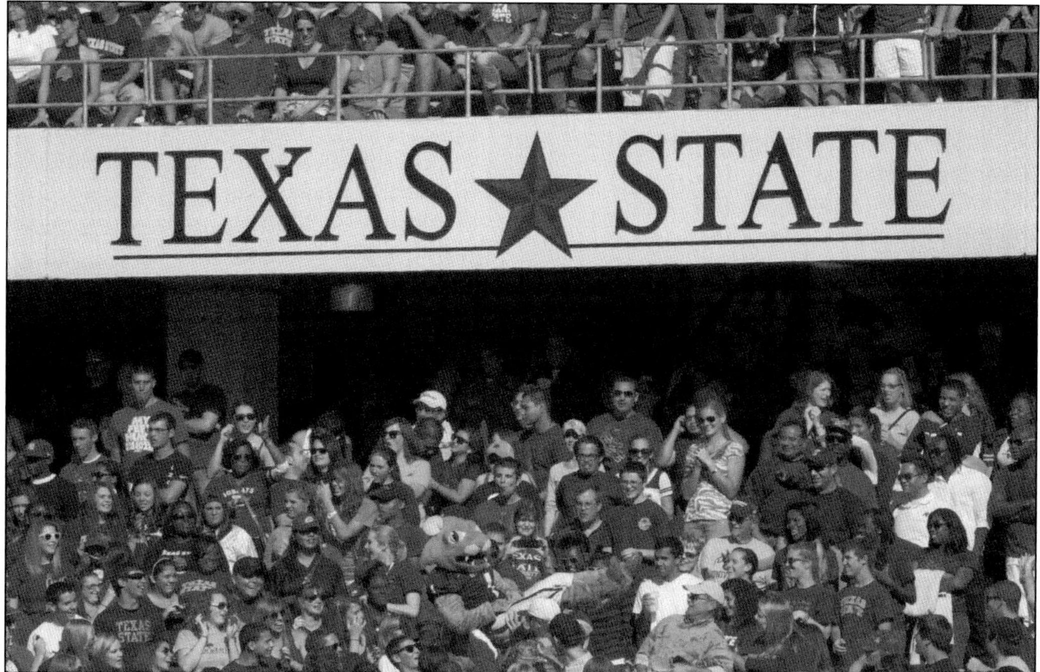

Student Section During Football Game. The university mascot, Boko the Bobcat, is shown crowd-surfing at a sold-out Texas State football game in Bobcat Stadium. When Texas State moved up to Division 1-A (FBS), it spent 2011 in the Western Athletic Conference and joined the Sun Belt Conference in 2012. In September 2012, the remodeled stadium hosted its largest crowd ever, with more than 33,000 spectators watching the Bobcats play Texas Tech University from the Big XII Conference. (TxSt.)

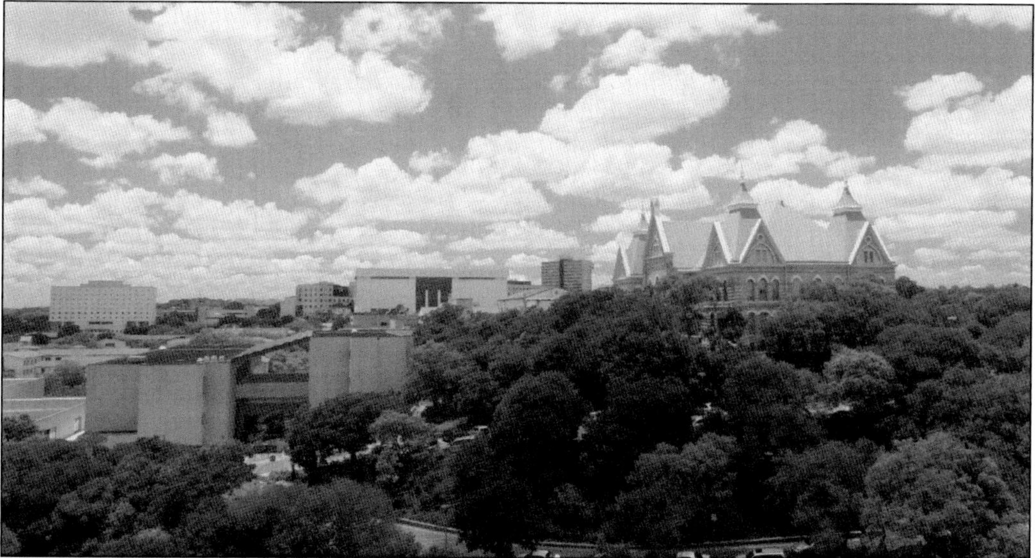

View of Campus from J.C. Kellam Building. A 21st-century view west from the top of the J.C. Kellam Building reveals an attractively landscaped campus that now serves over 36,000 students. Old Main dominates the view on the right, and the Alkek Library is near center. Downtown San Marcos, out of sight, is immediately to the south (left) of campus as seen here. (TxSt.)

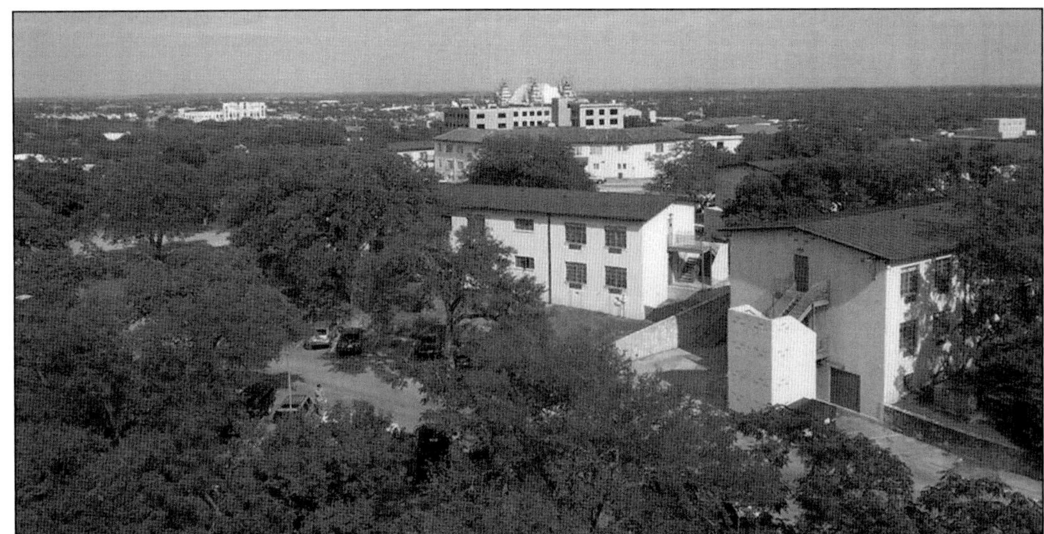

Campus View from Old Main. Looking northeast from near the ground floor of Old Main, low campus buildings built between the 1930s and 1950s are visible, and Bobcat Stadium is in the left-center distance. The numerous trees on campus, many of them live oaks that are green nearly year-round, make the campus a particularly attractive location. The trees also can provide welcome shade from the heat of a Texas summer afternoon. (Will Butler.)

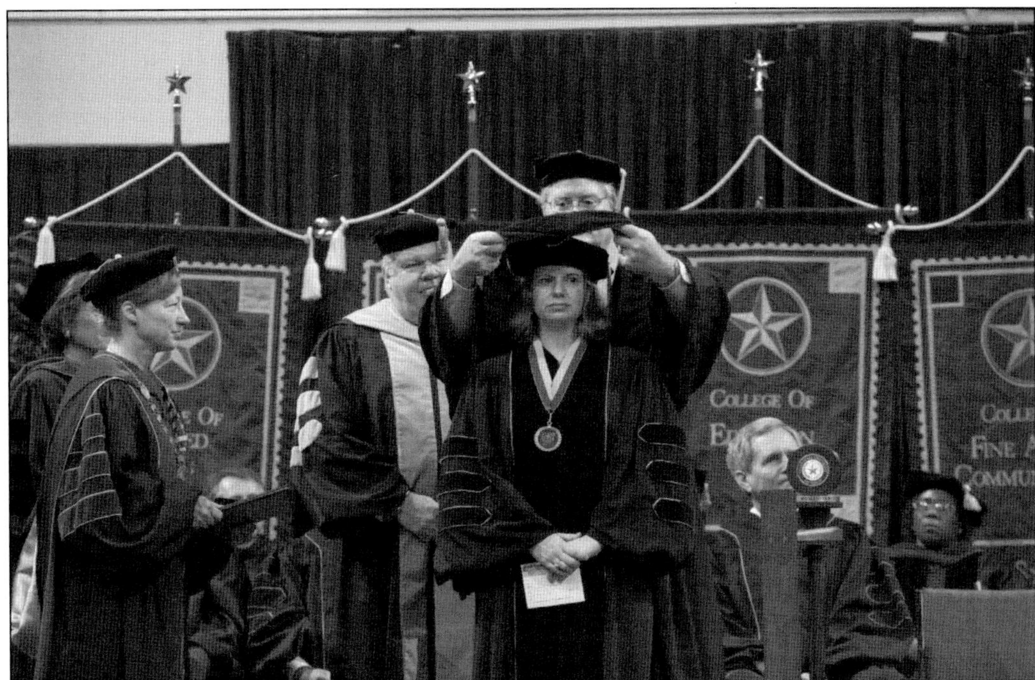

Doctoral Hooding Ceremony in Strahan Coliseum. As part of the growth of Texas State University, doctoral programs have become an integral part of the school's move to its current status as an emerging research university. Doctoral hooding ceremonies such as the one shown here are a key part of graduation exercises. Prof. David R. Butler is hooding Dr. Carol Sawyer in this December 2007 graduation, while university president Dr. Denise Trauth (left) and graduate dean Dr. Michael Willoughby look on. (TxSt.)

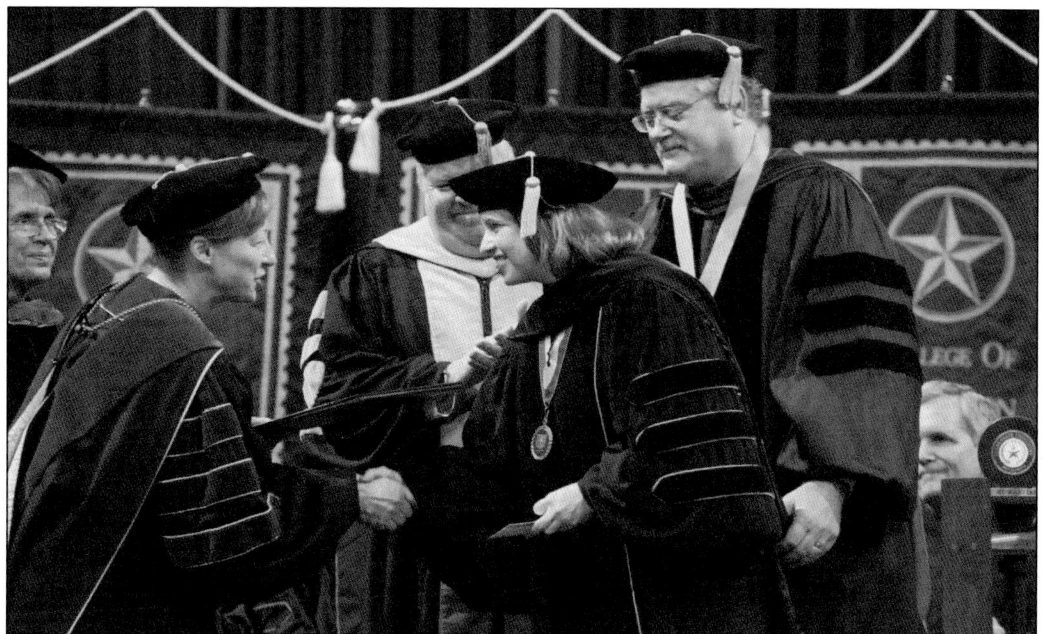

University President Congratulates Doctoral Recipient. University president Dr. Denise Trauth congratulates newly hooded Dr. Carol Sawyer, recipient of a doctorate in environmental geography at the December 2007 commencement ceremony. Looking on are dean of liberal arts Dr. Ann Marie Ellis, graduate dean Dr. Michael Willoughby, and Dr. Sawyer's doctoral advisor, Dr. David Butler. (TxSt.)

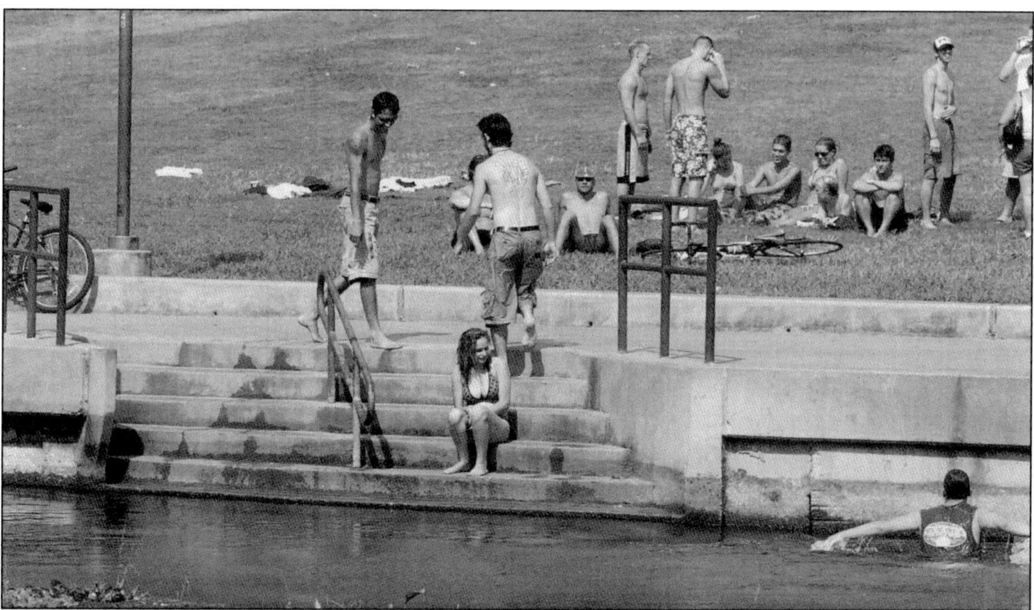

Students at Strahan Beach. The quality of life for students at Texas State University is frequently noted as being very high. In addition to access to a major university, students have the opportunity to take advantage of the university's location astride the San Marcos River (see chapter five). The river, a constant 72 degrees, draws many students to Strahan Beach, the grassy slope between Strahan Coliseum (out of sight at upper right) and the river below. (TxSt.)

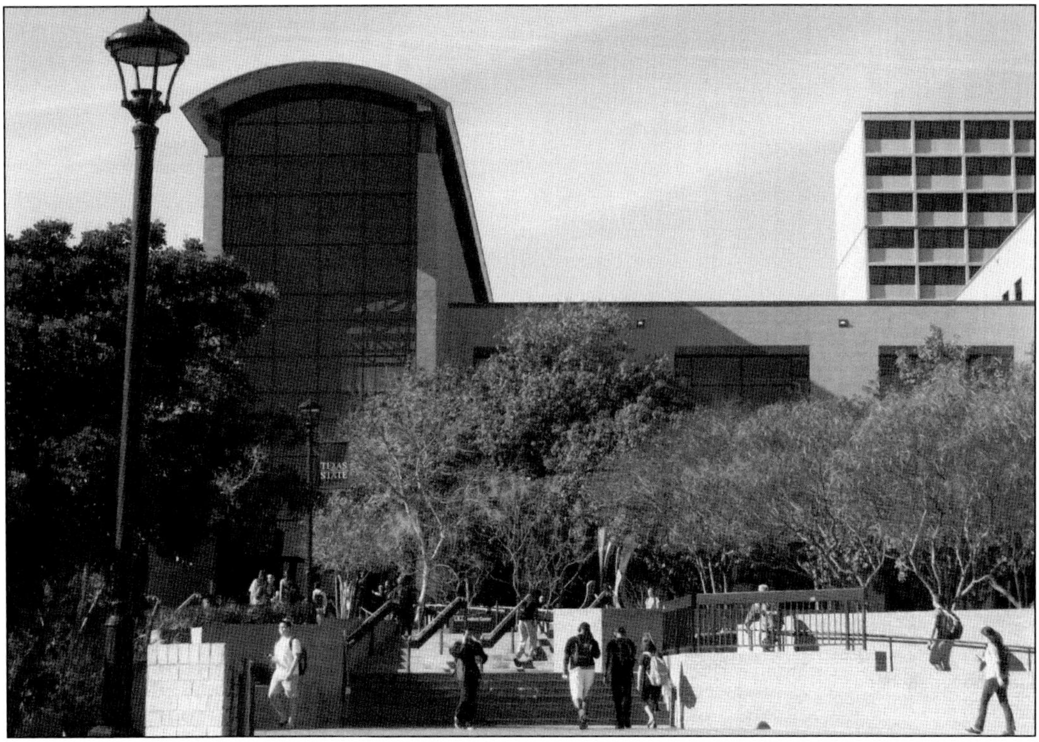

East Entrance, LBJ Student Center. The LBJ Student Center, opened in 1998, is named after former US president Lyndon B. Johnson (see chapter four). It is located near the center of campus west of Alkek Library. It is the newest location and structure housing the student center, with past student centers in a variety of places on campus, including the Lampasas Building in the 1950s and the Nueces Building starting in 1962. (TxSt.)

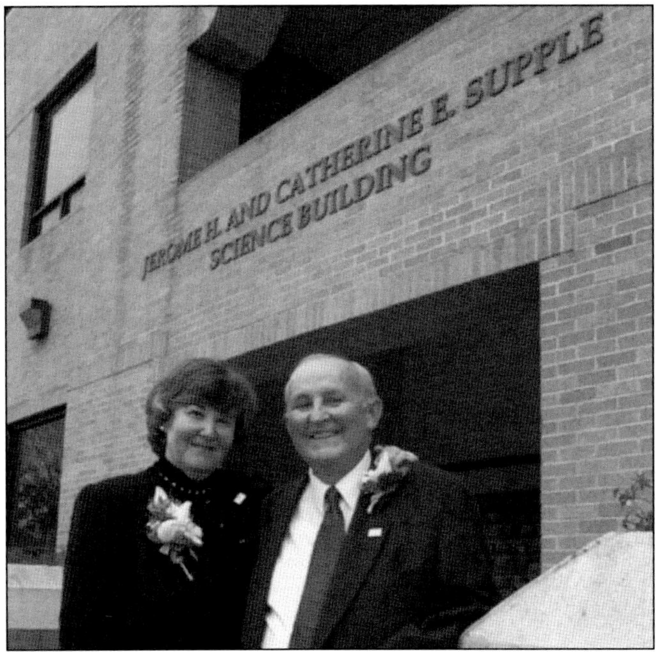

Supple Science Building Renaming Ceremony. The Jerome H. and Catherine E. Supple Science Building, established in 1991, was rededicated and renamed in 2003 after university president Jerome Supple and his wife, Catherine, shown here at the renaming ceremony. Dr. Supple was president of Texas State University from 1989 to 2002, during which time he oversaw the creation of university doctoral programs and the opening of numerous new campus buildings. (TxSt.)

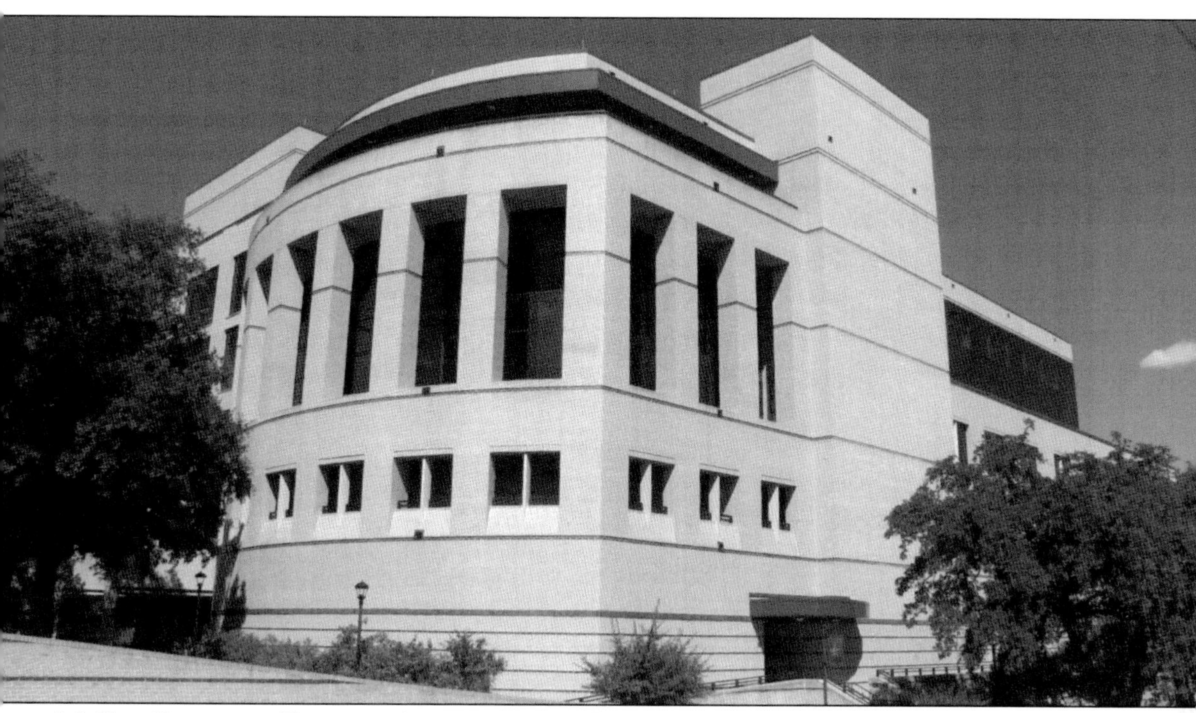

McCoy College of Business Administration Building. Texas State established its business school in 1968, and it was housed in Derrick Hall for many years. Local businessman Emmett McCoy and his wife, Miriam, donated $20 million for the construction of a new business college building. Named after the McCoys, the McCoy College of Business Administration building was opened and dedicated in 2006.

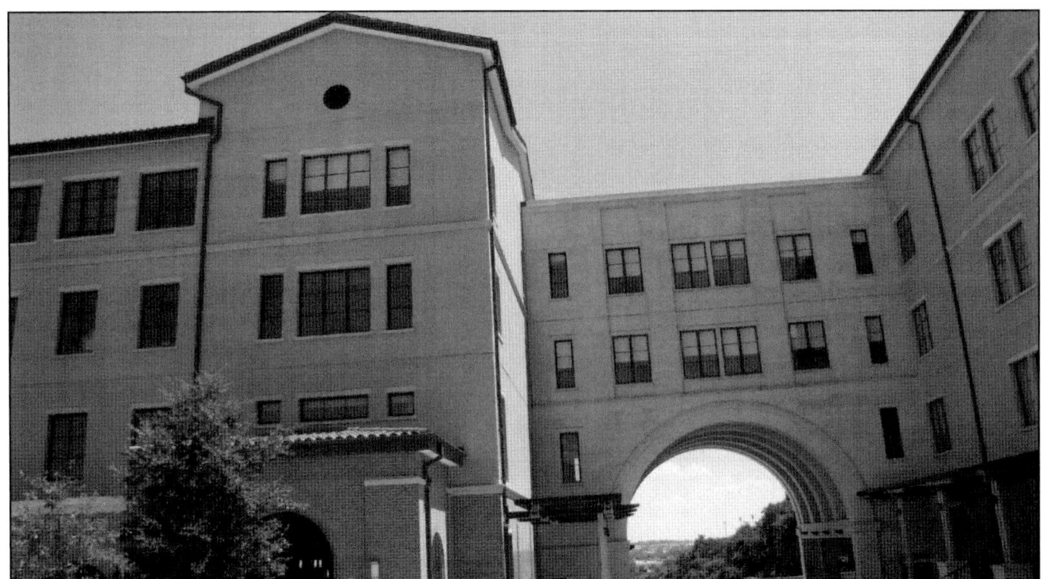

New Undergraduate Academic Center. Opened in 2013, the new undergraduate academic center houses University College, the Personalized Academic and Career Exploration (PACE) Center, and the Departments of Political Science, Psychology, and Sociology. The PACE Center provides freshman advising, mentoring, academic coaching, and career exploration. University College is home to the university's bachelor of general studies and university seminar programs.

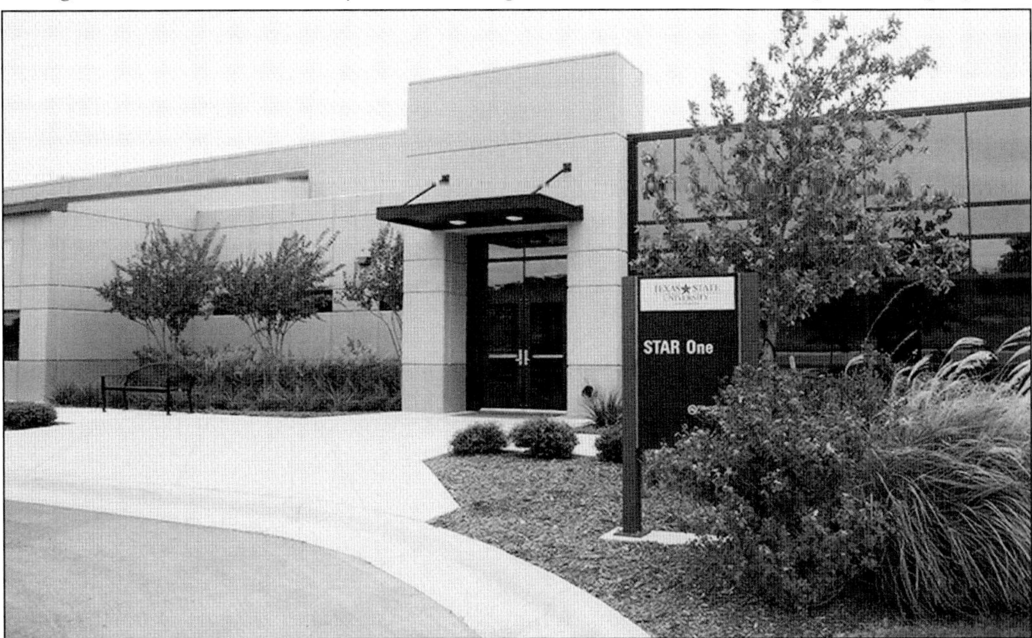

STAR One Building at University STAR Park. The newest initiative of Texas State University, STAR (Science, Technology and Advanced Research) Park is a 38-acre research park about five miles south of the main campus on Hunter Road. The first building in STAR Park is STAR One, shown here, a 20,000-square-foot facility opened in November 2012 and used as a technology incubator for early-stage businesses and collaboration space for joint research and development with industry. (TxSt.)

Four

San Marcos's Most Famous Citizen LBJ

Only one institution of higher learning in the state of Texas can boast of having a president of the United States as an alumnus, and that school is the present-day Texas State University in San Marcos. Lyndon Baines Johnson (famously known by his initials, LBJ) enrolled in what was then known as the Southwest Texas State Teachers College in 1927. While in college in San Marcos, LBJ participated in campus politics and was a standout member of the debate team. He also wrote for the *College Star*, the campus newspaper. During 1928–1929, LBJ paused from his studies to teach Hispanic students in Cotulla, Texas, south of San Antonio. Working with students from poor backgrounds, Johnson developed a lifelong commitment to enhancing educational opportunities for all citizens. This commitment was exemplified by his returning to Southwest Texas State College as president in 1965 to sign the Higher Education Act, a piece of legislation providing funding opportunities for disadvantaged students.

After leaving college, LBJ entered politics but returned to San Marcos during elections and as vice president, president, and former president. In 1962, Vice President Johnson was honored with the first honorary doctoral degree ever offered by Southwest Texas State College, receiving an honorary doctor of laws degree. As president, Johnson visited San Marcos several times, including a visit to the Gary Job Corps center in San Marcos in 1965. The job corps was a central piece of Johnson's War on Poverty. Johnson also visited his alma mater during homecoming and graduation activities during and after his presidency.

The LBJ Student Center on campus is named after Johnson, the most famous alumnus of Texas State University. A statue of Johnson as a young student occupies a central position in front of the College of Liberal Arts building on campus. In the city of San Marcos, the former Austin Street was renamed LBJ Drive in Johnson's honor. In late 2006, the LBJ Museum of San Marcos opened on Guadalupe Street on the courthouse square. The museum focuses on Johnson's student days and his efforts as president to expand educational opportunities for all Americans.

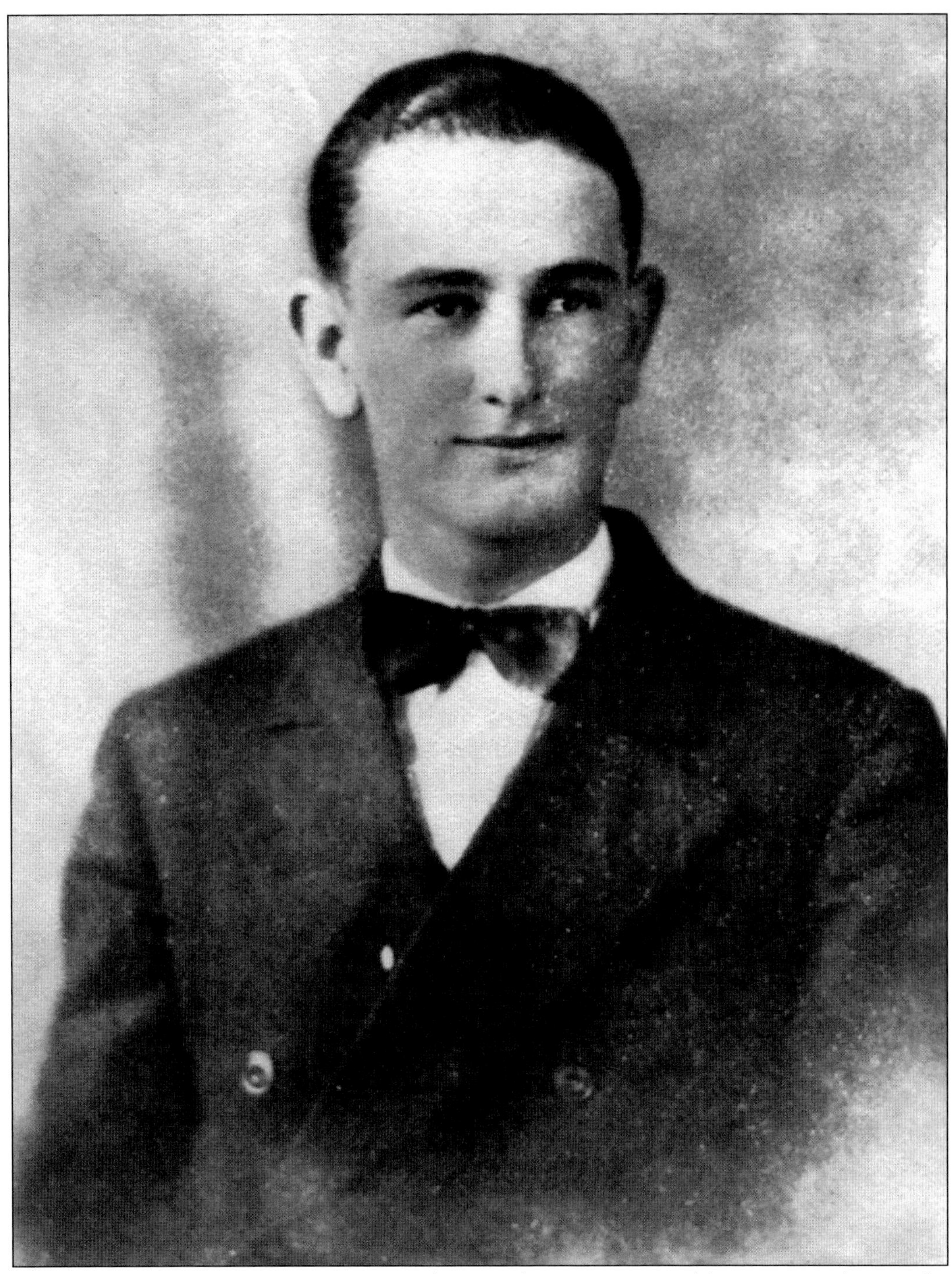

LBJ as a College Student. Young Lyndon B. Johnson is pictured here as a student at the Southwest Texas State Teachers College. Johnson was 19 years old when he enrolled in 1927, hitchhiking from Johnson City to San Marcos. (LBJSM).

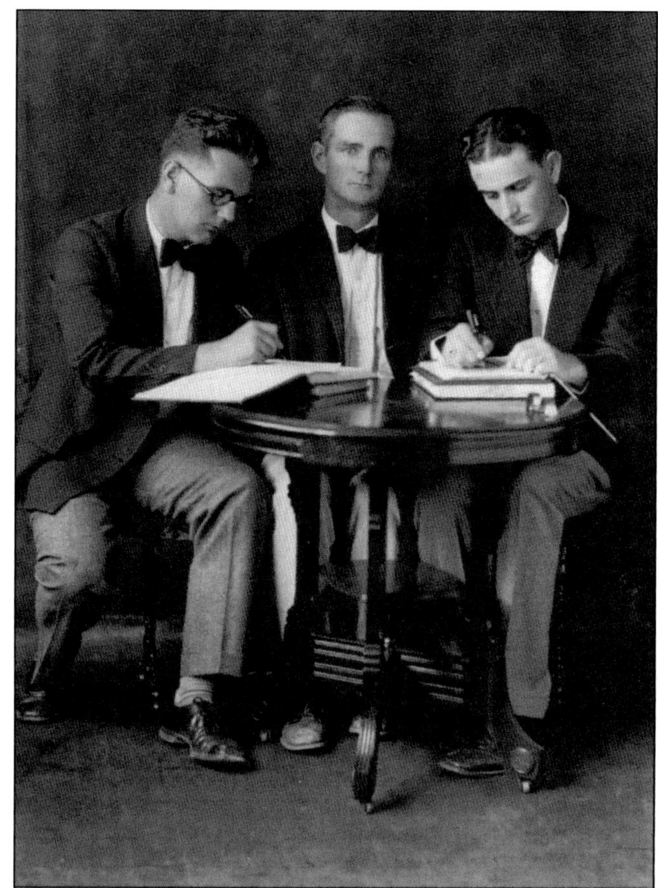

LBJ and the College Debate Team, 1928. Johnson was a member of the debate team at Southwest Texas State Teachers College during a time when intercollegiate debates were more popular campus events than athletics. Pictured here from left to right are fellow student debate team member Elmer Graham, debate coach Prof. Howard Mell Greene, and Johnson. (LBJPL).

Johnson Reunited with 1928 Debate Team. In this undated photograph, Johnson is reunited with the members of his 1928 debate team, Elmer Graham (left) and debate coach Prof. Howard Mell Greene (center) during a visit to San Marcos. (SMPL.)

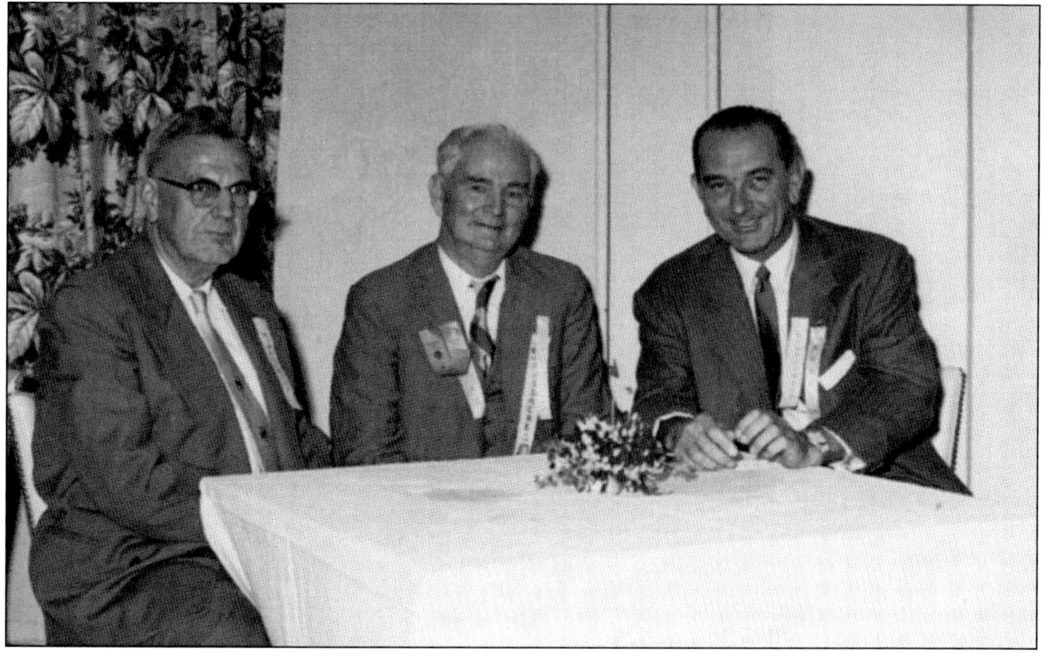

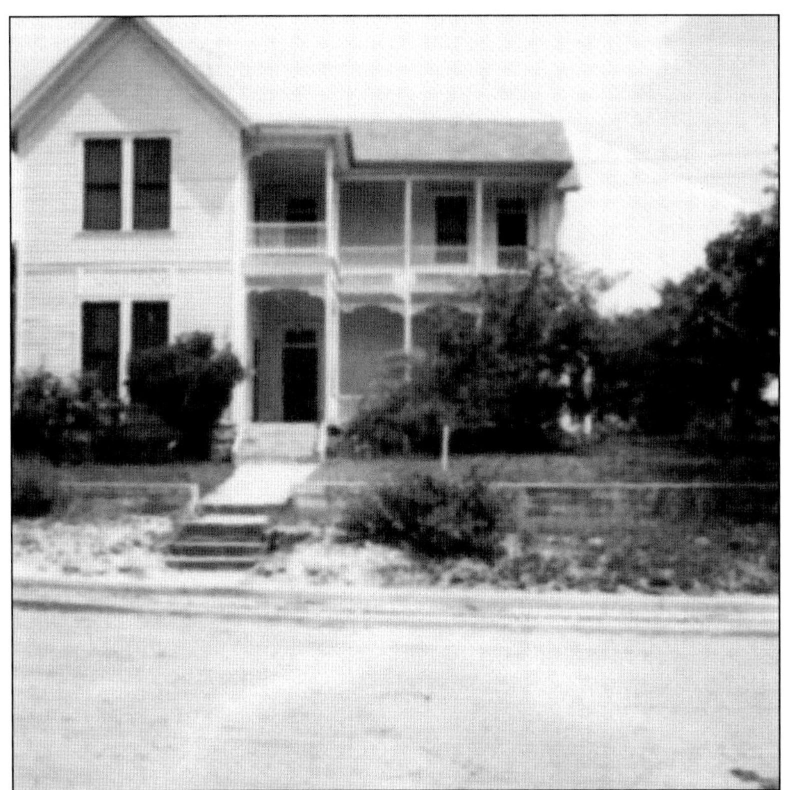

House where LBJ Lived as a Student. Pictured here is the former residence of LBJ on Woods Street in San Marcos, where he lived while a student at Southwest Texas State Teachers College. Johnson graduated from Southwest Texas State Teachers College in 1930 with a bachelor's degree in history. (SMPL.)

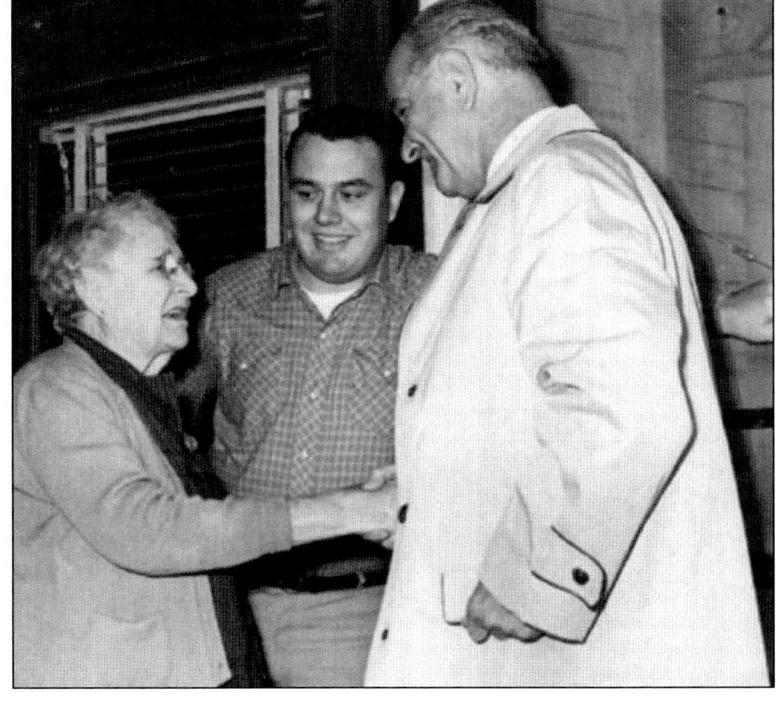

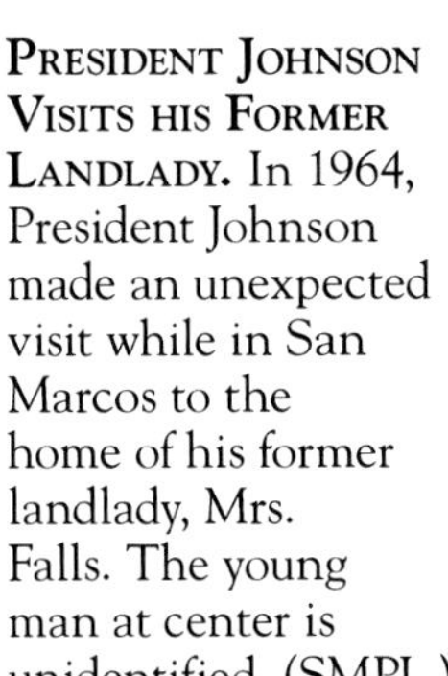

President Johnson Visits his Former Landlady. In 1964, President Johnson made an unexpected visit while in San Marcos to the home of his former landlady, Mrs. Falls. The young man at center is unidentified. (SMPL.)

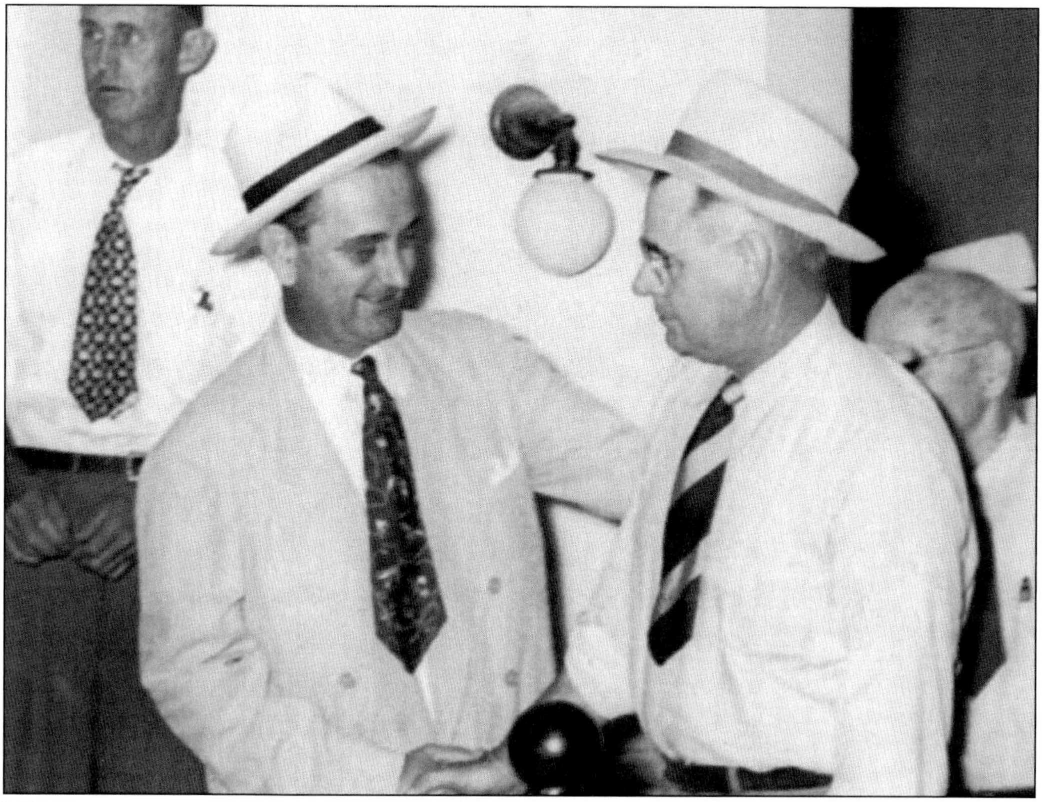

LBJ Campaigns in San Marcos. LBJ was famous for his campaigning abilities. Here he is greeting potential voters in San Marcos during his 1948 senatorial campaign. (SMPL.)

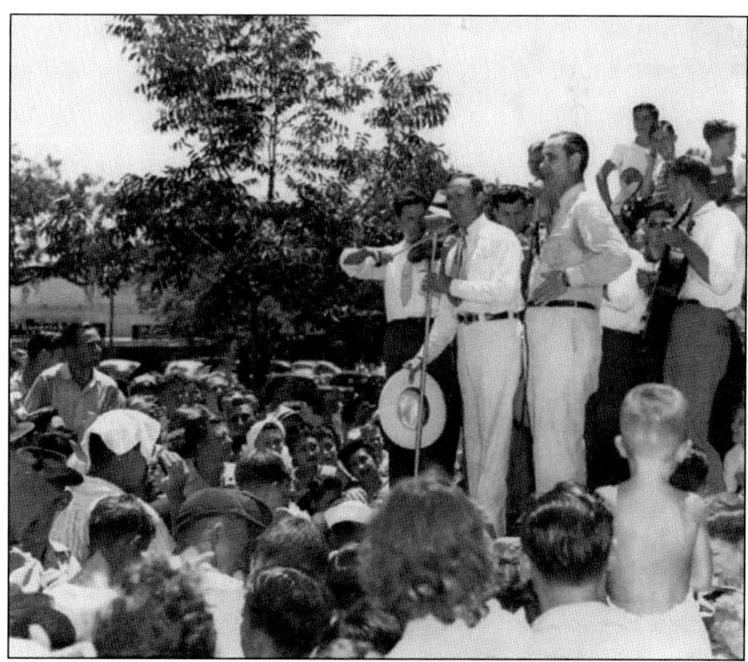

LBJ with Gene Autry in Senate Campaign. Lyndon Johnson visited San Marcos in 1948 as a candidate for the US Senate. He is shown here at a campaign rally complete with cowboy movie star Gene Autry with the white hat and Autry's band of musicians. Although the site of the photograph is unidentified, it appears to be on the central courthouse square in downtown San Marcos. (SMPL.)

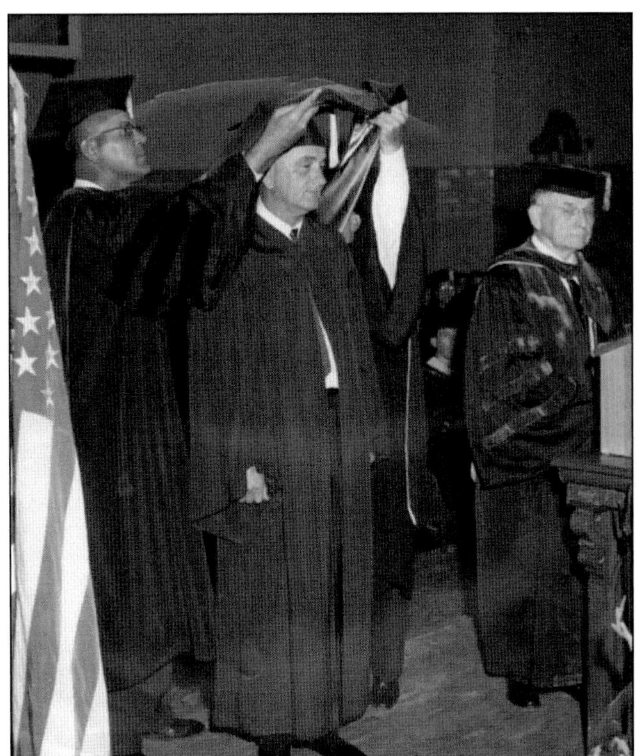

Vice President Johnson Receives Honorary Doctorate. In 1962, then-vice president Lyndon Johnson visited Southwest Texas State College to receive an honorary doctor of laws degree. Johnson was the first individual at what is now Texas State University to receive an honorary doctorate. (SMPL.)

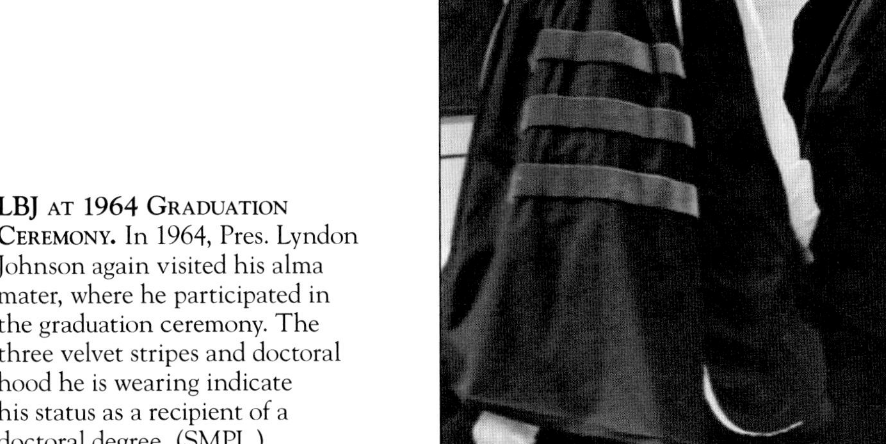

LBJ at 1964 Graduation Ceremony. In 1964, Pres. Lyndon Johnson again visited his alma mater, where he participated in the graduation ceremony. The three velvet stripes and doctoral hood he is wearing indicate his status as a recipient of a doctoral degree. (SMPL.)

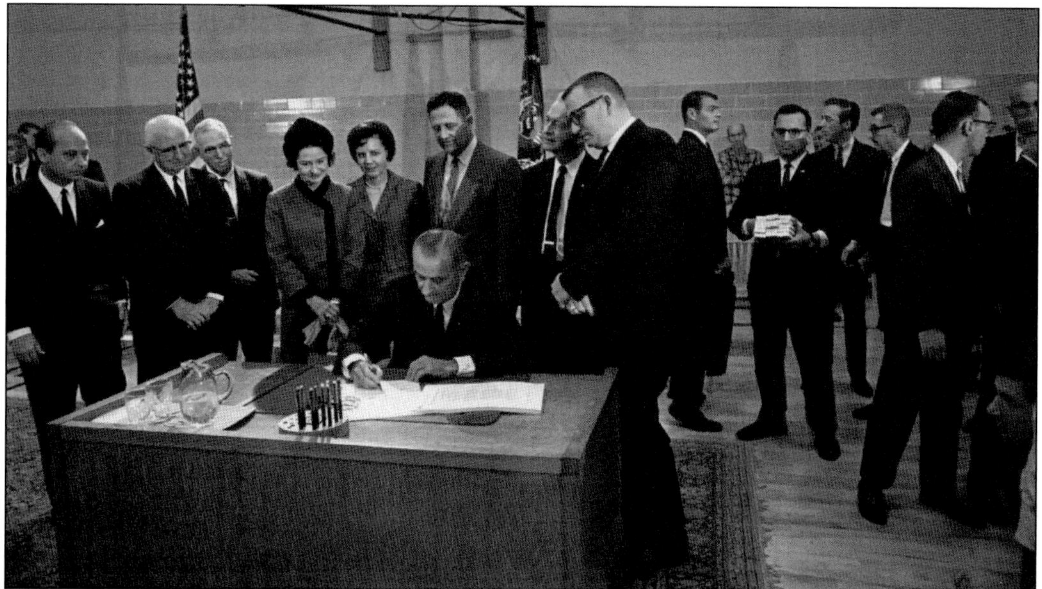

LBJ Signs the Higher Education Act. On November 8, 1965, President Johnson signed the Higher Education Act on the campus of his alma mater, Southwest Texas State College. From left to right behind President Johnson are three unidentified, Lady Bird Johnson, unidentified, Congressman Jake Pickle, Jesse C. Kellam, and James McCrocklin. (LBJPL.)

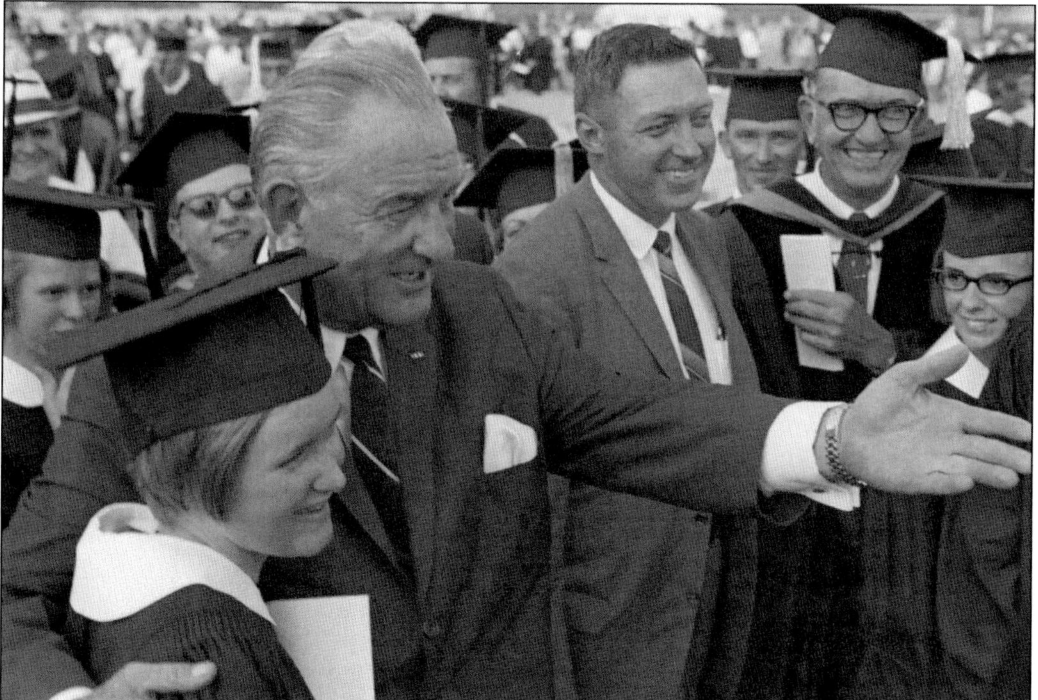

President Johnson Attends 1968 Graduation Ceremony. President Johnson visited Southwest Texas State College and attended the August commencement ceremony in 1968 in San Marcos. He is shown here posing for a photograph with an unidentified female student who was graduating. (TxSt.)

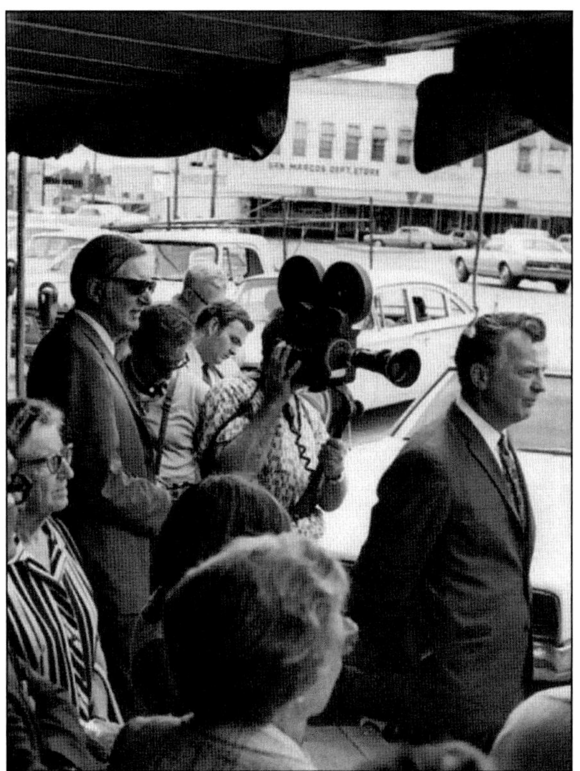

PUBLICITY AND SECURITY DURING PRESIDENTIAL VISIT. A presidential visit like this one in August 1968 entails a great deal of publicity and security. Security and publicity men stand in front of onlookers in downtown San Marcos on the central square during a visit by LBJ. (SMPL.)

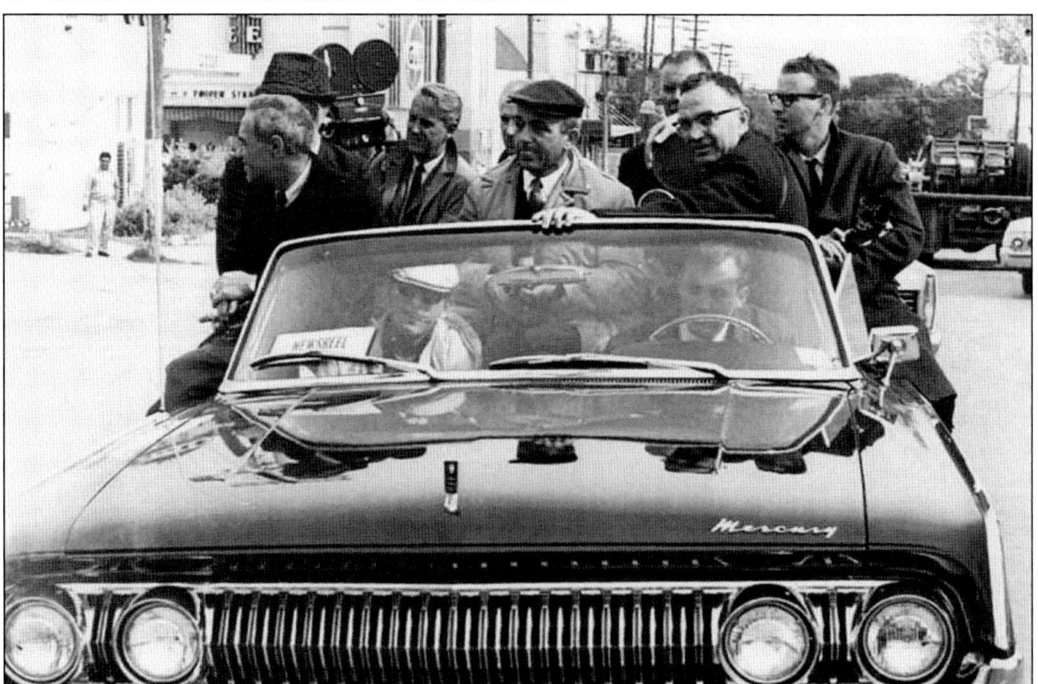

SECURITY AND PUBLICITY IN CROWDED CAR. Presidential security men and cameramen, including one shooting newsreel footage, are crowded into a car during President Johnson's visit to San Marcos in August 1968. (SMPL.)

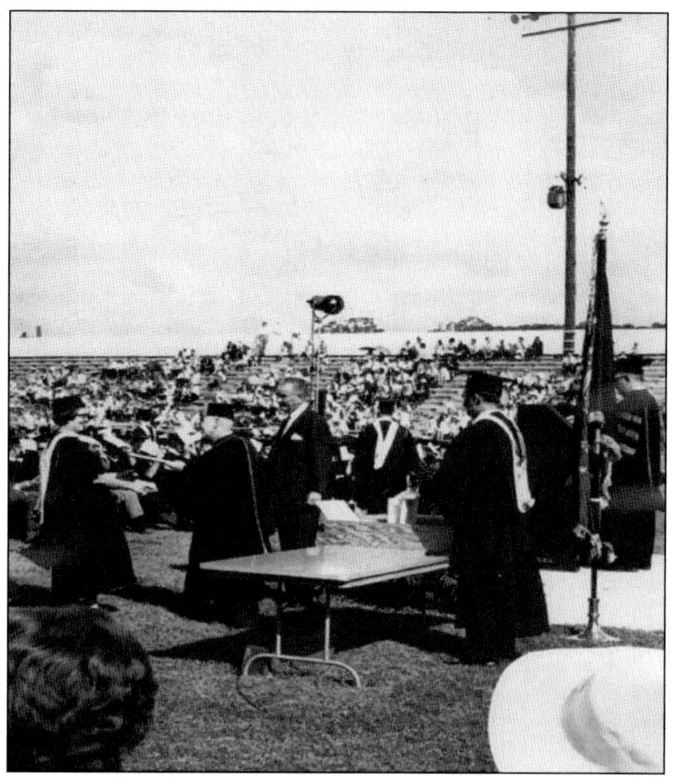

LBJ at 1968 Graduation Ceremony. President Johnson attended the Southwest Texas State College graduation in 1968. The ceremony appears to be located on the football field. Modern graduations take place in the air-conditioned comfort of Strahan Coliseum. (SMPL.)

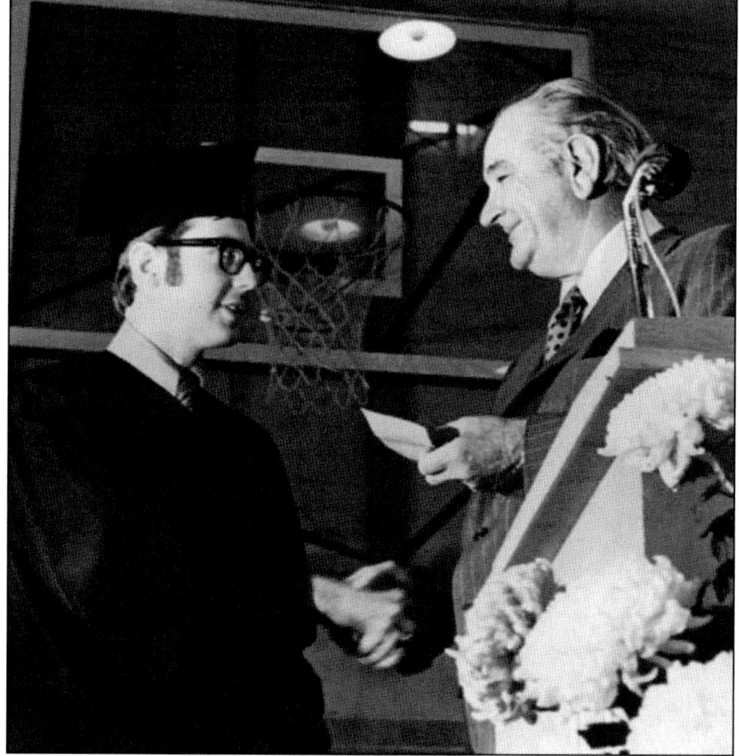

President Johnson Greets College Graduate. In another segment of the 1968 graduation ceremonies at Southwest Texas State College, President Johnson greets an unidentified graduate. The 1968 graduation ceremonies were the last that LBJ took part in while still president; he left office with the inauguration of Pres. Richard Nixon in January 1969. (SMPL.)

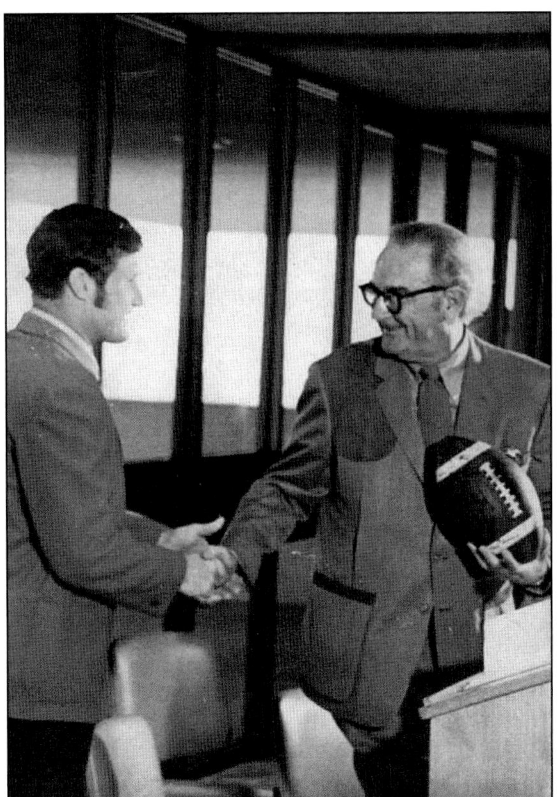

President Johnson Greets Bobcat Athlete. President Johnson shakes hands with an unidentified Southwest Texas State Bobcat athlete in this undated photograph. A big football fan, Johnson occasionally attended games at the nearby University of Texas at Austin stadium after he had left the presidency. (SMPL.)

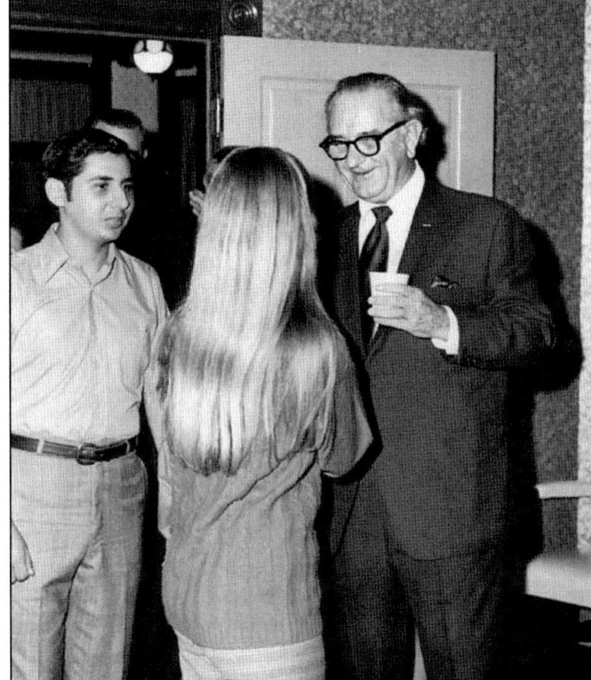

Students Greet President Johnson. LBJ visits with unidentified students during a visit to Southwest Texas State University. Although the photograph is undated, President Johnson's hair length suggests that this photograph was taken after he left the office of the presidency. (SMPL.)

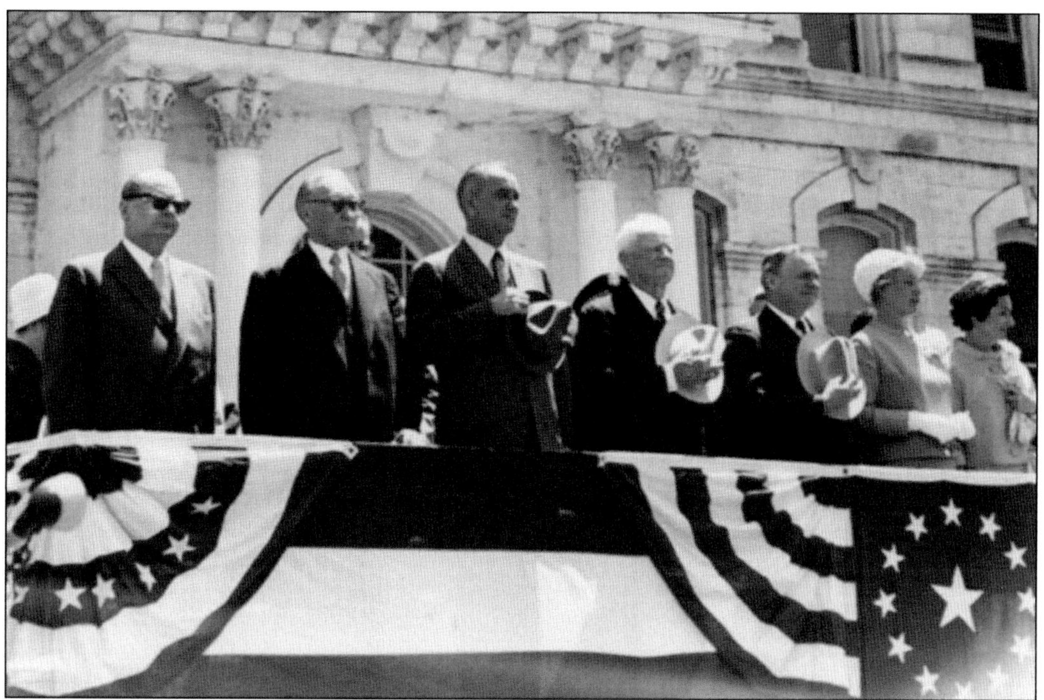

LBJ and First Lady Attend San Marcos Parade. President Johnson and the first lady (at far right) stand with other unidentified people for the passing of the colors during a parade in San Marcos during a visit to campus in 1968. (SMPL.)

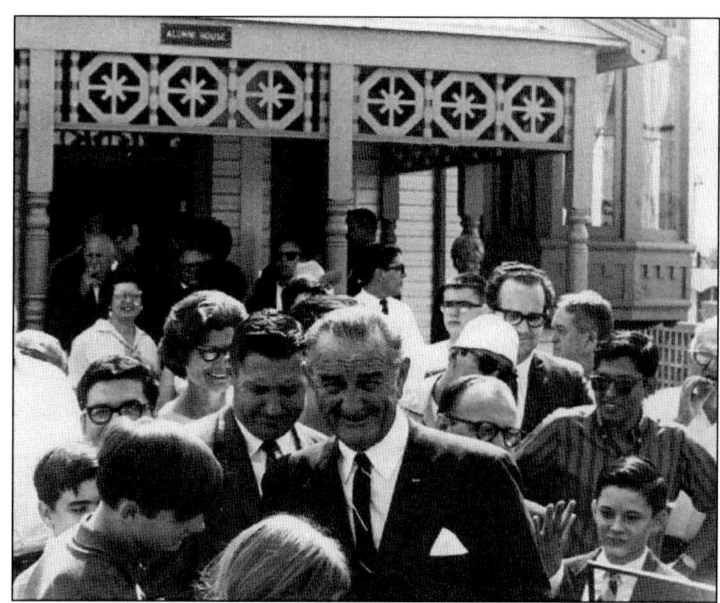

Alumni House Ceremony. LBJ meets the people on the southern edge of Southwest Texas State College outside of Alumni House during the dedication ceremony in 1968. The home was relocated from its original location in San Marcos to the Texas State campus sometime in the 1940s or 1950s. It was recommended to the Texas State Alumni Association by the San Marcos Urban Renewal Agency in 1966 and formally dedicated two years later. (SMPL.)

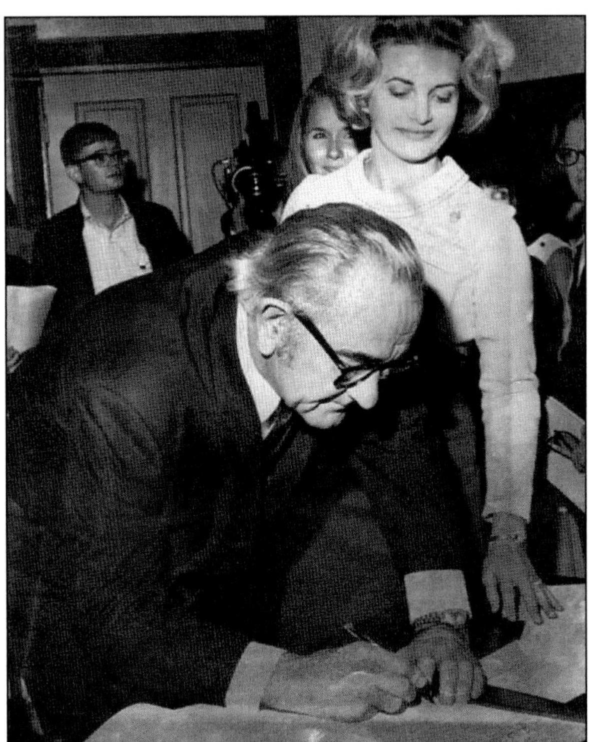

Former President Johnson Again Visits Campus. Former president Lyndon Johnson visited the newly renamed Southwest Texas State University during homecoming in 1970. The name change from Southwest Texas State College to University occurred in 1969. (SMPL.)

LBJ and Former First Lady Attend 1970 Homecoming. Former President Johnson is shown here with his wife, Lady Bird Johnson, on his immediate left, during the homecoming visit in 1970. Note how Johnson allowed his hair to grow longer in the rear after leaving the White House. (SMPL.)

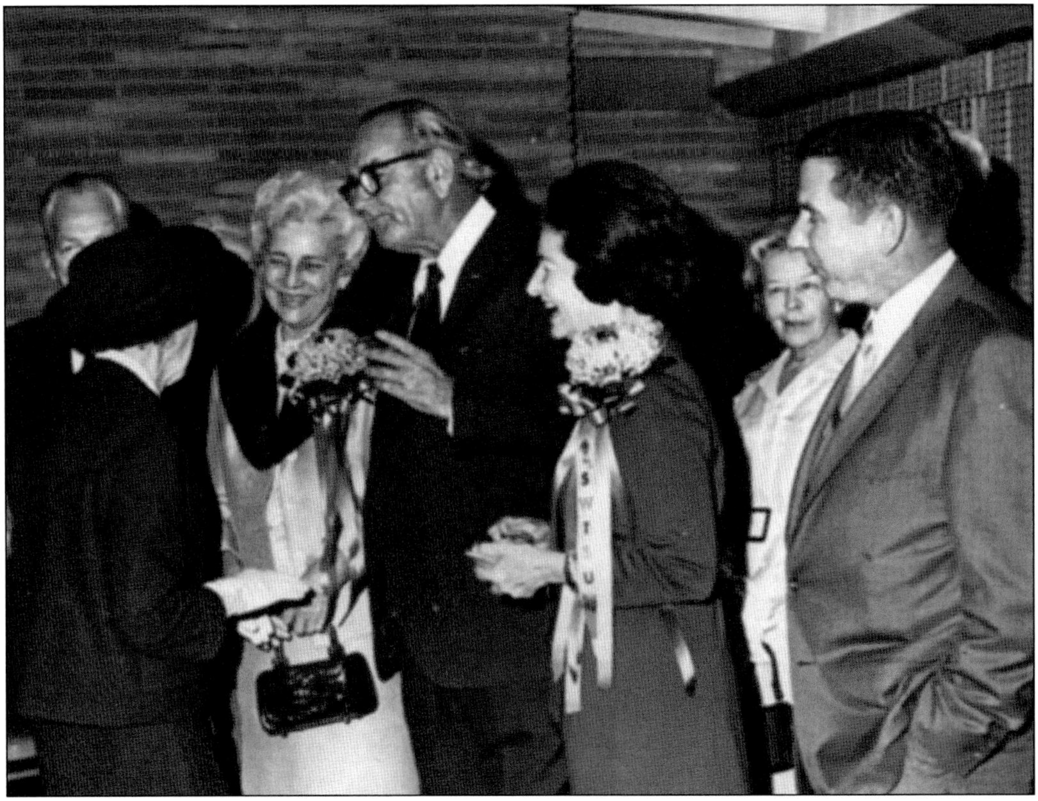

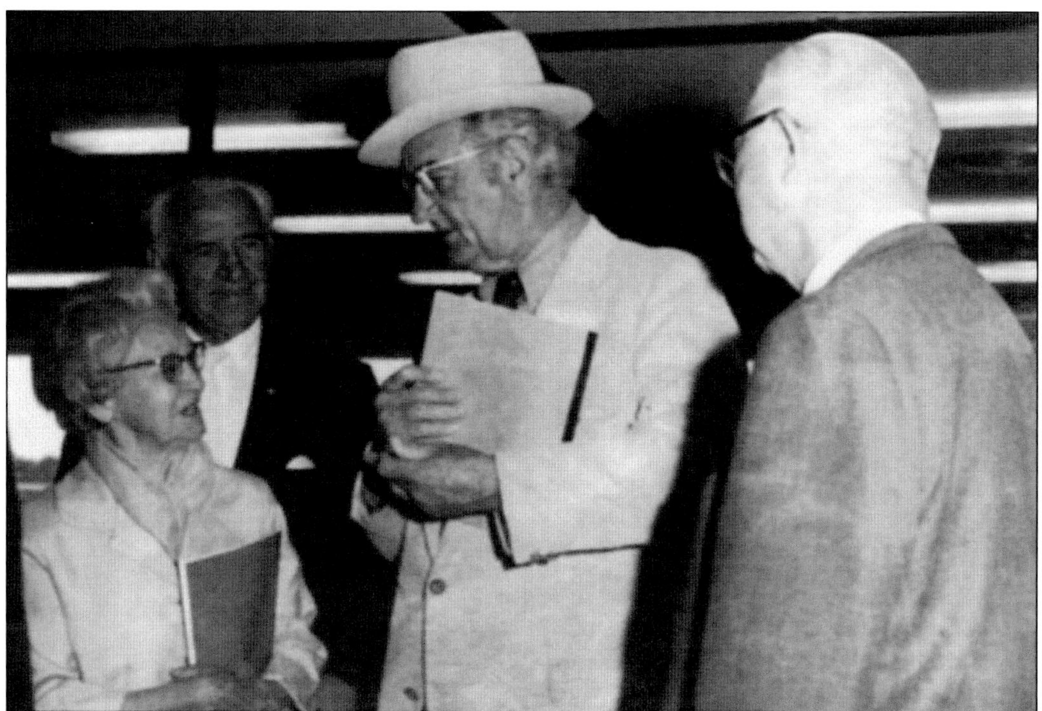

Former President Visits Campus in 1971. During one of his last visits to his alma mater, the former president is seen here visiting with Mrs. Ed Cape. This visit to Southwest Texas State University took place on November 8, 1971. (SMPL.)

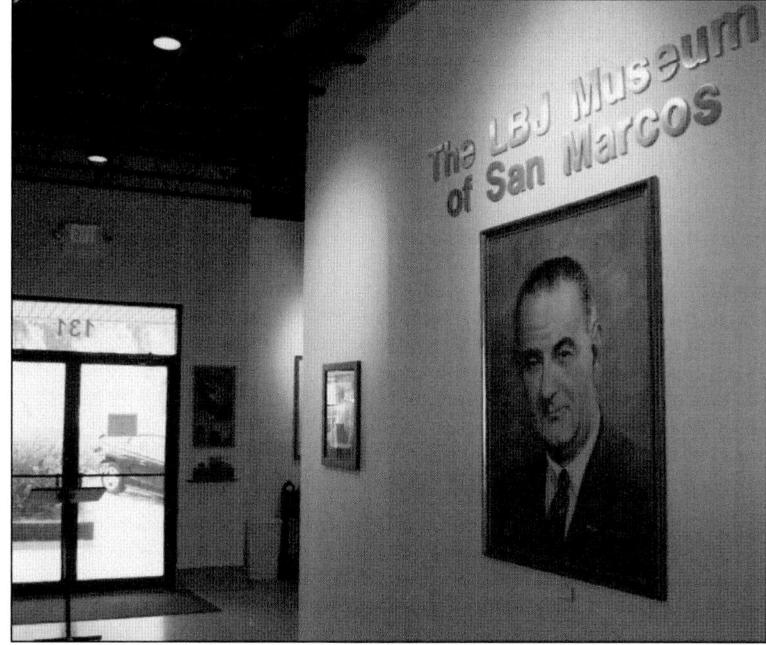

LBJ Museum in San Marcos on Courthouse Square. Located at 131 North Guadalupe Street on the courthouse square in downtown San Marcos, the LBJ Museum of San Marcos opened on December 6, 2006, with Johnson's daughter Luci Baines Johnson as a keynote speaker at the opening ceremony. The museum is the only Johnson-related site in Texas that focuses on his university student years. (LBJSM.)

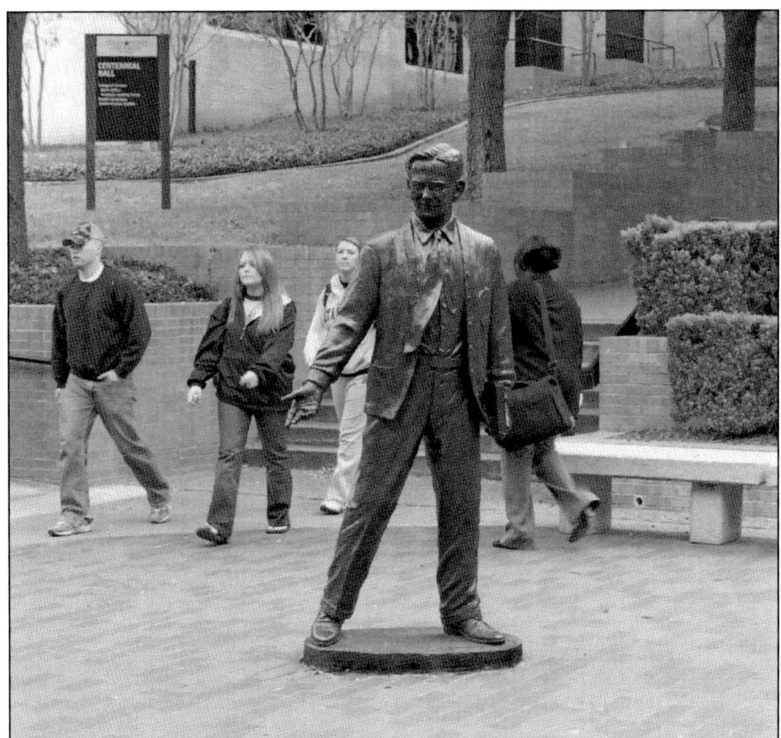

LBJ STATUE SHOWS JOHNSON AS A STUDENT. The LBJ statue on the campus of Texas State University was unveiled in September 2006 and illustrates how Johnson looked while a student at the then–Southwest Texas State Teachers College. The statue was commissioned by the associated student government and was created by sculptor Lawrence Ludtke of Houston. Here it is shown before it was permanently placed on its pedestal. (TxSt.)

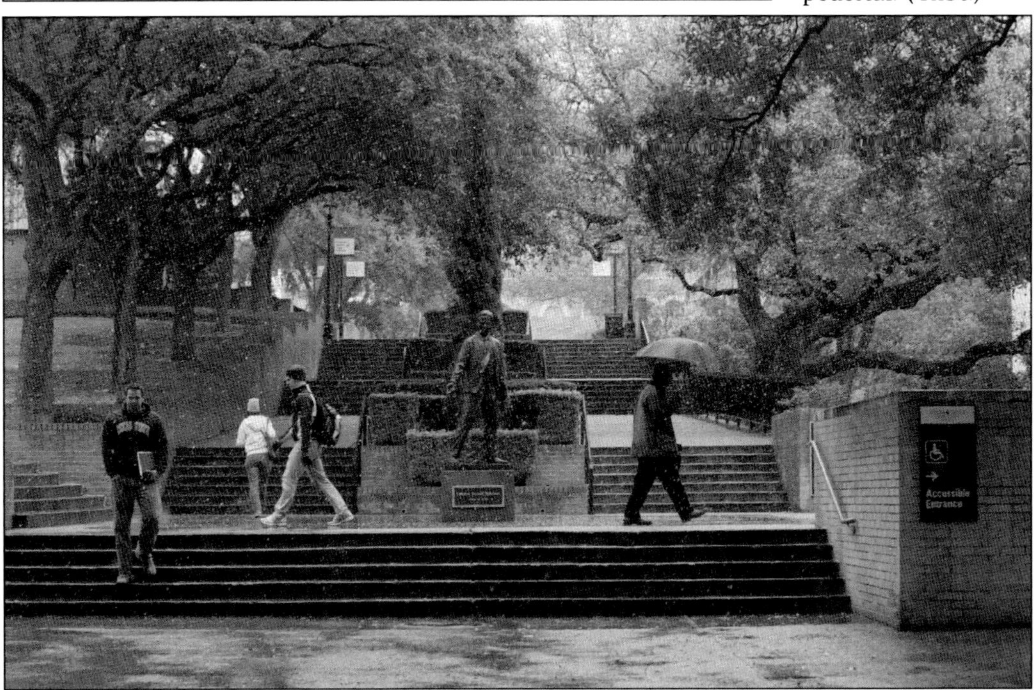

LBJ STATUE IN FRONT OF FLOWERS HALL. On a rare snowy day on the Texas State University campus, the LBJ statue dominates the quad in front of Flowers Hall, home of the College of Liberal Arts from which Johnson graduated in 1930 with a degree in history. The placard on the statue's pedestal reads simply "Lyndon Baines Johnson Class of 1930." (TxSt.)

Five

The Town Lifeline

Spring Lake and the San Marcos River

The San Marcos River originates at the foot of the Balcones Escarpment through a series of springs collectively known as the San Marcos Springs. The springs are now submerged under Spring Lake, a manmade feature created by the damming of the river in 1849. The dam was built by former Republic of Texas vice president Edward Burleson, one of the first settlers of San Marcos. The water feeding the springs originates in the Edwards Aquifer, an underground reservoir fed from the surface by stream flow and rainfall on exposed outcrops of Edwards limestone. Because of its spring-fed nature, the San Marcos River has never ceased to flow in recorded history—even during times of severe drought.

From Spring Lake, the river meanders past and through the campus of Texas State University and through town in a southeasterly direction. The river's temperature through most of San Marcos is a constant 72 degrees, characteristic of a spring-fed river. The water flows clear and swift, making for excellent recreational activities, including swimming, canoeing, and kayaking, as well as other recreational activities in several university and city parks along the river's banks. One seasonal activity that has become a student favorite is the graduation jump, in which students who have received their degree from Texas State jump while still in cap and gown into the river in Sewell Park.

In 1994, then–Southwest Texas State University acquired the former Aquarena Springs resort and theme park at Spring Lake. Aquarena Springs, established as a resort by A.B. Rogers in 1928, served for several decades as a tourist destination associated with its renowned underwater theater. This theater was removed in May 2012 as the university continued the process of transitioning the former tourist resort into a scientific center preserving and protecting the headwaters of the San Marcos River for future generations. Now called the Meadows Center for Water and the Environment, the 90-acre university property is the site of a wide variety of educational and research pursuits. The Meadows Center, Spring Lake, and the upper headwaters of the San Marcos River are home to several endangered species of plants and animals that exist nowhere else in the world.

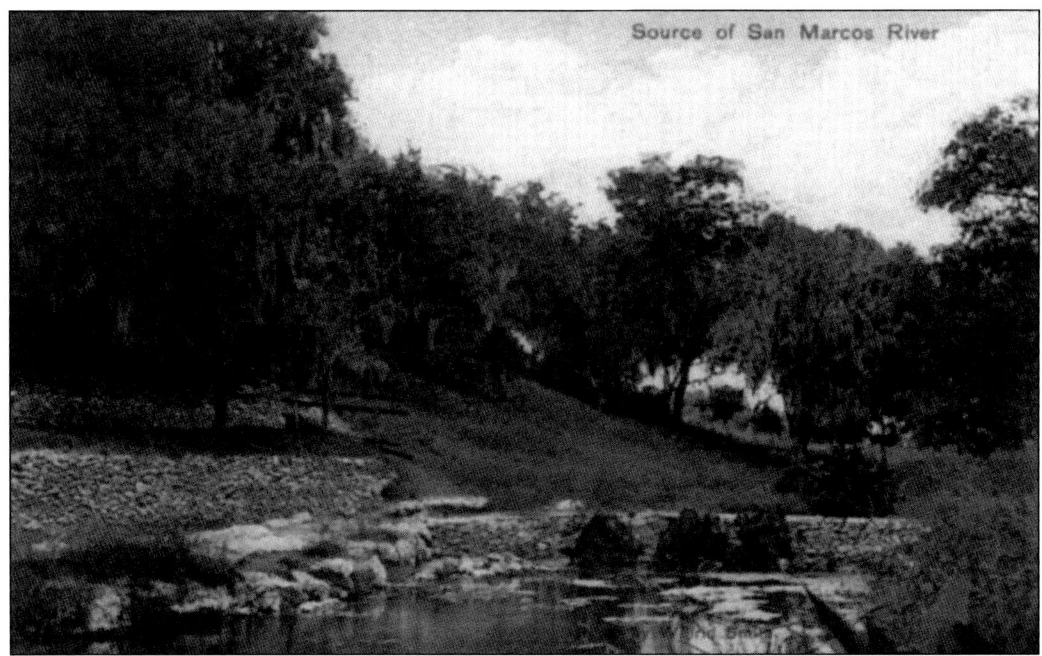

Source of the San Marcos River. The headwaters of the San Marcos River arise in Spring Lake, which was formed by damming by San Marcos pioneer settler Edward Burleson in 1849. Burleson's homestead was on the bluff above the lake he created. The area is now owned by Texas State University as part of its Meadows Center for Water and the Environment. (SMPL.)

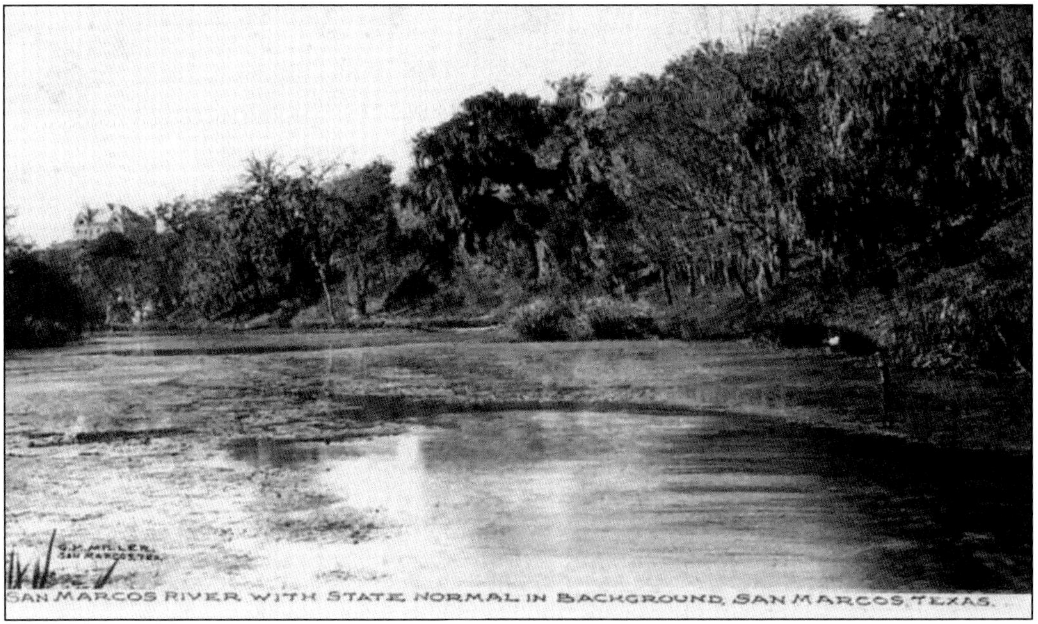

San Marcos River with State Normal School in Background, c. 1908. This photograph was taken near the headwaters of the San Marcos River with the Southwest Texas State Normal School (now Texas State University) on the hill at center left. Many large cypress and oak trees line the banks of the San Marcos River. Texas wild rice, an endangered species, is found only in the upper two miles of the river. (SMPL.)

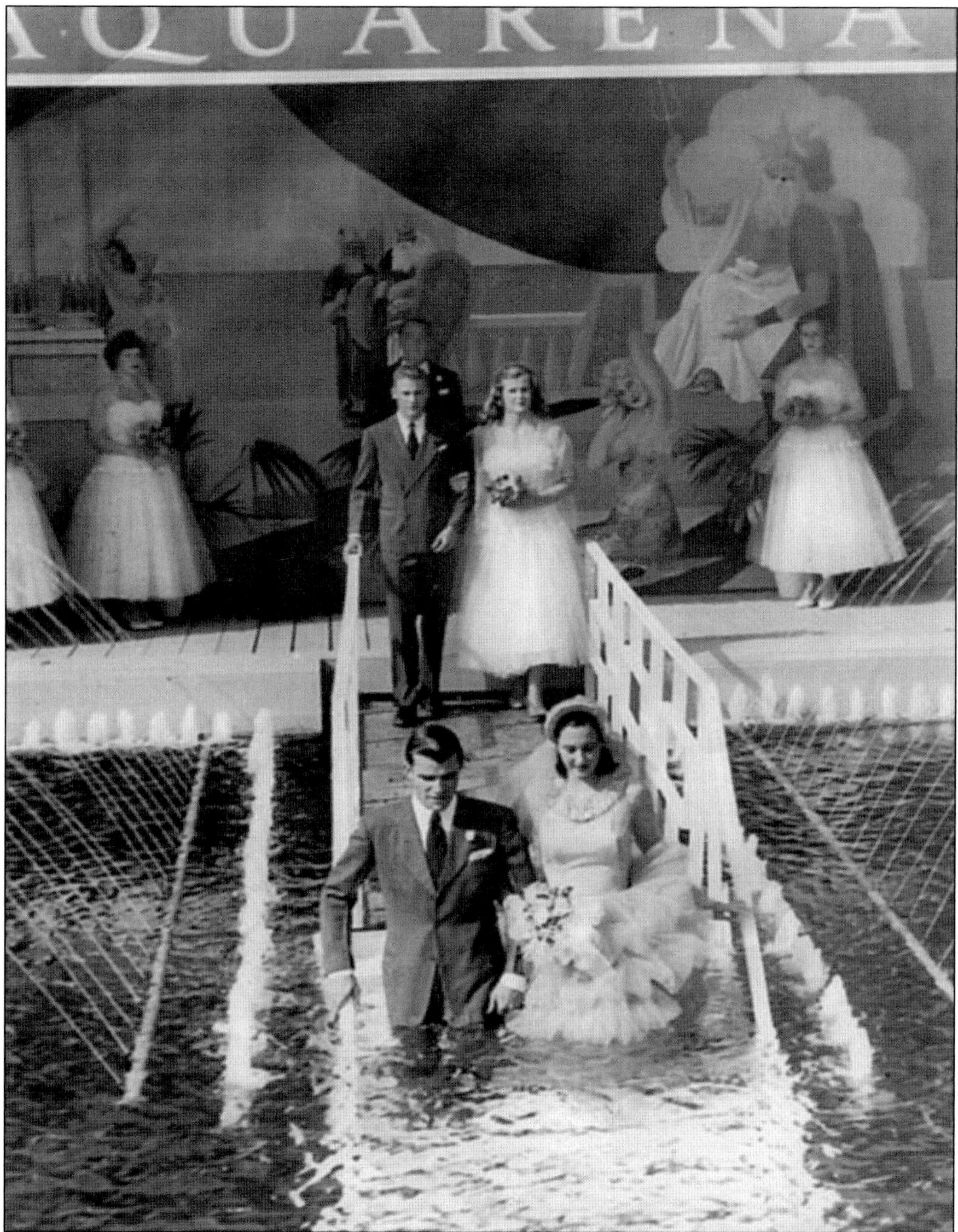

Underwater Wedding at Aquarena Springs. An underwater wedding took place at the Aquarena Springs resort on March 8, 1954. The bride and groom were Mary Beth Sanger and Bob Smith. The maid of honor was Margaret Russell, who was an Aquamaid in the Submarine Theater at the resort. The other people are unidentified. Aquamaids performed artistic routines and dances while underwater in the theater, breathing occasionally through an underwater air hose. (SMPL.)

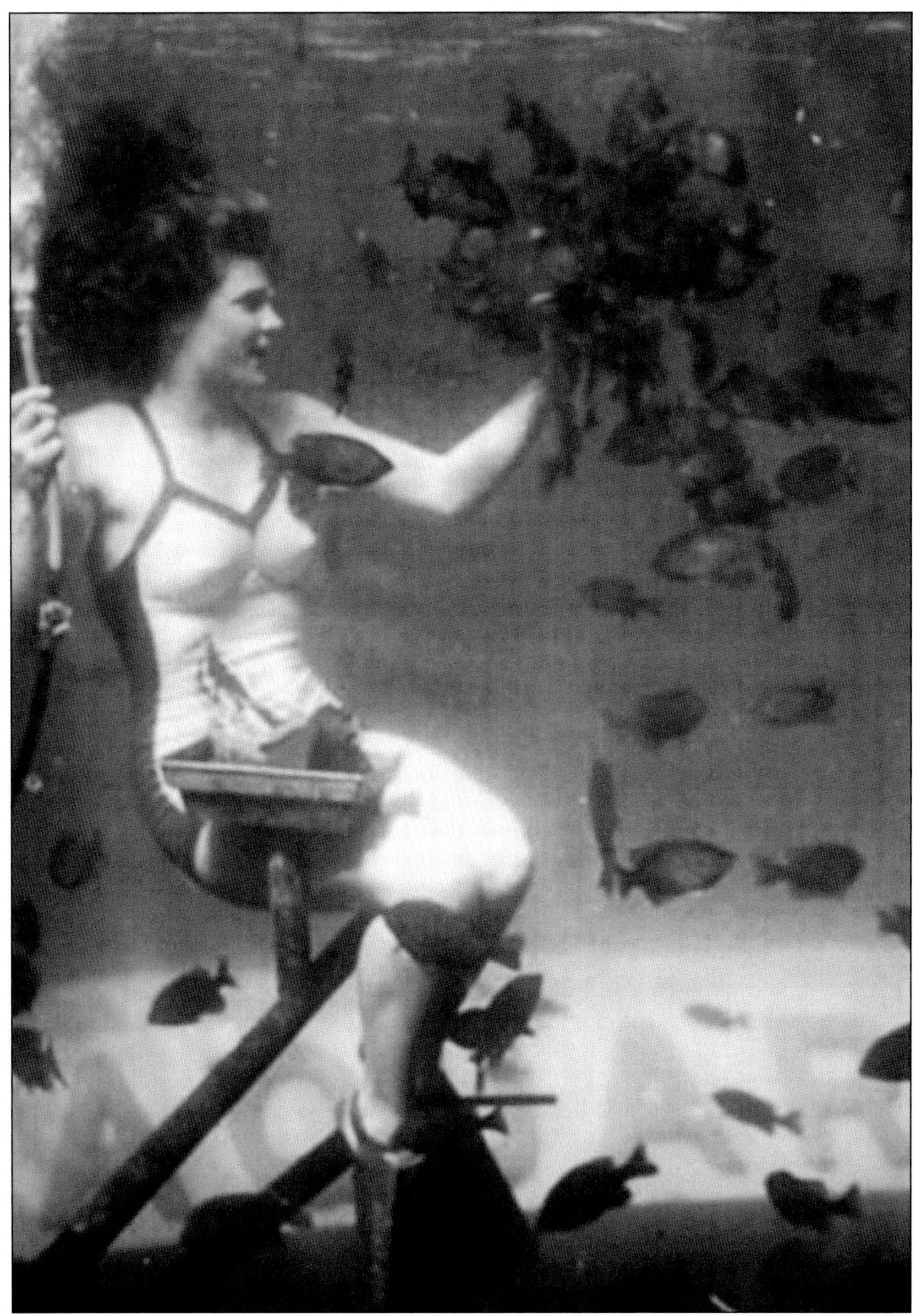

Aquamaid Margaret Russell in Submarine Theater. Margaret Russell, an Aquamaid in the Submarine Theater at the Aquarena Springs resort, is shown here with a school of fish during a typical performance underwater. Russell is holding her air-supply hose in her right hand. Note the swim fins on her feet. (SMPL.)

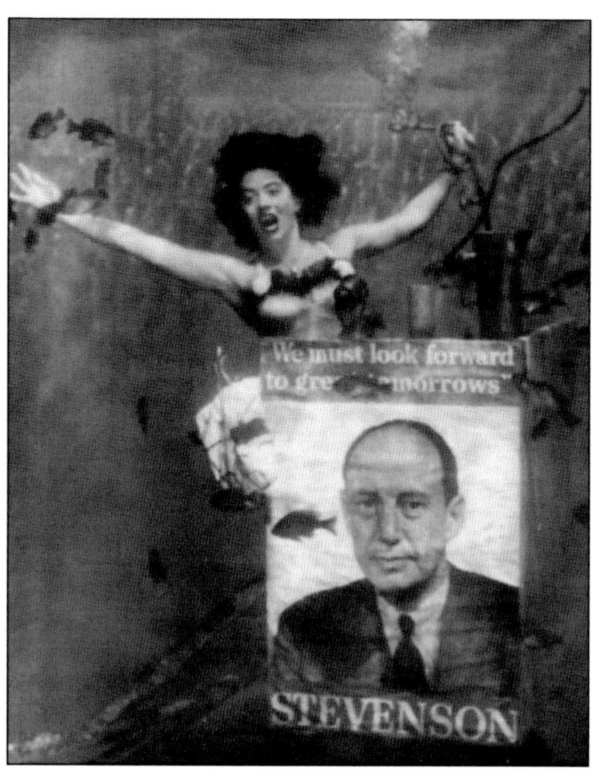

Aquamaid Skit During Presidential Campaign. During the 1952 presidential campaign, an Aquamaid performed skits associated with both the Democratic challenger Adlai Stevenson and the Republican nominee, soon-to-be Pres. Dwight Eisenhower. It would be interesting to know the purposes of the moneybags seen in each photograph and why the Aquamaid is holding a moneybag in the shot with the image of Republican Eisenhower but not in the image posing with the campaign image of Democrat Stevenson. The Aquamaid is holding her breathing hose in her left hand in both photographs. (Both, SMPL.)

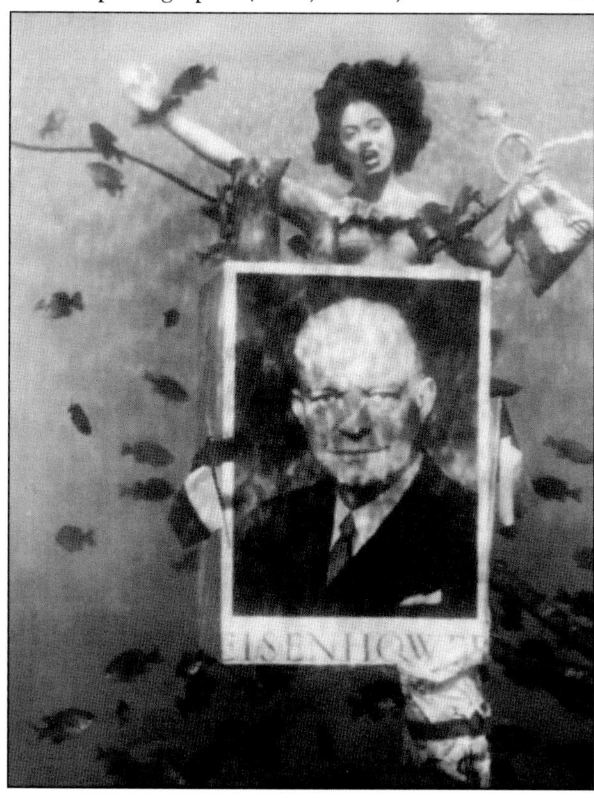

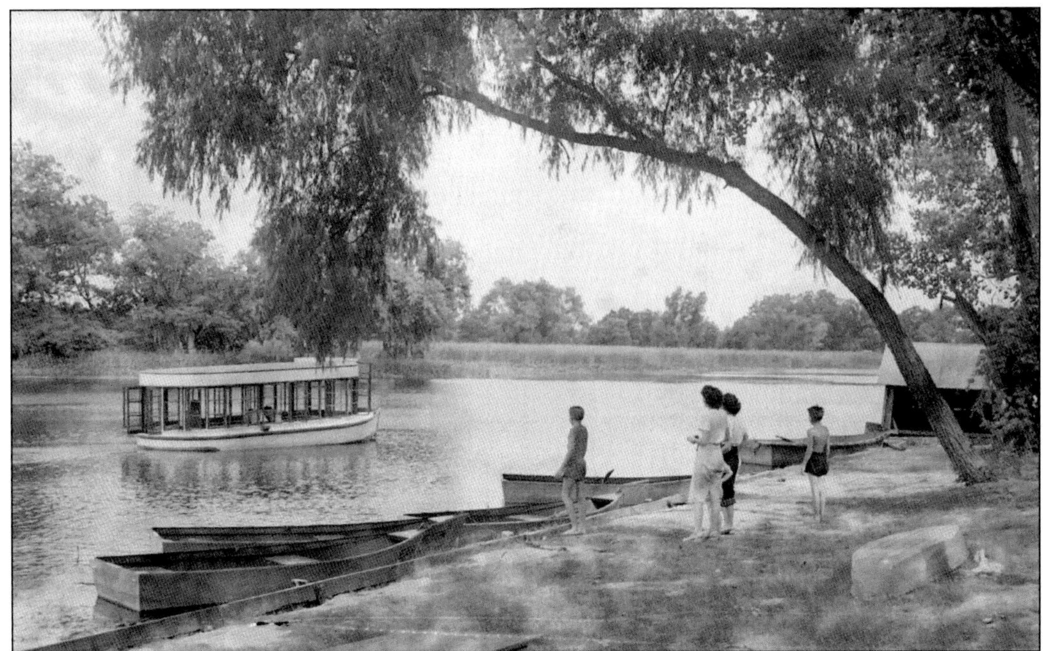

Glass-Bottom Boat on Spring Lake. Visitors at the Aquarena Springs resort look on as one of the famous glass-bottom boats glides by on Spring Lake. The glass-bottom boats have been a staple of tourism, and, since Texas State University assumed ownership, education on Spring Lake since 1945. The first glass-bottom boat, built by resort owner Paul Rogers, was a converted paddleboat. (SMPL.)

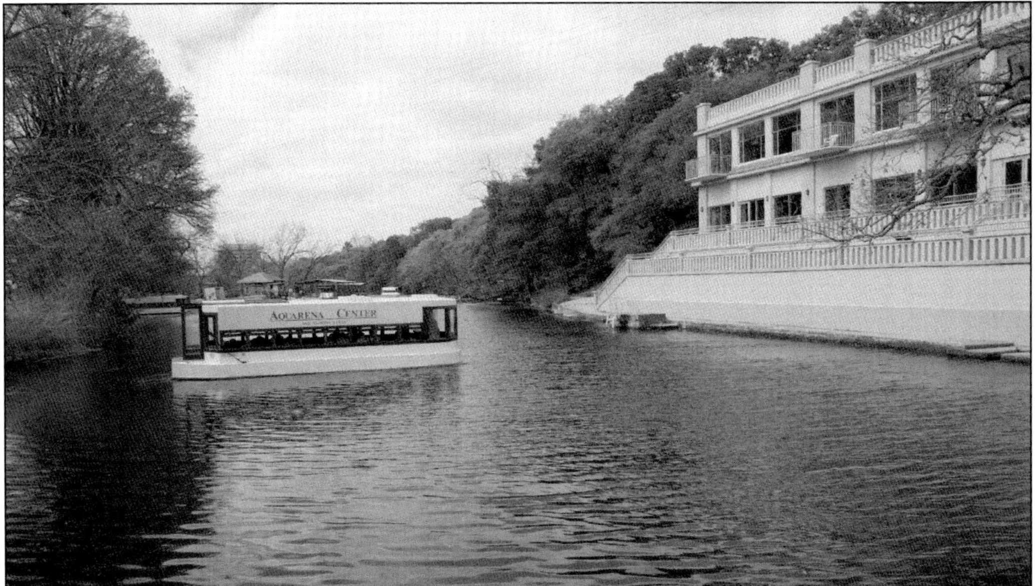

Glass-Bottom Boat Adjacent to Former Resort Hotel. One of the Aquarena Center glass-bottom boats glides past the former resort hotel, now home to the offices of Texas State University's Meadows Center for Water and the Environment. Between 1945 and 1994, when the university acquired the Aquarena Springs resort, eight glass-bottom boats were built using the same design. (TxSt.)

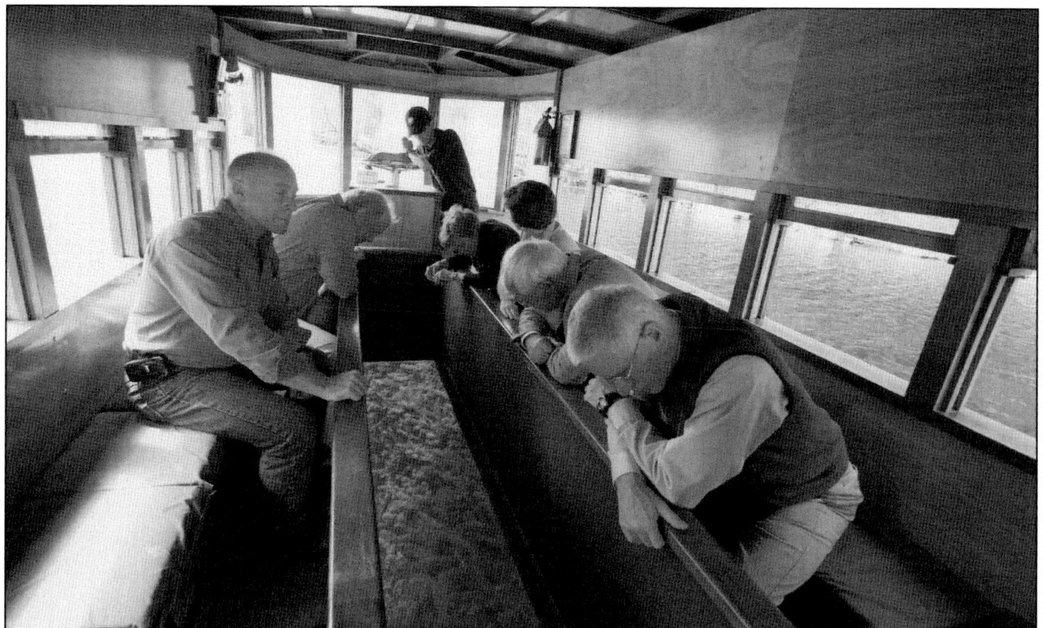

INTERIOR OF GLASS-BOTTOM BOAT ON SPRING LAKE. An interior view of one of the glass-bottom boats illustrates how visitors get to see through the crystal-clear waters to the floor of Spring Lake. Fish and other wildlife are typically observed on every boat ride in the lake, as are springs bubbling up from the bottom of the lake. The person on the right closest to the camera is professor emeritus James Kimmel of the Department of Geography at Texas State University, but the other people are unidentified. (TxSt.)

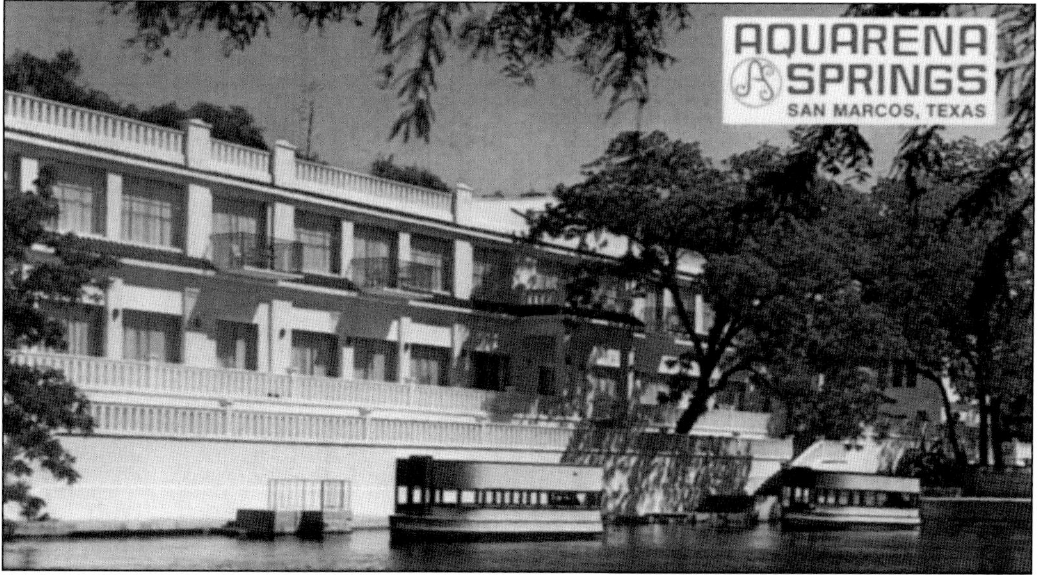

AQUARENA SPRINGS RESORT HOTEL AND GLASS-BOTTOM BOATS. This is an undated view of the Aquarena Springs resort hotel with two of the famous glass-bottom boats on Spring Lake. This postcard, advertising the resort, was distributed widely throughout the state and region. The current offices of the Meadows Center for Water and the Environment at Texas State University occupy much of the first floor of the former hotel. (SMPL.)

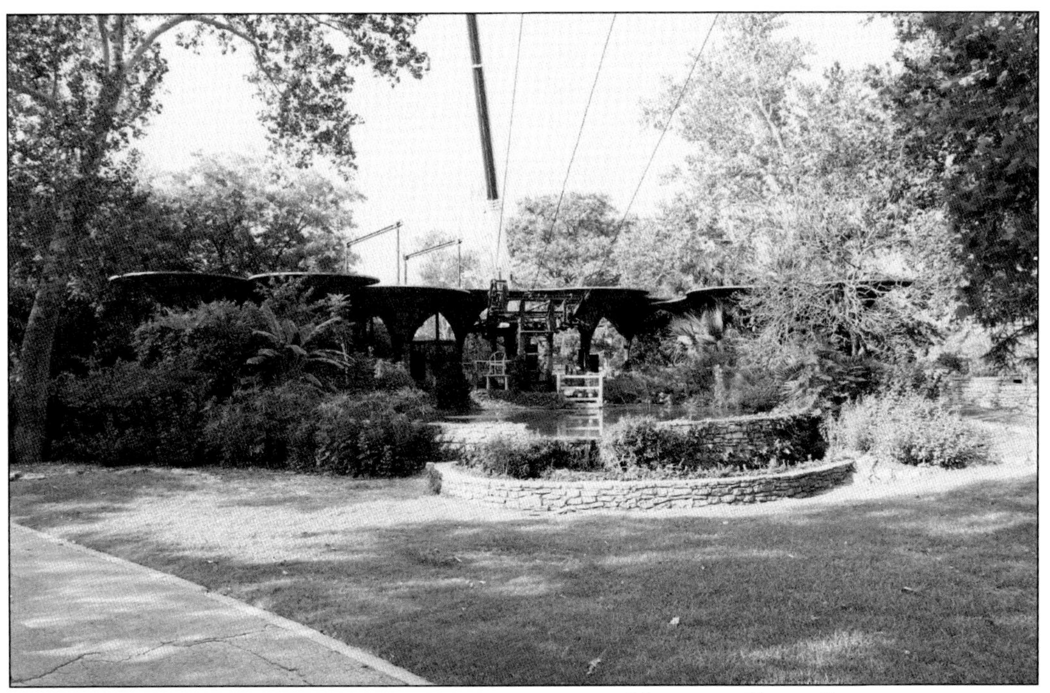

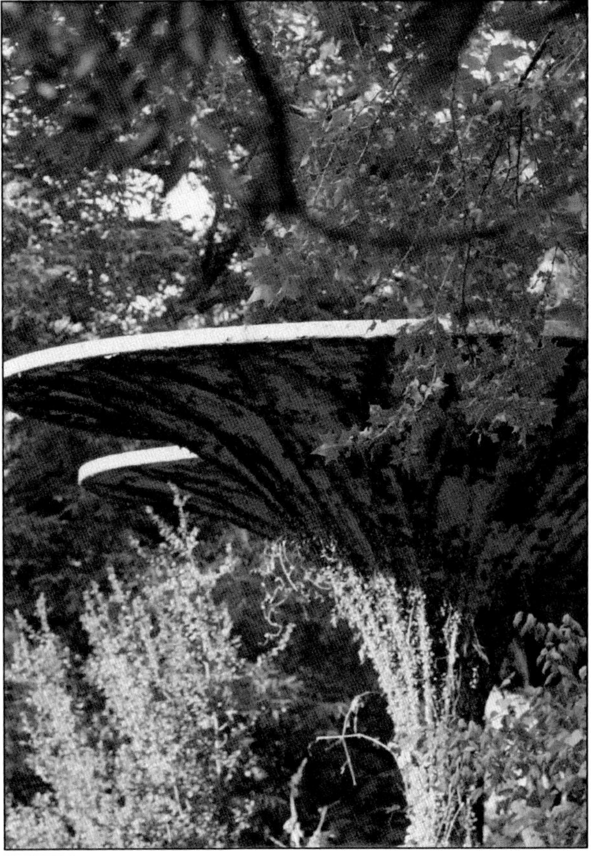

Morning Glory Sculptures at Aquarena Springs Resort. In 1963, sculptures of morning glories, created by Texas artist Buck Winn, were installed at the Aquarena Springs resort. Winn's grandson, Andrew Winn, negotiated with Texas State University for their preservation rather than being bulldozed as a part of the university's plan to restore the natural environment at Spring Lake. The sculptures were removed and relocated in August 2011. (TxSt.)

Morning Glory Sculptures Prior to Removal. The 16 morning glory sculptures at Aquarena Springs offered shade to visitors who were waiting for a ride on the (now removed) resort cable car ride. The size of the sculptures, too tall and wide to be removed safely by truck, posed a conundrum for how the university could have them safely removed and transported to Andrew Winn's ranch. (TxSt.)

Morning Glory Sculpture Removal, 2011. The solution for the removal of Buck Winn's morning glories was transport by helicopter. Texas State University honored Andrew Winn's request not to destroy the sculptures by paying for their removal to the Winn family ranch in the small nearby town of Wimberley, where they reside today. (TxSt.)

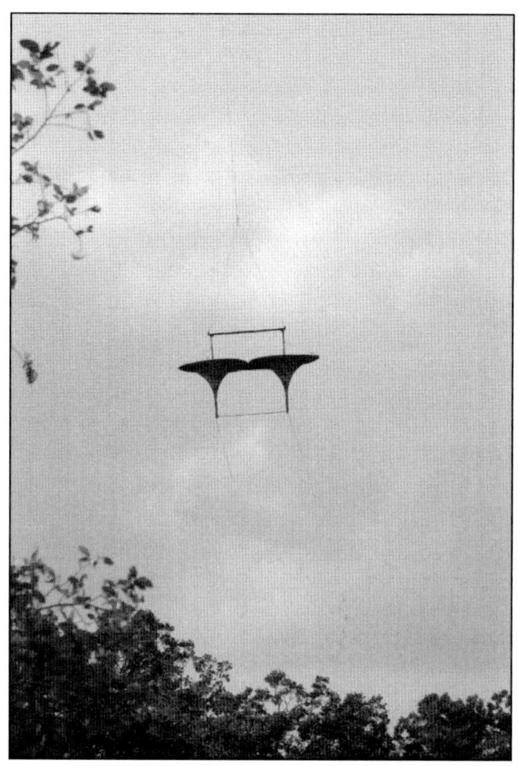

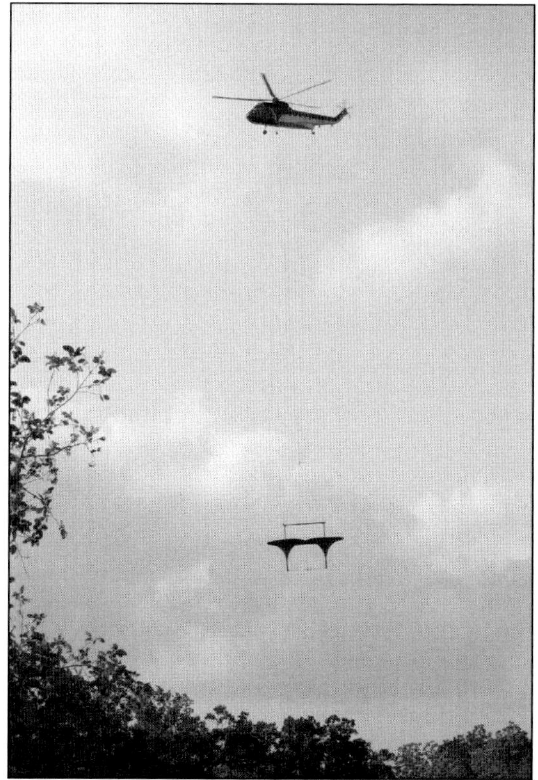

Helicopter Removal of Morning Glory Sculptures. This helicopter is removing two of Buck Winn's morning glory sculptures from the former Aquarena Springs resort in August 2011. Placed on Andrew Winn's ranch in Wimberley, several of the sculptures were blown over by a windstorm in April 2012. Efforts to restore the sculptures will require additional funding sources. (TxSt.)

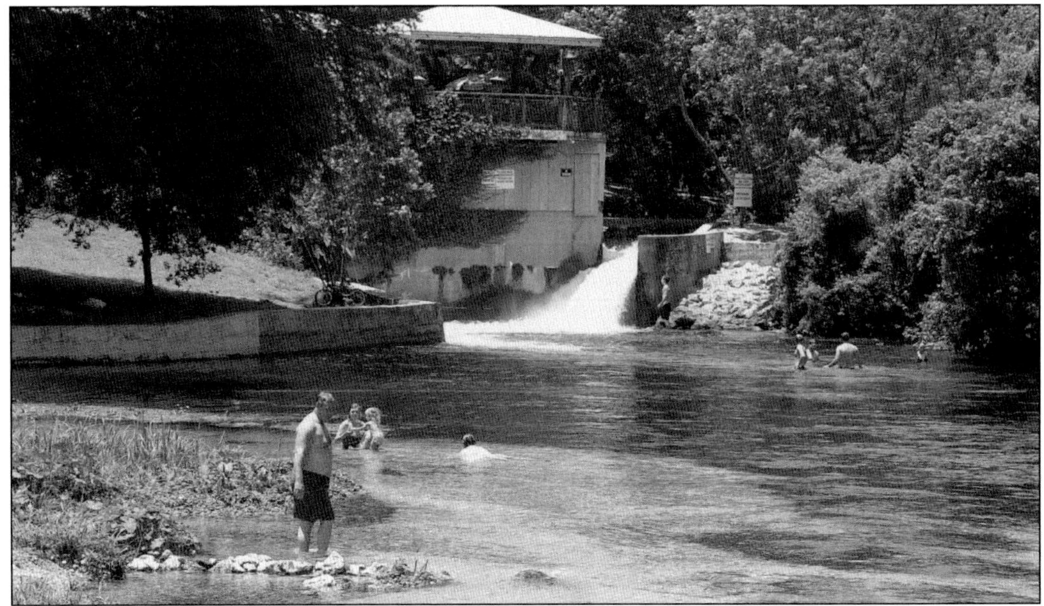

People Enjoying the San Marcos River below the Spring Lake Spillway. At the left spillway of the Spring Lake Dam, which impounds Spring Lake, a popular swimming pool in the San Marcos River entices people to enjoy its warm, clear waters. The building above and to the left of the spillway is a popular local restaurant with deck seating, which allows customers to sit outside over the spillway. (TxSt.)

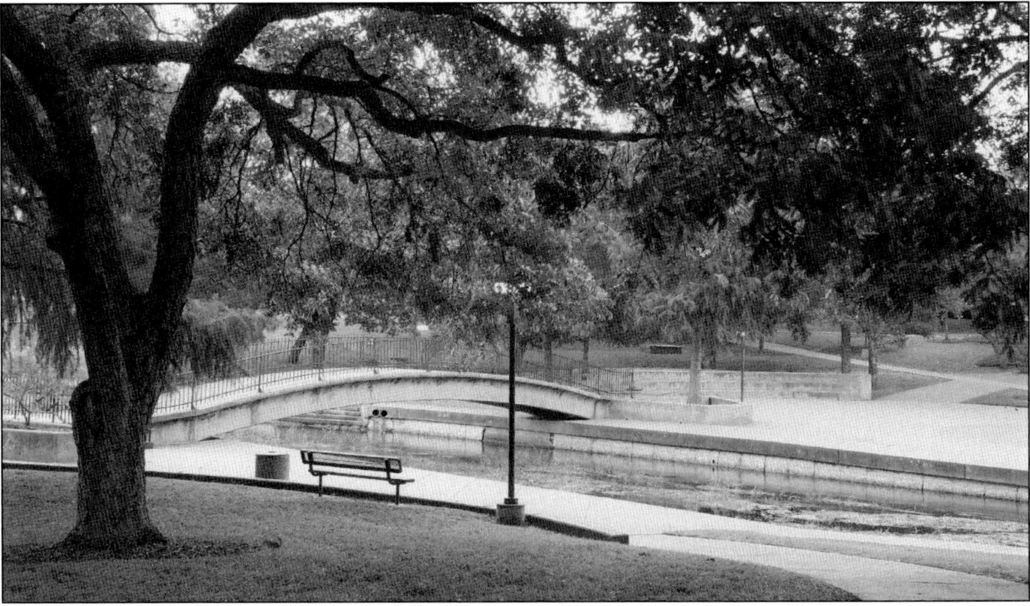

Sewell Park and the San Marcos River. Sewell Park, owned and administered by Texas State University, is just downstream of the swimming pool beneath the Spring Lake Dam shown in the previous photograph. Named after university mathematics professor S.M. Sewell, Sewell Park is adjacent to Strahan Coliseum, which hosts university sporting events as well as university graduation exercises. Sewell Park is a popular location for sunbathing, swimming, and other recreational activities. (TxSt.)

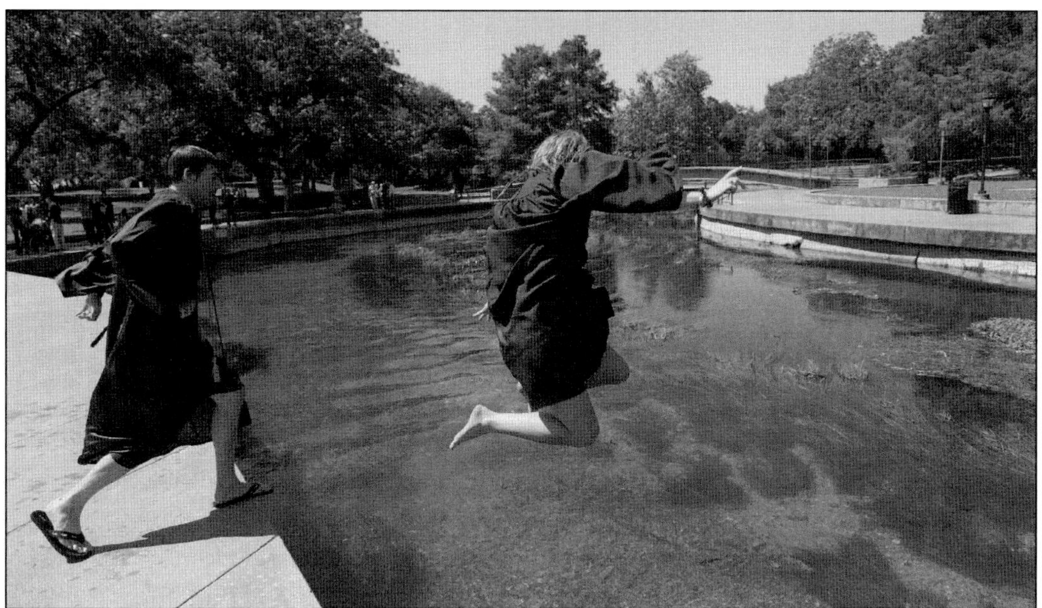

Graduation Plunge into the San Marcos River. A graduation tradition at Texas State University is the post-graduation leap into the San Marcos River at Sewell Park while still wearing the ceremonial graduation gown. These unidentified students are continuing the tradition of the post-ceremony recessional march out of Strahan Coliseum and directly into the river. The author's son participated in this very tradition when he graduated from the university in 2010. (TxSt.)

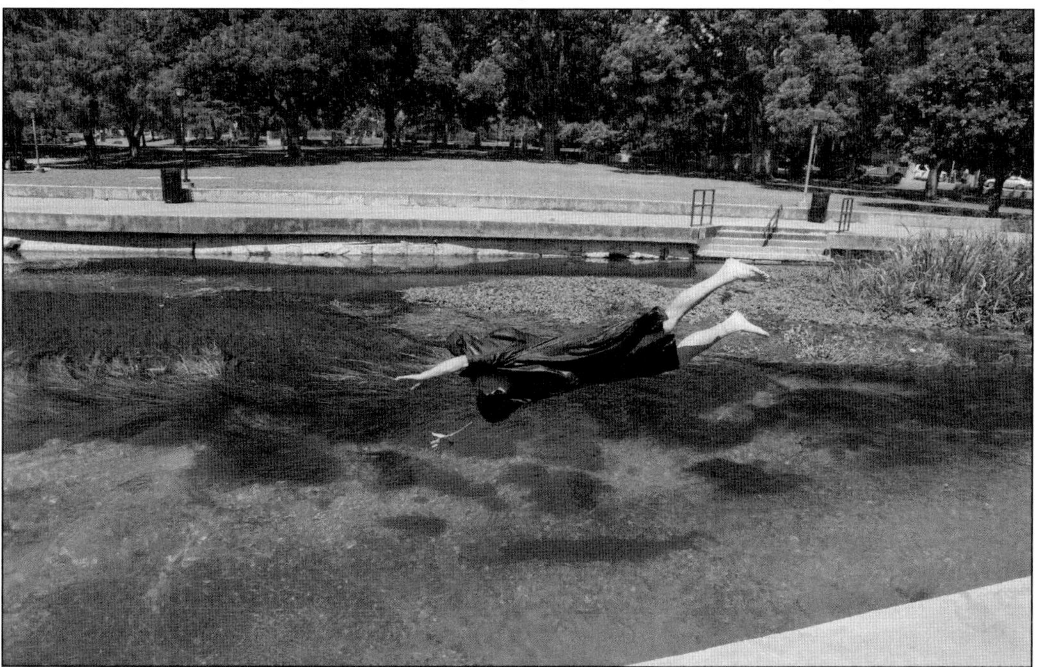

Graduated Student Plunges into the San Marcos River. Still wearing both mortarboard cap and gown, another unidentified student takes the plunge into the clear waters of the San Marcos River at Sewell Park. The grassy slopes of the park across the river serve as an ideal area for sunbathing as well as for volleyball games (a volleyball net is visible at upper left). (TxSt.)

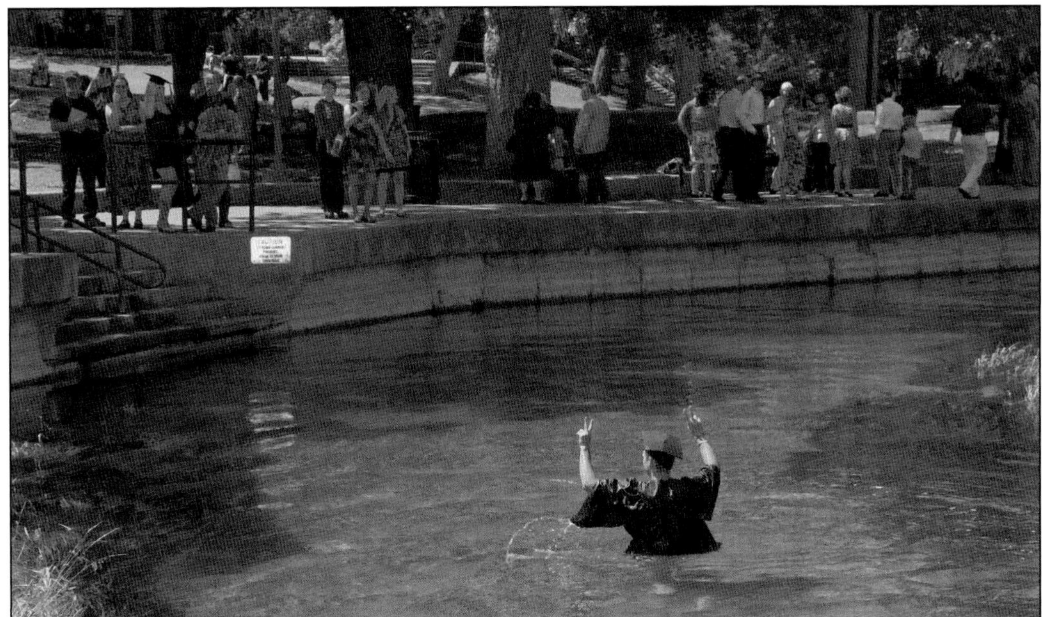

ONLOOKERS OBSERVE SOAKED GRADUATE. Family and friends gather on the Strahan Coliseum banks of the San Marcos River to observe the antics of the newly minted college graduates who have taken the river plunge. The stairs at left allow swimmers and waders a more subtle method of entry into the clear water of the river. (TxSt.)

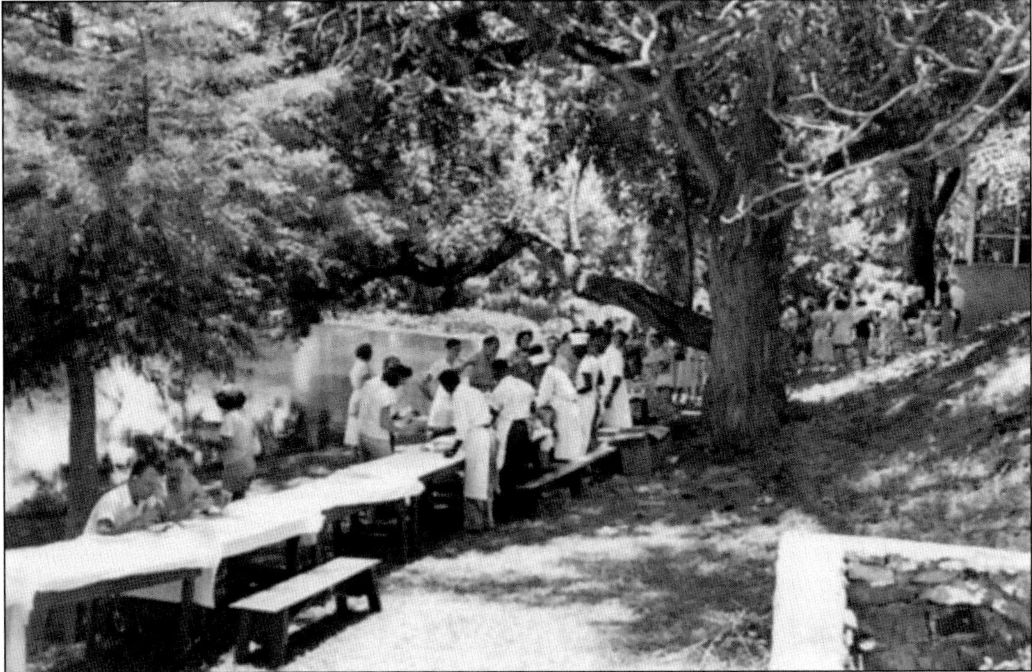

RIO VISTA PARK PICNIC, 1950. Pictured here is a Fourth of July picnic in Rio Vista Park along the San Marcos River. Rio Vista Park is a favorite location for large family and group gatherings in the shade beside the river. The park is approximately a quarter of a mile downstream from Sewell Park. It is also a very popular park for swimming and kayaking on the river. (SMPL.)

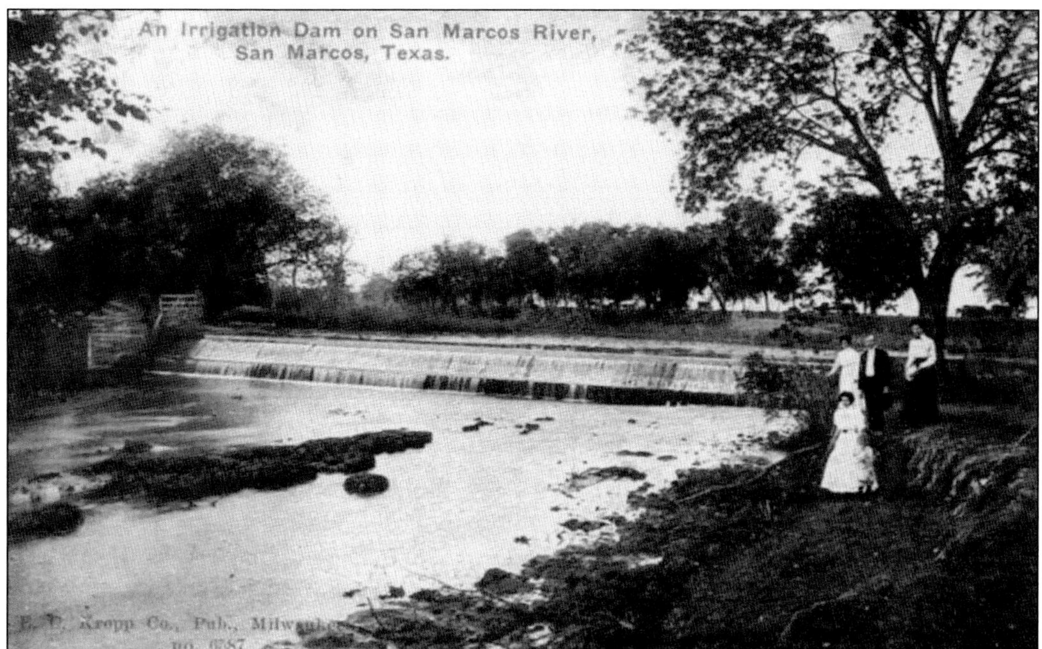

ROGERS DAM, BUILT FOR IRRIGATION AND POWER. This is an early 20th century view of Rogers Dam, which was later renamed Rio Vista Dam. The dam was built by W.D. Malone and P.T. Bost in 1904 for irrigation via a canal and to power a mill. The headworks of the diversion canal for irrigation purposes can still be seen on the east edge of the dam. (SMPL.)

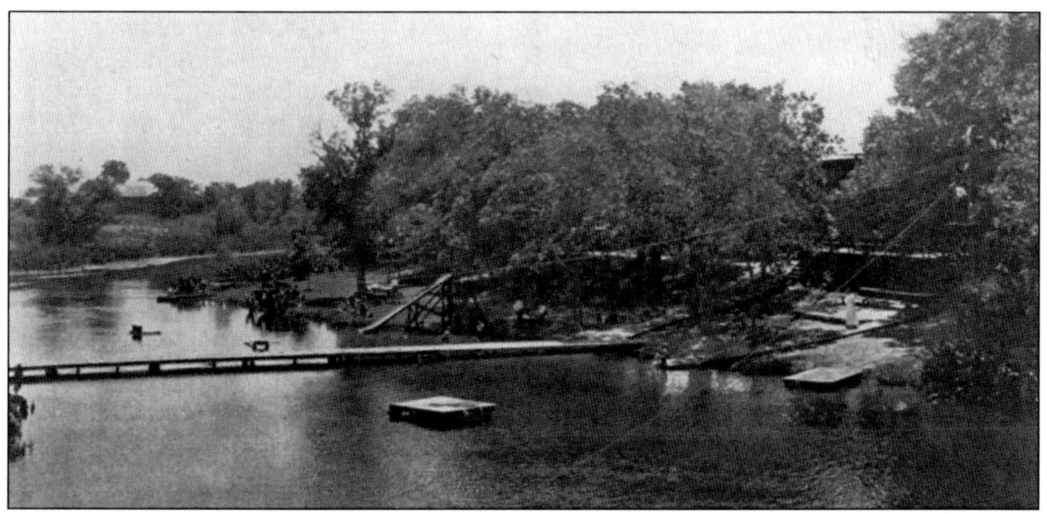

ROGERS RIVER RESORT IN PRESENT-DAY RIO VISTA PARK. Prior to operating the Aquarena Springs Resort, A.B. Rogers first operated San Marcos's first river park, known as Rogers River Resort. This resort was at the site of Rogers Dam. (SMPL.)

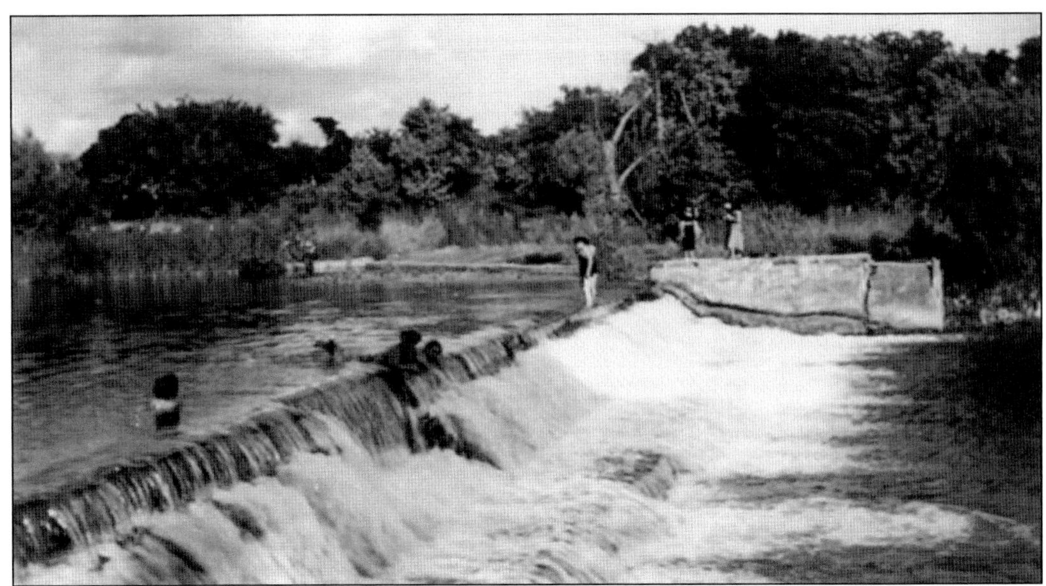

Rogers Dam, San Marcos River, 1948. The pool above the dam quickly became a popular swimming hole on the San Marcos River. By the 1950s, Rogers Dam had become known as Rio Vista Dam, in association with the surrounding land being established as Rio Vista Park. (SMPL.)

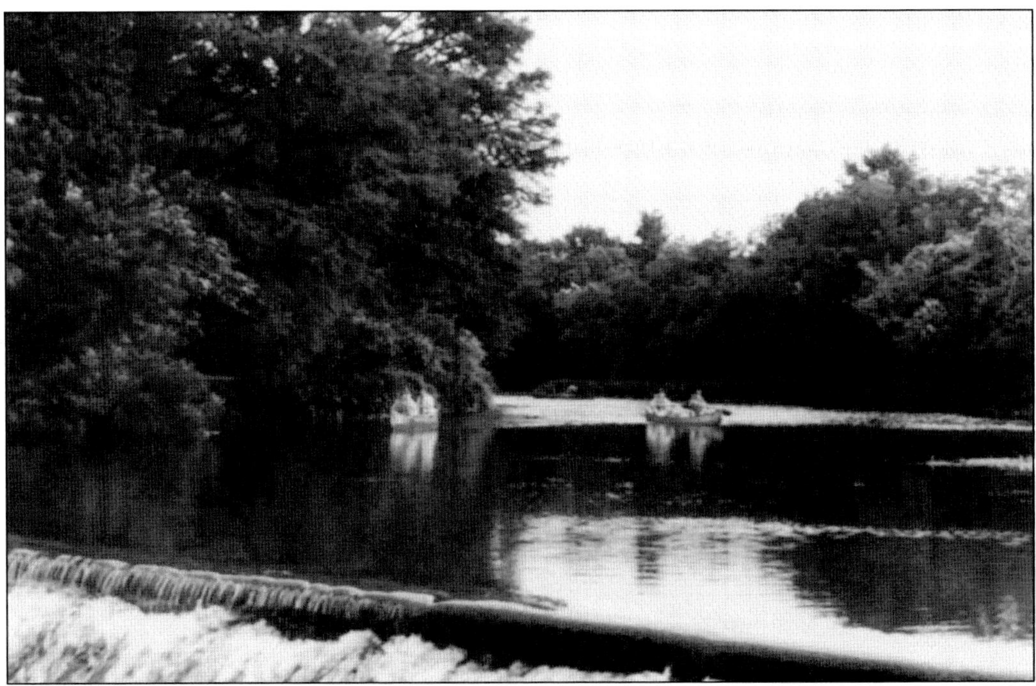

Canoers Above Rio Vista Dam, San Marcos River, 1993. The former Rogers Dam, now known as the Rio Vista Dam, created a deep pool popular not only with swimmers but also with canoers, kayakers, and tubers. This view shows people in canoes enjoying the pool in 1993. (SMPL.)

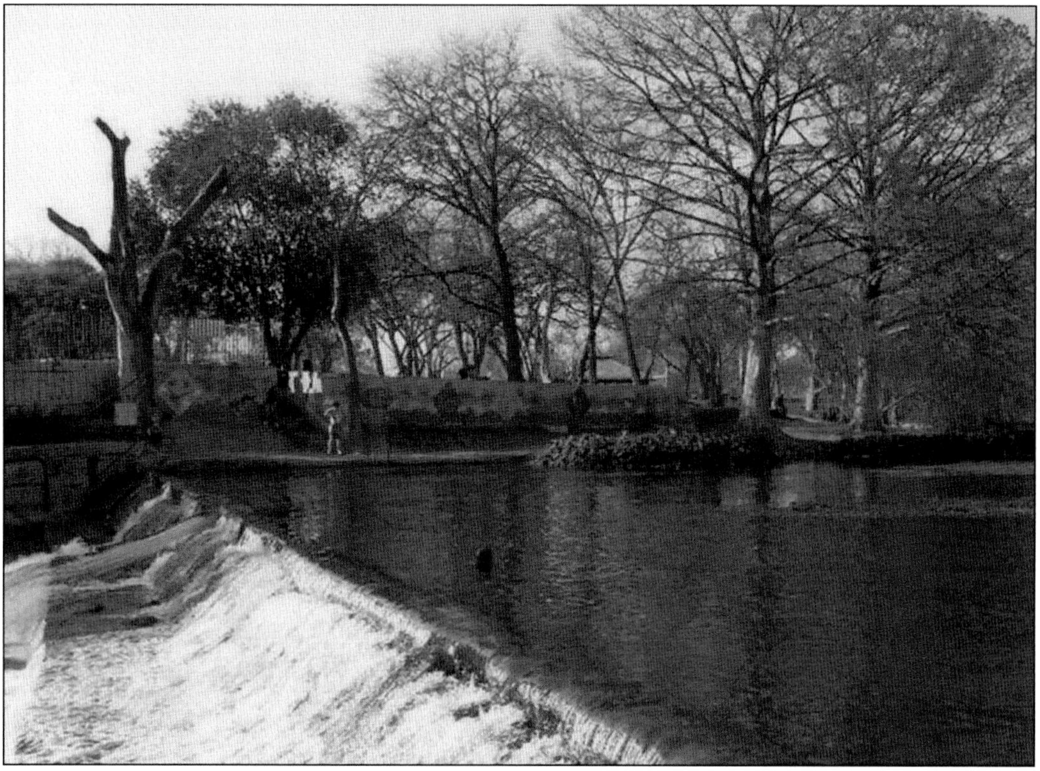

Rio Vista Dam Prior to Reconstruction, 2006. By 2006, the Rio Vista Dam was showing its age, having been damaged over the years and especially by a flood in 1998. Cracks and areas of undermining were becoming of increasing public concern. A plan was put in place to redesign the dam and expand recreational capabilities at the site. (Michelle Bussemey.)

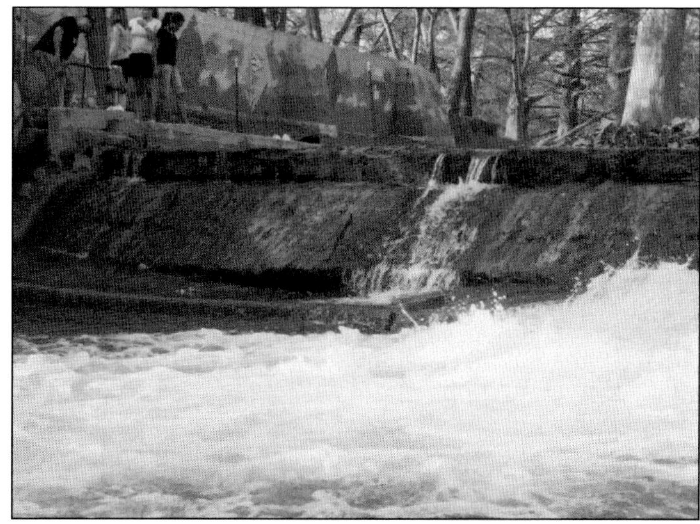

Rio Vista Dam Structural Damage, March 2006. This close-up view of the left side of the Rio Vista Dam shows where the dam had become cracked as well as undermined by water action, hence the need for redesigning and reconstructing the structure. (Michelle Bussemey.)

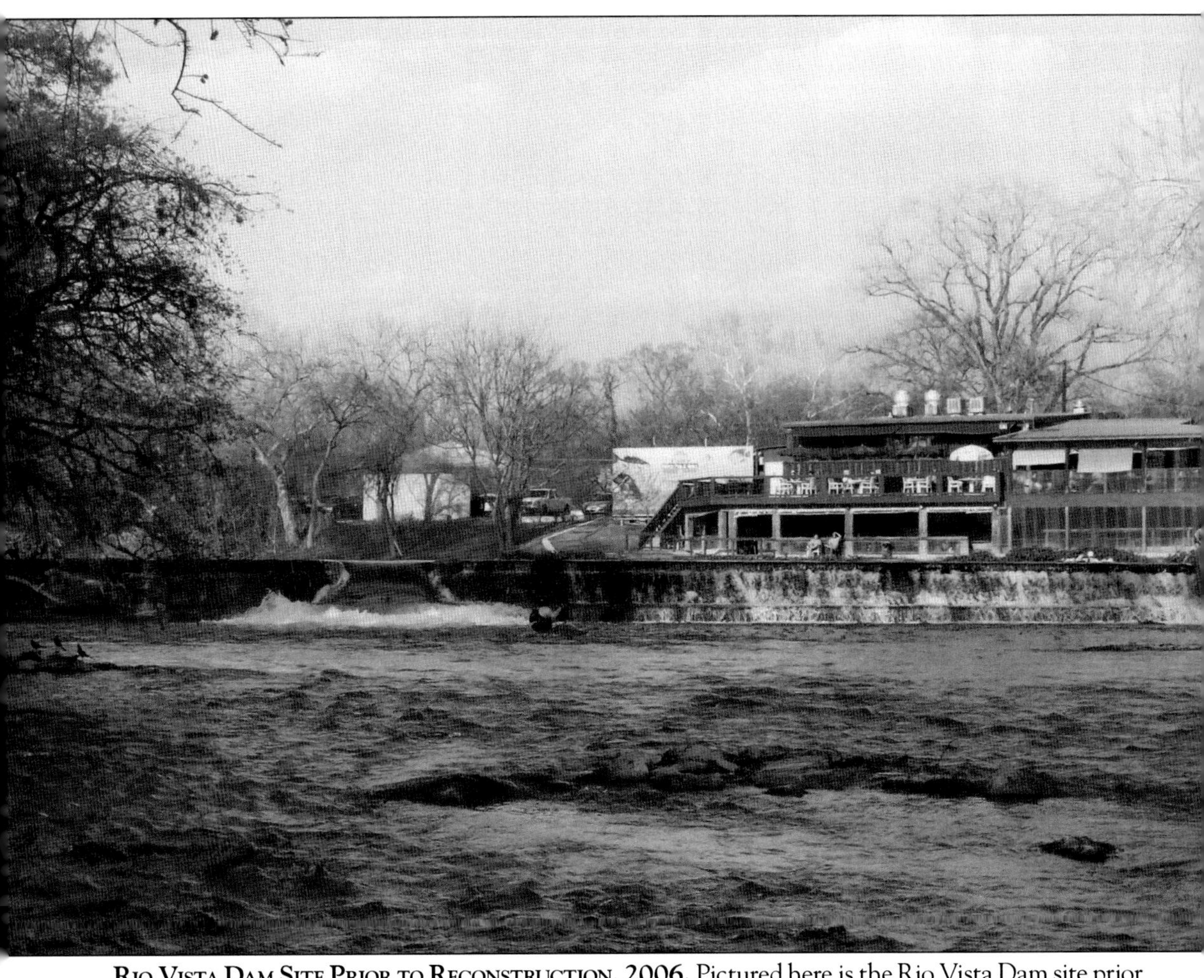

Rio Vista Dam Site Prior to Reconstruction, 2006. Pictured here is the Rio Vista Dam site prior to reconstruction, illustrating the attractive setting of the structure. A popular local restaurant with a deck sitting out over the edge of the San Marcos River is at the right. (Michelle Bussemey.)

View Across Rio Vista Dam Prior to Reconstruction, 2006. This view across the Rio Vista Dam prior to reconstruction was specifically taken to contrast with the next photograph, which illustrates the same site after redesign and reconstruction. (Michelle Bussemey.)

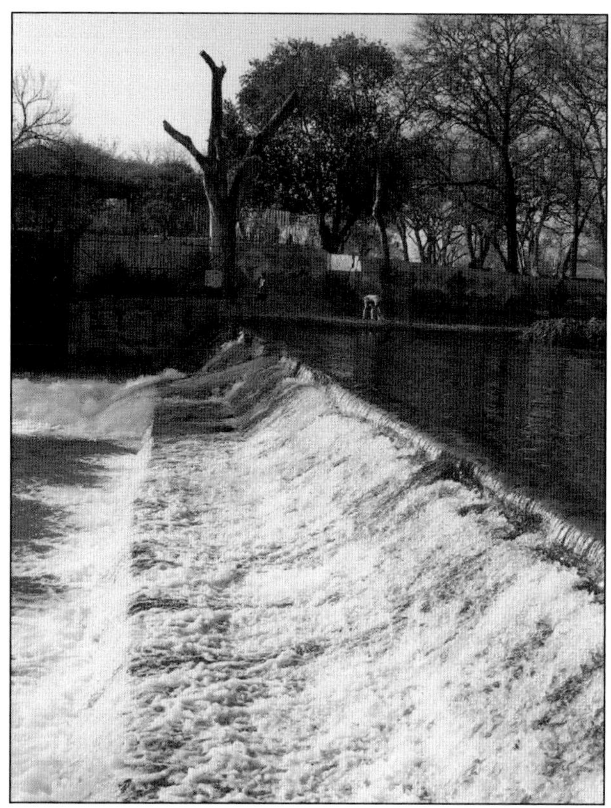

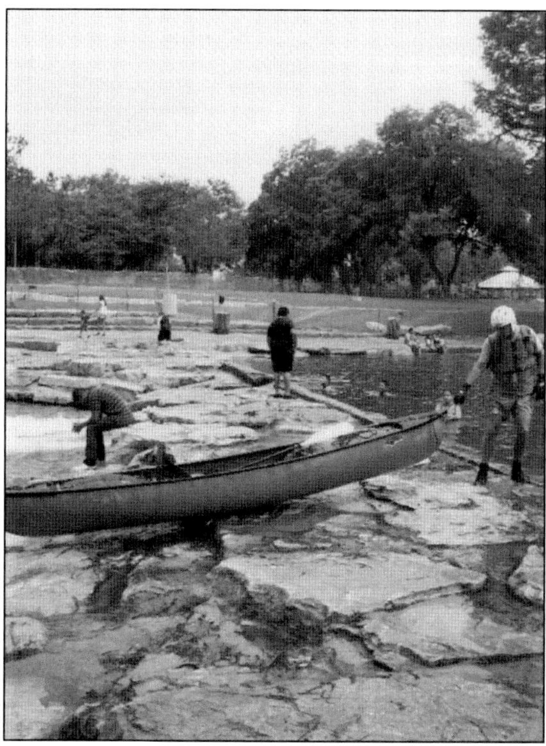

Post-reconstruction and Re-design, Rio Vista Dam, June 2006. The new redesigned damsite incorporates steps and water chutes designed to challenge kayakers enjoying the river. Canoes are best portaged over the steps rather than taken through the chutes. Compare this view across the damsite with the previous photograph, taken prior to reconstruction. (Michelle Bussemey.)

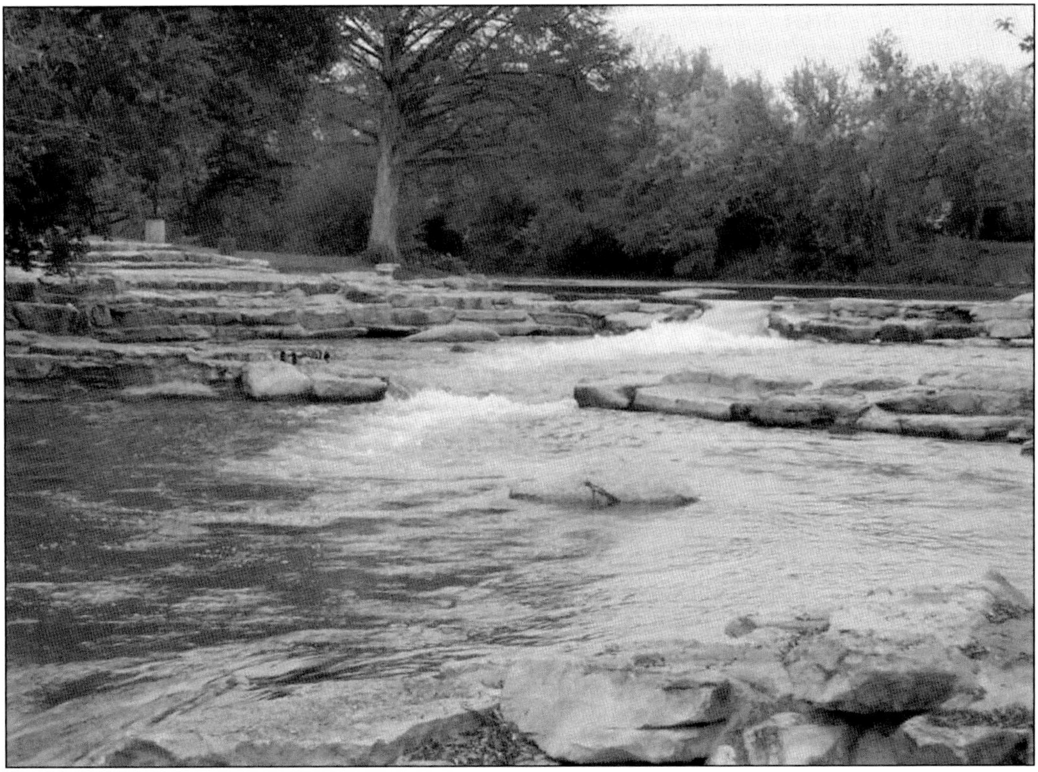

RECONSTRUCTED RIO VISTA FALLS, JUNE 2006. Chutes for kayaking are visible in this upstream view of the redesigned and reconstructed dam site. These features have proven very popular with local as well as regional kayak aficionados. (Michelle Bussemey.)

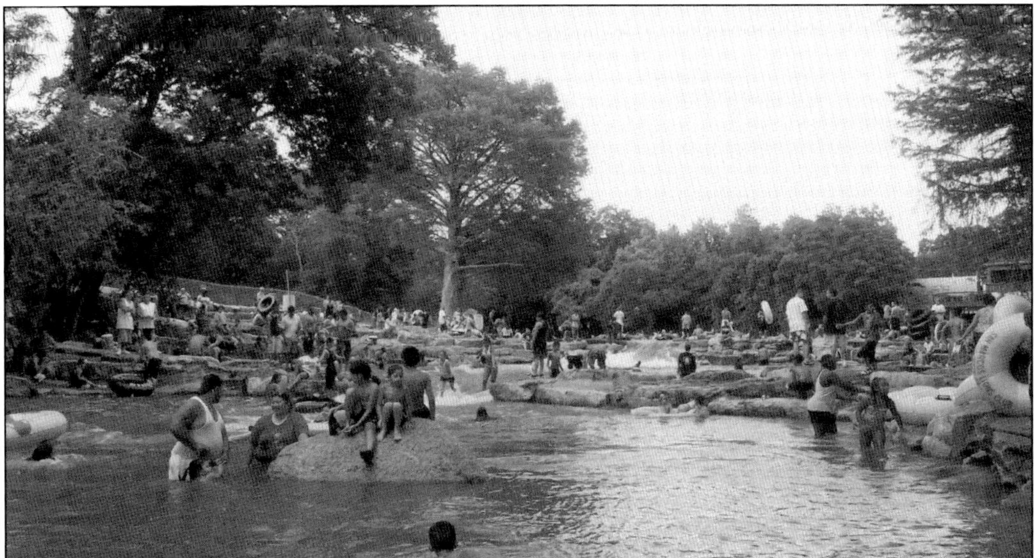

CROWD ENJOYS REDESIGNED RIO VISTA DAM SITE, 2006. The reconstructed Rio Vista Dam attracts hundreds of visitors on hot summer days, of which San Marcos has an ample supply. Swimming and wading, in addition to kayaking, canoeing, and tubing, are popular on the river. (Michelle Bussemey.)

Six

Around Town
Icons and Landmarks

Beyond downtown and the Texas State campus, San Marcos has many other distinctive landmarks and iconic neighborhoods. One of the oldest historic landmarks in town is El Camino Real de los Tejas National Historic Trail. Recognized by Congress in 2004, the trail connected a series of outposts and missions and was the primary overland route from the Rio Grande to the Red River Valley in Louisiana during the Spanish Colonial Period, from 1690 to 1821.

The Belvin and San Antonio Street Historic Districts in San Marcos preserve fine examples of Southern style and Victorian 19th-century homes. The Belvin Street District, created in 1974, is in the 700–800 blocks of Belvin Street and adjacent Mitchell Street. Lot and home sizes are large in scale, many with distinctive front yard fences. The San Antonio District, created in 1982, has a collection of Craftsman as well as Southern-style homes, and the district has unique concrete street markers located at San Antonio Street intersections, which designate the block number and street name.

Another historic area is the Dunbar Historic District, designated in 2003, which recognizes and preserves aspects of the local African American community heritage. The recently renovated Cephas House of Ulysses Cephas (1884–1952), the son of former slaves who became a prominent blacksmith in the San Marcos area, and the Calaboose Museum, housed in Hays County's first jailhouse, are prominent structures in the Dunbar District.

Several historic churches and church-related schools are part of the past and present in San Marcos. The San Marcos Baptist Academy, established in 1907 and now known simply as San Marcos Academy, has a long history of strong education in the town. The Coronal Institute was a private coeducational school affiliated with the Methodist Church.

The cemeteries of San Marcos also preserve the town's history. San Marcos Cemetery, often referred to as City Cemetery, preserves much of the history of the town's Anglo community. The San Pedro Cemetery, off of Old Bastrop Road, was a primary burial place for the local Hispanic community. The San Marcos–Blanco Cemetery, north of town on Post Road, was established in 1893 by five African American men—Wyatt Newman, James Landon, Henry Richardson, Lucky McQueen, and Miles Bowen.

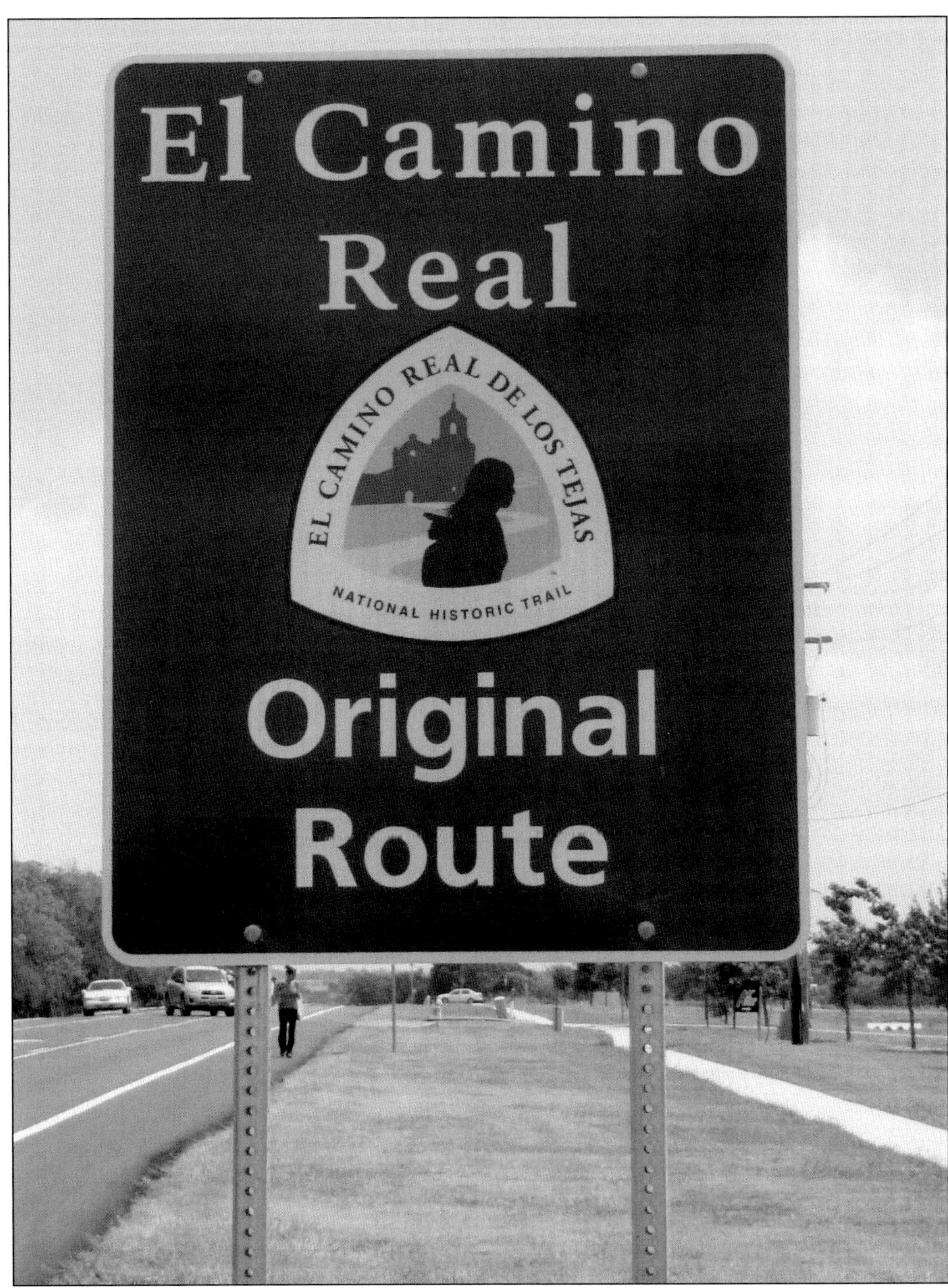

Marker Sign for El Camino Real. The El Camino Real de los Tejas National Historic Trail runs through San Marcos, here by San Marcos High School. Recently, signs designating this significant history of the Spanish colonial period in what is now the state of Texas have been installed in town. The El Camino Real de los Tejas fostered a mix of Spanish and Mexican traditions, laws, and cultures with those of Texas and America.

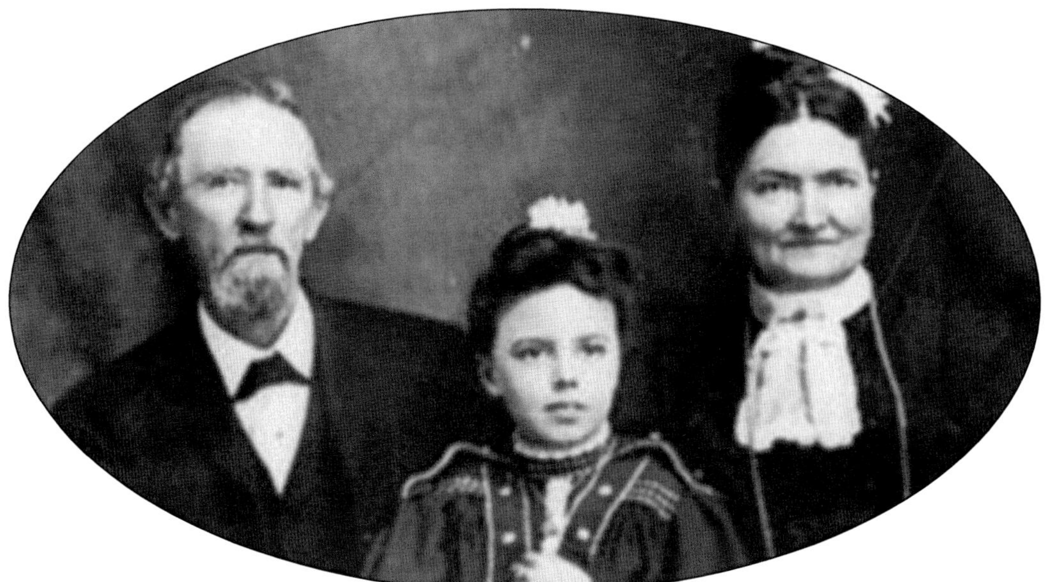

GEORGE AND SARAH MCGEHEE AND DAUGHTER. George Thomas and Sarah Cherokee Woods McGehee and their daughter Clara Belle are shown in this undated photograph. McGehee's parents were among the earliest settlers of San Marcos, and he grew up in Hays County. McGehee, born in 1836, was 90 years old when he died in 1926. He is buried in the San Marcos Cemetery. (SMPL.)

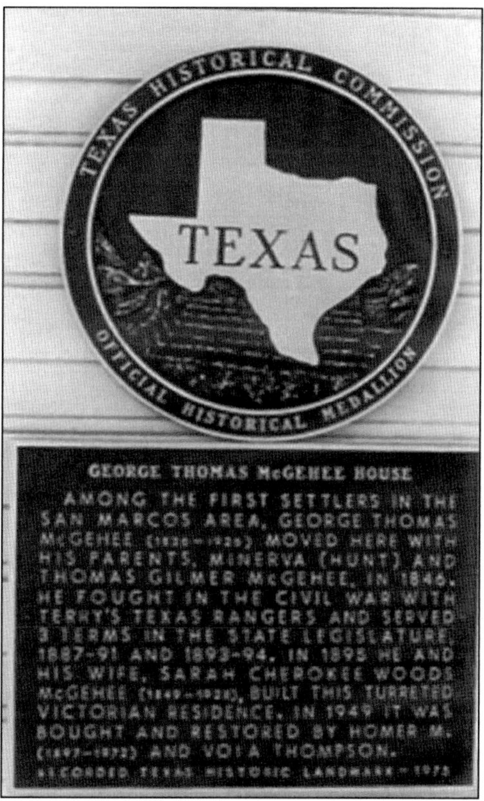

HISTORIC MARKER FOR MCGEHEE HOUSE ON BELVIN STREET. McGehee and his wife built a classic turreted Victorian home on Belvin Street in San Marcos, and this plaque illustrates the historical status of their home. The house is a Texas Historical Landmark, as recorded by the Texas Historical Commission, achieving that status in 1975. (SMPL.)

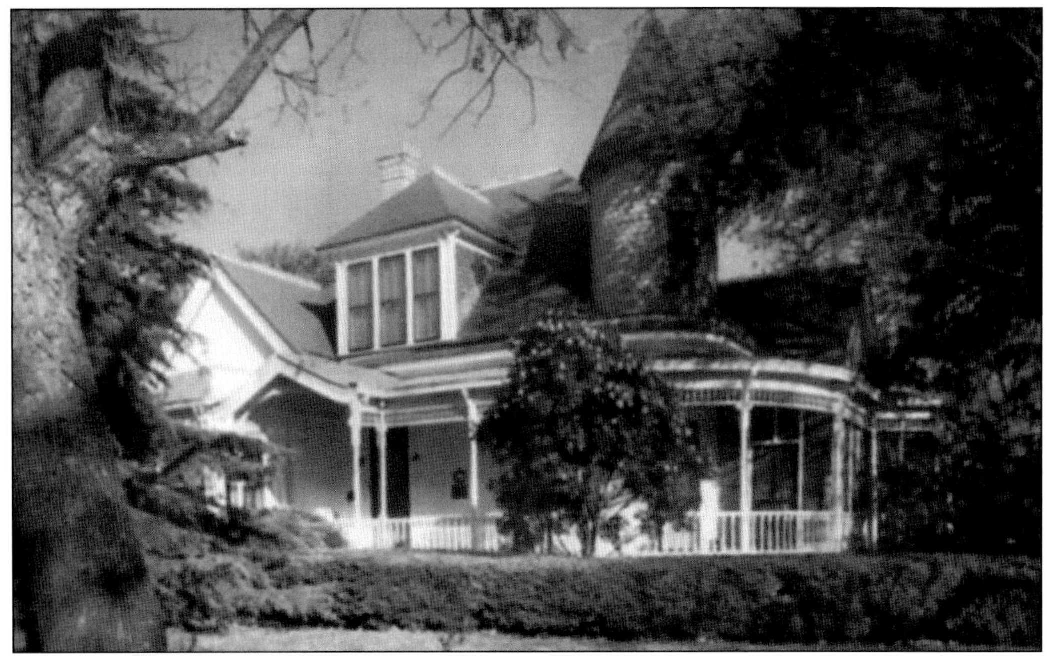

Historic McGehee Home on Belvin Street. The McGehee home, as restored, is one of the centerpieces of the Belvin Street Historic District in San Marcos. Located at 727 Belvin Street, the peach-colored house was built by S.B. McBride. It is a two-story asymmetrical Victorian house with a wraparound porch featuring spindle trim and a redbrick chimney. (SMPL.)

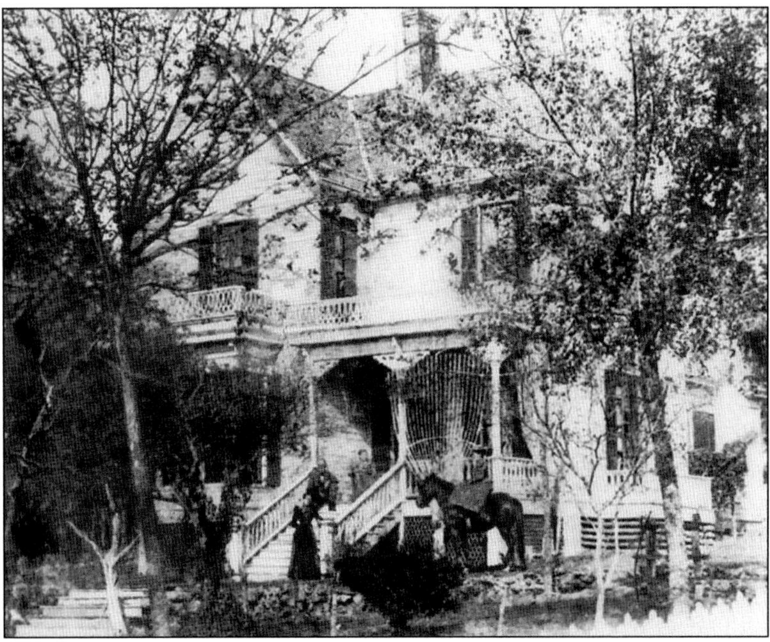

Historic Talmadge House on Belvin Street. At 802 Belvin Street, the George Henry Talmadge House was built in 1889 by a Union army soldier who had skills as a carpenter. The Talmadge House in the Belvin Street Historic District is an asymmetrical two-story Victorian L-shaped house. It has a one-story encircling porch and a railed porch roof on the second floor. (SMPL.)

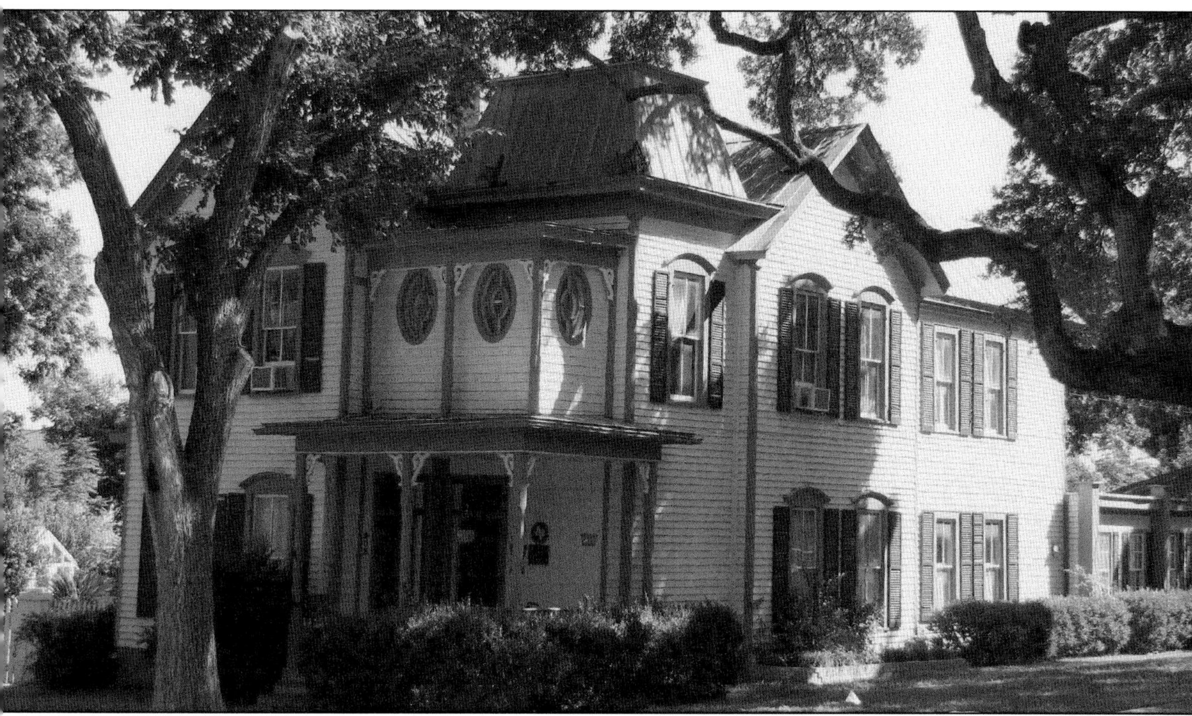

KONE HOUSE ON BELVIN STREET. The Sam R. Kone Jr. House, at 903 Belvin Street, was built by S.B. McBride in 1886. It is a striking pink Victorian frame house with an unusual central chimney. Sam R. Kone Jr. (1855–1941), was a successful merchant, active Mason, and member of the San Marcos City Council from 1914 to 1915. His wife, Laura (Smith) Kone, taught at the Coronal Institute in San Marcos before their marriage.

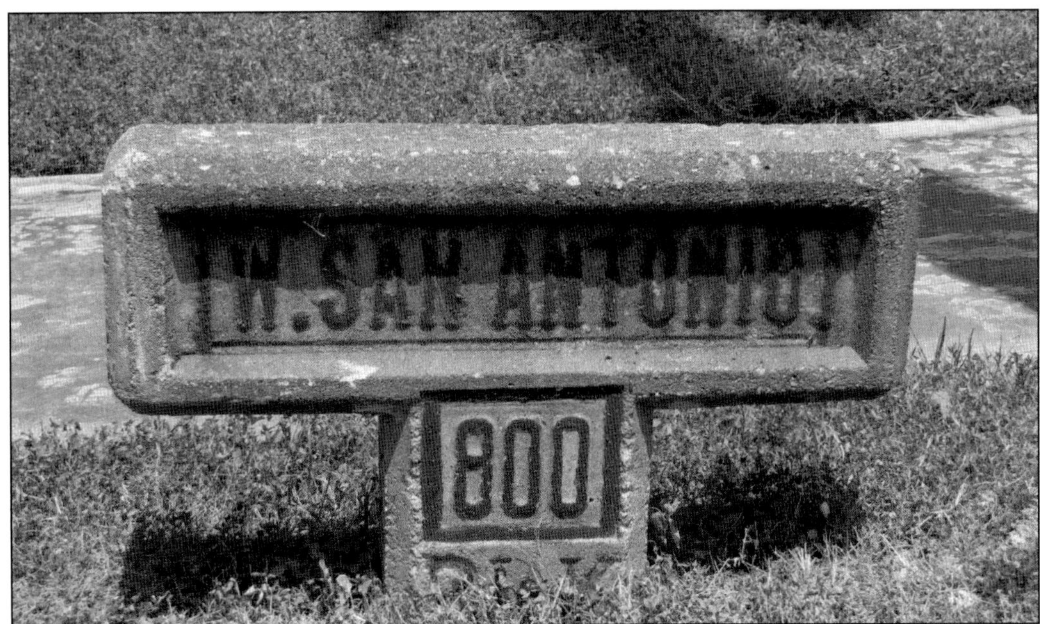

Concrete Street Marker on San Antonio Street. The San Antonio Street Historic District, established in 1982, has a larger collection of housing styles than does the Belvin Street District. The density of homes on San Antonio Street is also larger than the Belvin District as a result of differences in lot size and development pattern. The concrete street markers shown here are a unique feature of the San Antonio Street Historic District.

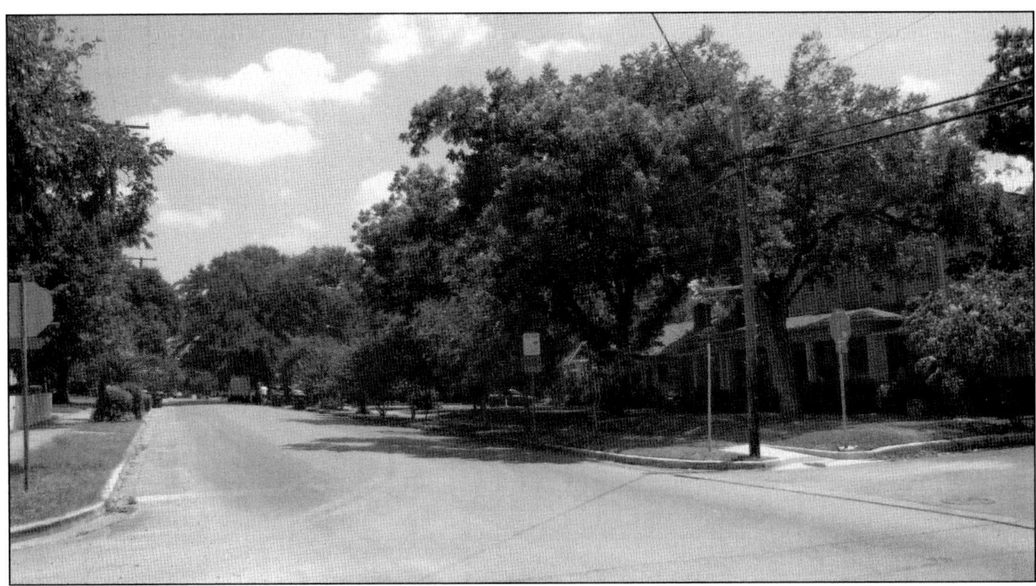

San Antonio Street Historic District. The San Antonio Street Historic District features a more eclectic mix of homes than the Belvin Street District. Houses includes Southern-style mansions, Craftsman homes, and homes from a variety of time periods.

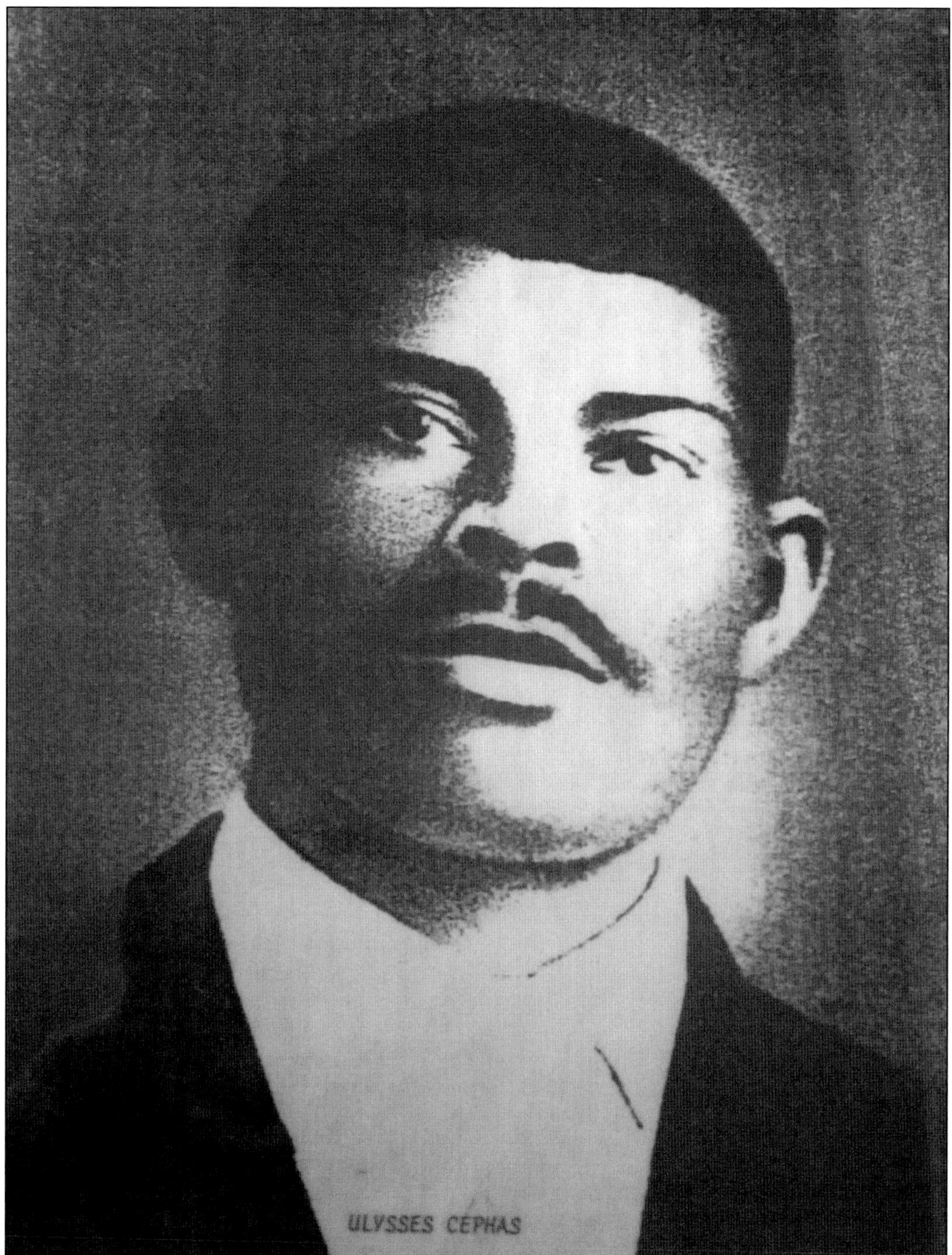

Ulysses Cephas, Famous San Marcos Blacksmith. Ulysses Cephas, born in San Marcos in 1884, was the son of former slaves Joe and Elizabeth Cephas. He was trained as a blacksmith and became a respected leader in the local African American community. He owned his own blacksmith shop and was renowned for his skills in shoeing horses and creating farm implements and superior wagons. He passed away in 1952. (TxSt.)

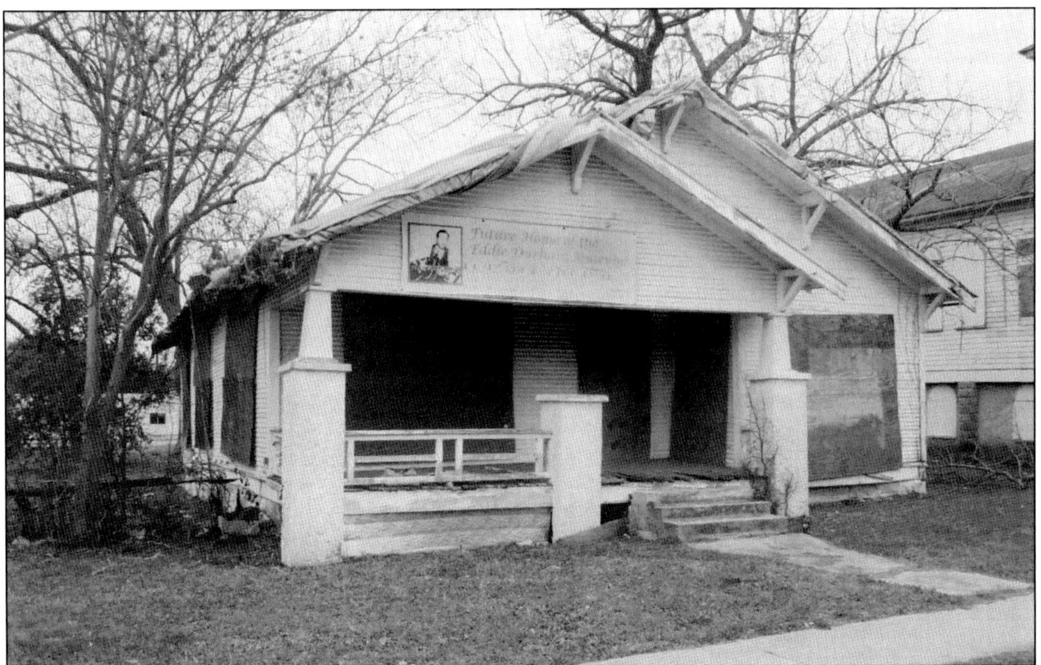

CEPHAS HOUSE IN HISTORIC DUNBAR DISTRICT. The Cephas House, former home of Ulysses Cephas, is located at 217 West Martin Luther King Drive, across the street from the Calaboose African American History Museum. Shown here prior to renovation, the house was purchased by the City of San Marcos in 2002 with community-development block grant funds and restored as a focal point in the Dunbar Historic District. (TxSt.)

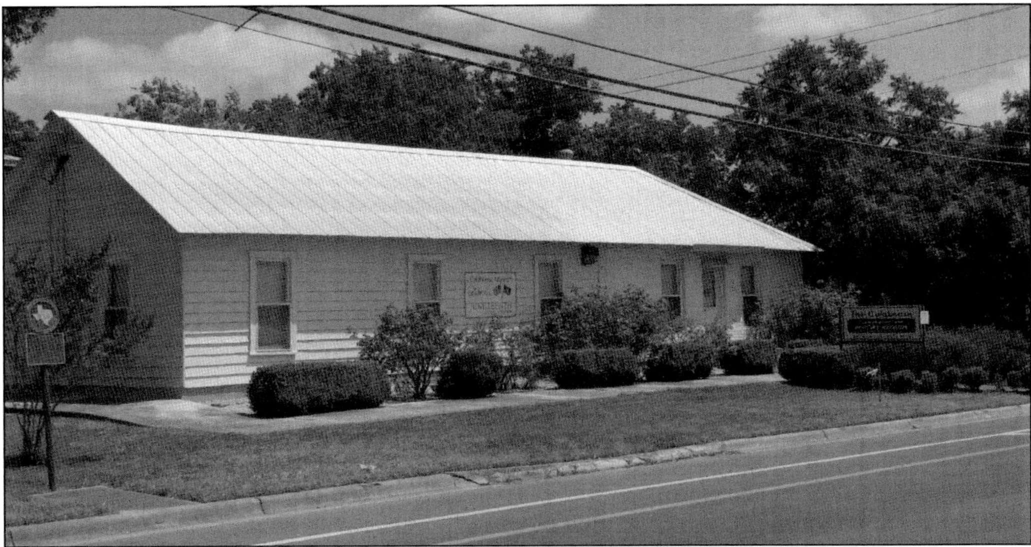

CALABOOSE AFRICAN AMERICAN HISTORY MUSEUM IN FIRST COUNTY JAIL. The Calaboose African American History Museum, on the corner of West Martin Luther King Drive and Fredericksburg Street, occupies the first Hays County Jail. Constructed in 1873, the building was later used as an annex for black prisoners and known as the Calaboose. The museum was founded by Mrs. Johnnie Armstead, and recognizes the history and importance of the African American community and experience in San Marcos and across the state and nation.

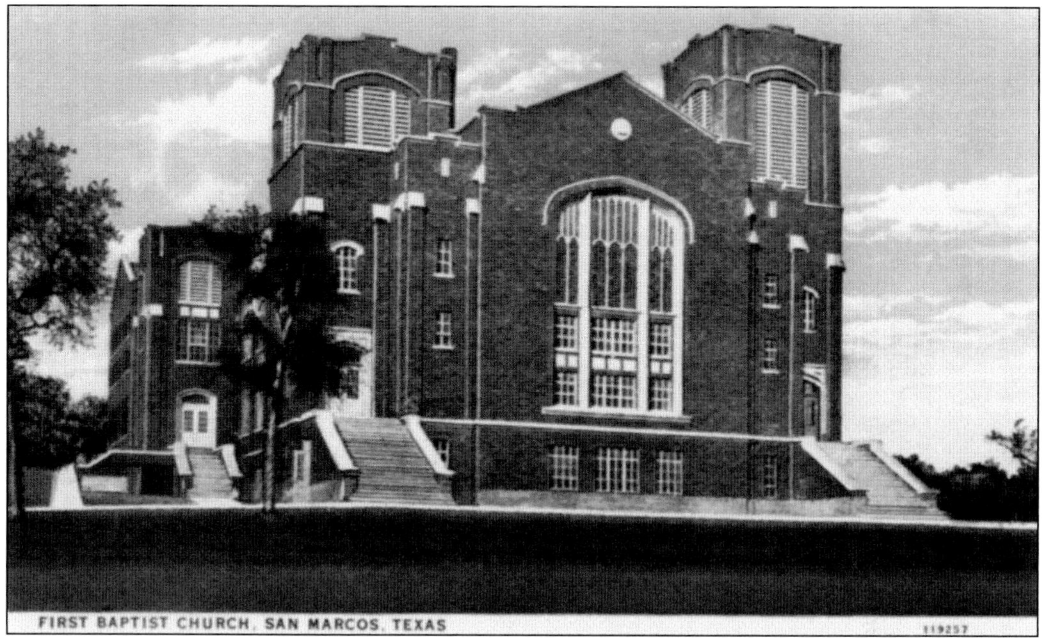

FORMER FIRST BAPTIST CHURCH OF SAN MARCOS. First Baptist Church of San Marcos, located on the corner of North and West Hutchinson Streets, was a brick-clad, steel-roofed church with a concrete frame built in 1927. Located only a few blocks from the university, the church was a vibrant part of the area northwest of the downtown square, where several large churches are located. (SMPL.)

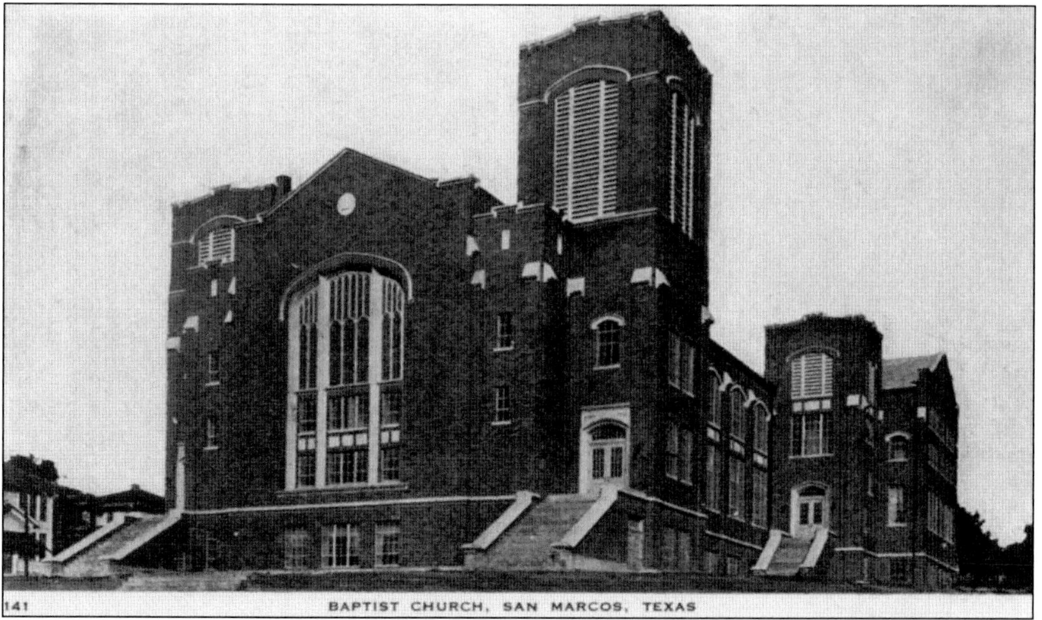

ANOTHER VIEW OF FORMER FIRST BAPTIST CHURCH. This postcard of First Baptist Church from an angle different from the previous view provides a feeling for the large size and height of the building. The church was only a few hundred feet from San Marcos's First Presbyterian Church, on the corner of North and West Hutchinson Streets. (SMPL.)

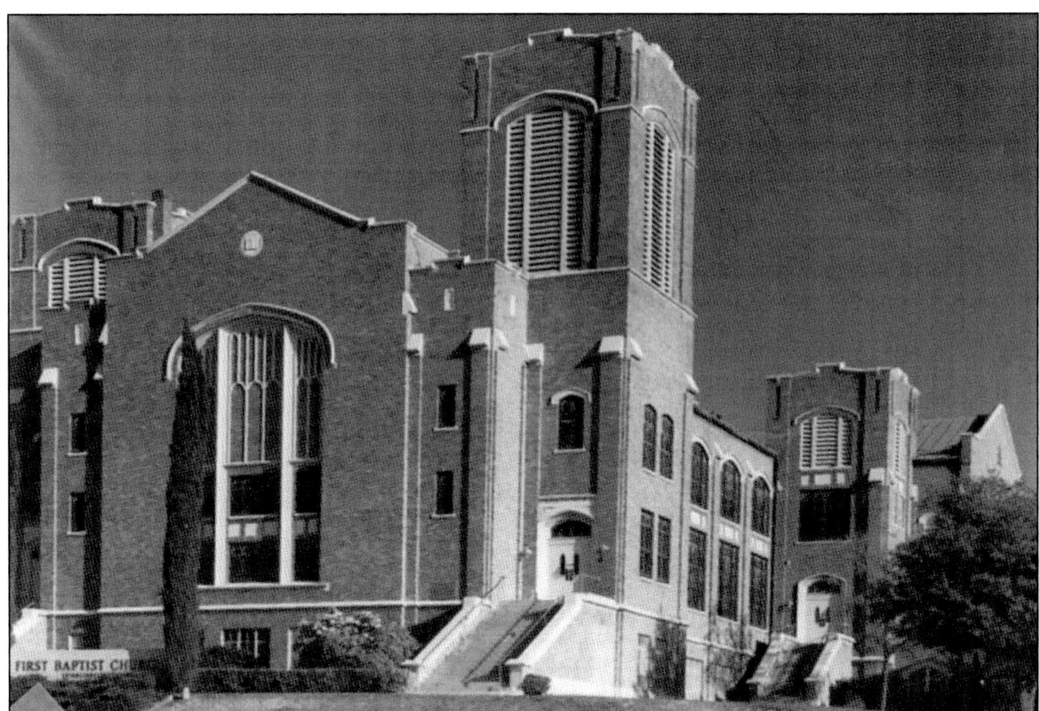

FORMER FIRST BAPTIST CHURCH, 1983. Seen here in 1983, First Baptist Church eventually became constrained by the growth of its congregation. The parish of First Baptist moved to a more spacious location with ample parking on West McCarty Lane on the south end of San Marcos, where it resides today. (SMPL.)

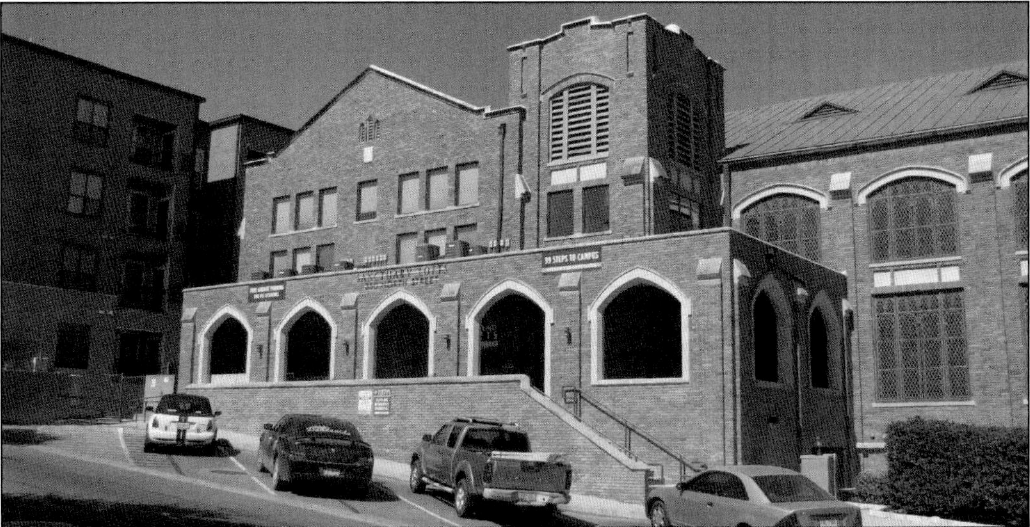

FORMER CHURCH CONVERTED INTO STUDENT LOFT APARTMENTS. A concern for preserving the historic First Baptist Church structure led the city, parish, and a developer to preserve the church as a part of a student living complex only a block from the campus of Texas State University. The project incorporated the shell and parts of the interior of the old church into an apartment complex that preserved a small chapel and the church's stained glass windows. The Sanctuary Lofts apartments opened in August 2006.

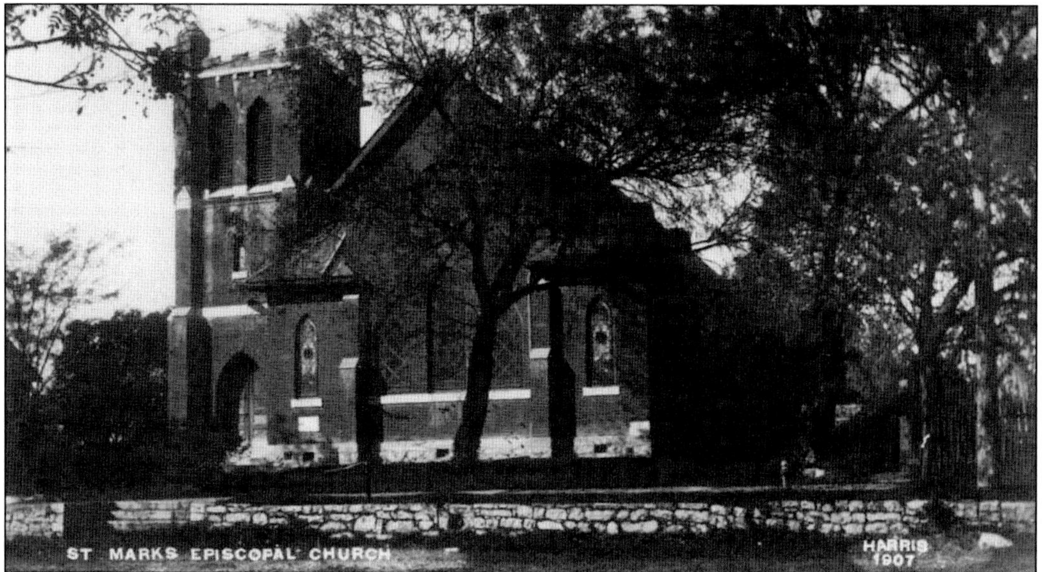

ST. MARK'S EPISCOPAL CHURCH. St. Mark's Episcopal Church has had several homes in San Marcos. Established in 1874, services were first held in the Presbyterian church. A subsequent small wooden structure gave way to the large brick building shown here, completed in 1904 and located on Hopkins and Comanche Streets, which was used until 1951. The next iteration of St. Mark's was immediately adjacent to the university campus on Guadalupe Street, where it remained until the congregation moved to a new, expansive 20-acre tract west of town on Ranch Road 12 in 2010. (SMPL.)

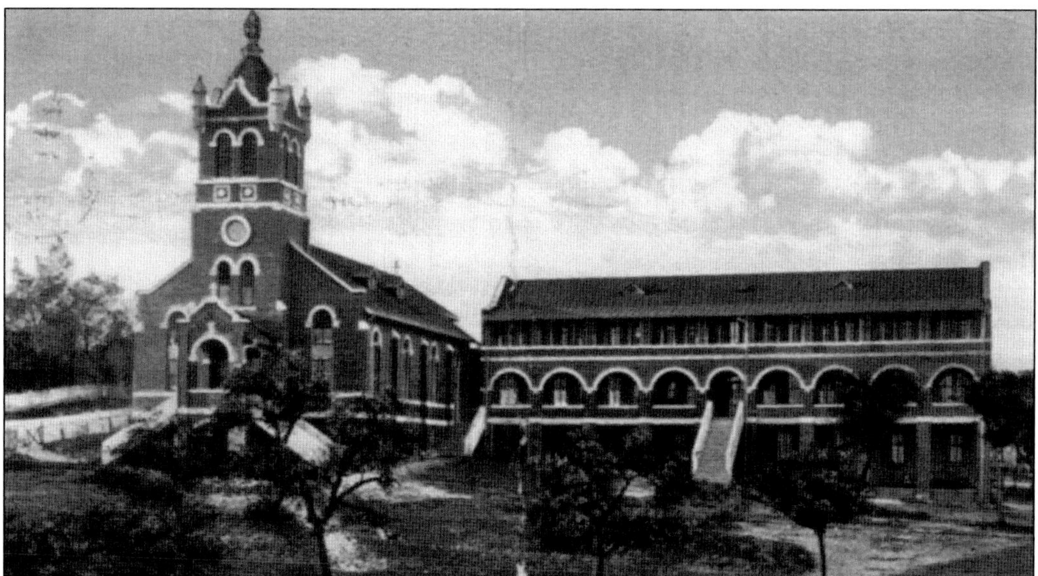

FORMER BUILDING OF ST. JOHN'S CATHOLIC CHURCH. St. John's Catholic Church began with the construction of a small wooden chapel in 1883. Fire destroyed this structure in 1915, and later that same year a new church and rectory, pictured here, was initiated on Guadalupe Street. This building was also destroyed by fire in 1970, subsequently torn down, and the land sold to the university. The current St. John's is located on East Hopkins Street near city hall and the San Marcos Public Library. (SMPL.)

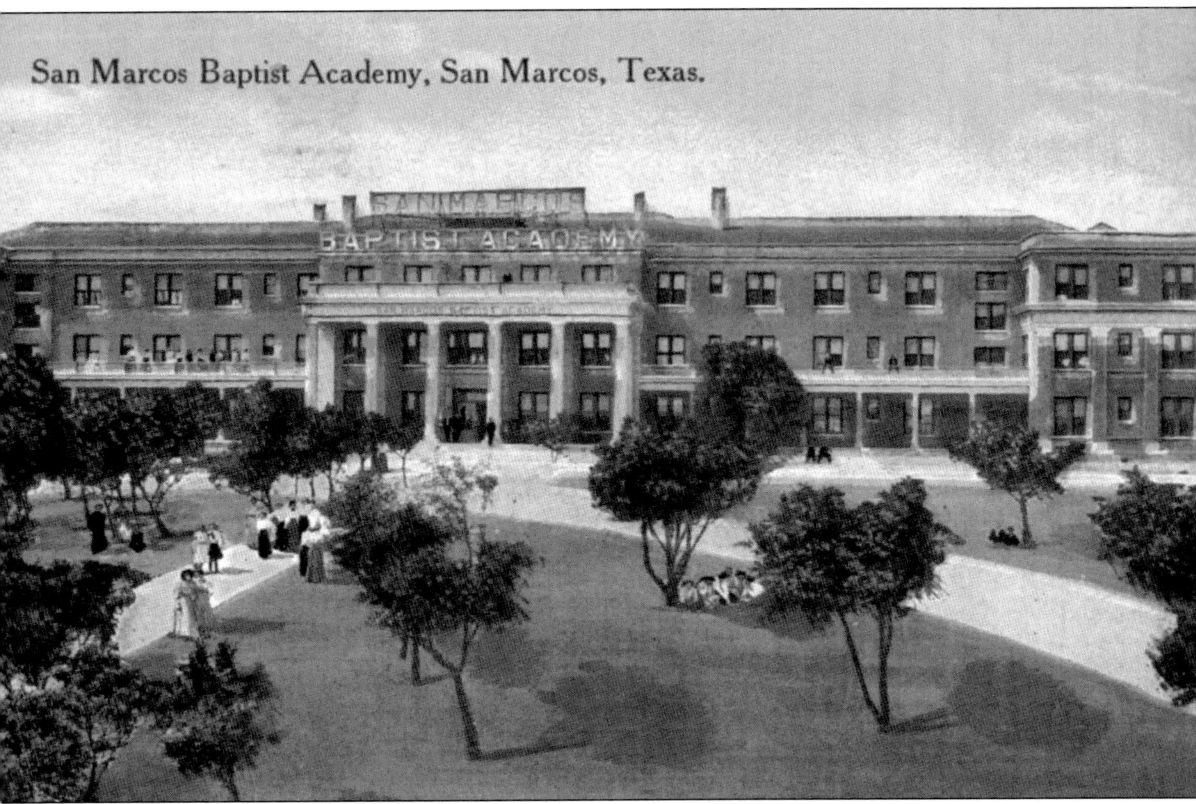

San Marcos Baptist Academy. This is an early 20th century postcard view of the San Marcos Baptist Academy, which was located on land that is now part of the southwest edge of Texas State University. The school opened for the first time in September 1908 with 200 students. (TxSt.)

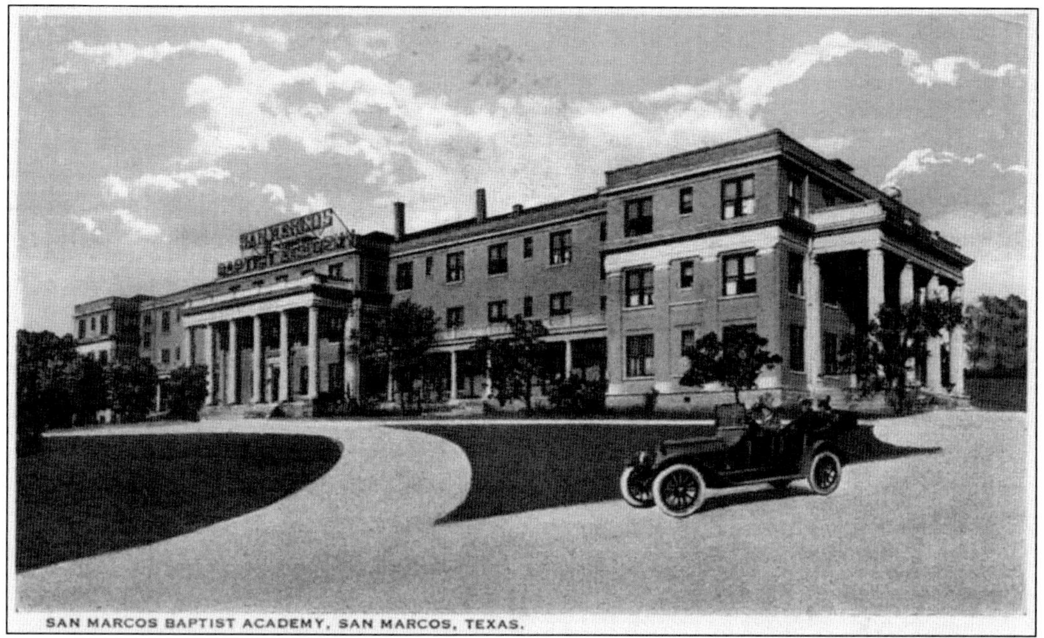

SAN MARCOS BAPTIST ACADEMY AND EARLY AUTOMOBILE. This is another early 20th century postcard view of the San Marcos Baptist Academy; in 1910, the school became affiliated with the Baptist General Convention of Texas. The school remains affiliated with the general convention and offers a fully accredited college-preparatory curriculum. (SMPL.)

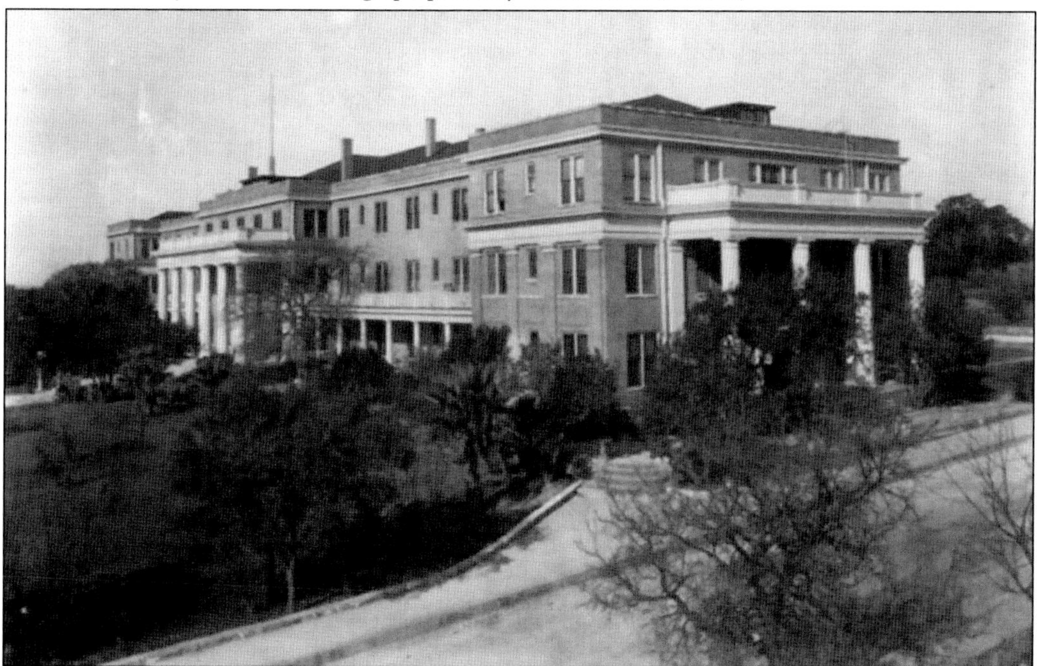

CARROLL HALL, SAN MARCOS BAPTIST ACADEMY. This undated photograph shows Carroll Hall at the former site of the San Marcos Baptist Academy. Carroll Hall was named after Dr. J.M. Carroll, the first president of the San Marcos Baptist Academy, who served from its founding until 1911. (SMPL.)

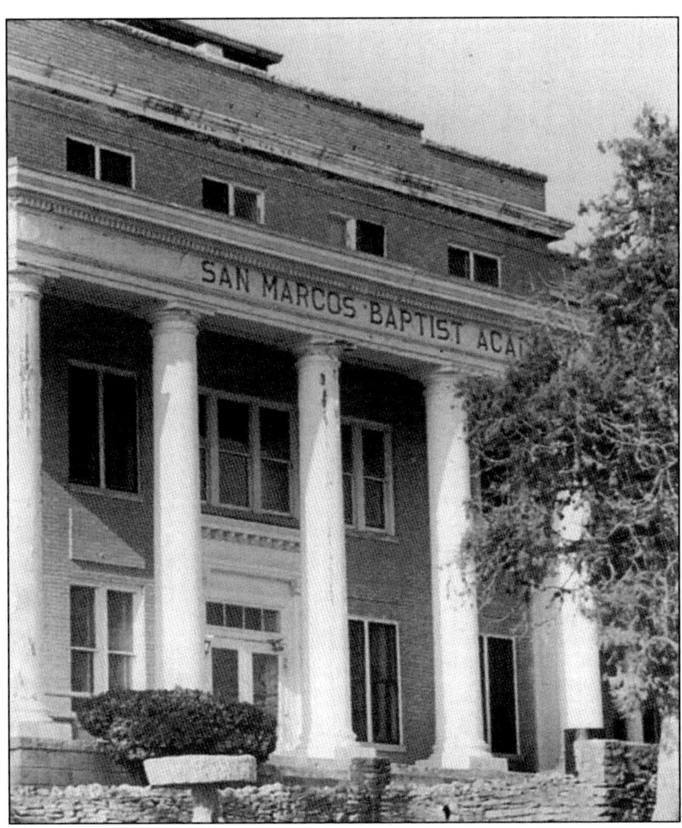

Front View of Carroll Hall. Carroll Hall was located on what is now the southwest edge of the Texas State University campus. San Saba Hall, a three-story student dormitory on the Texas State campus, was built at this same location. San Saba Hall was subsequently demolished in spring 2014 to make room for the new Moore Street Housing Project on the Texas State campus, due to be completed in 2016. (SMPL.)

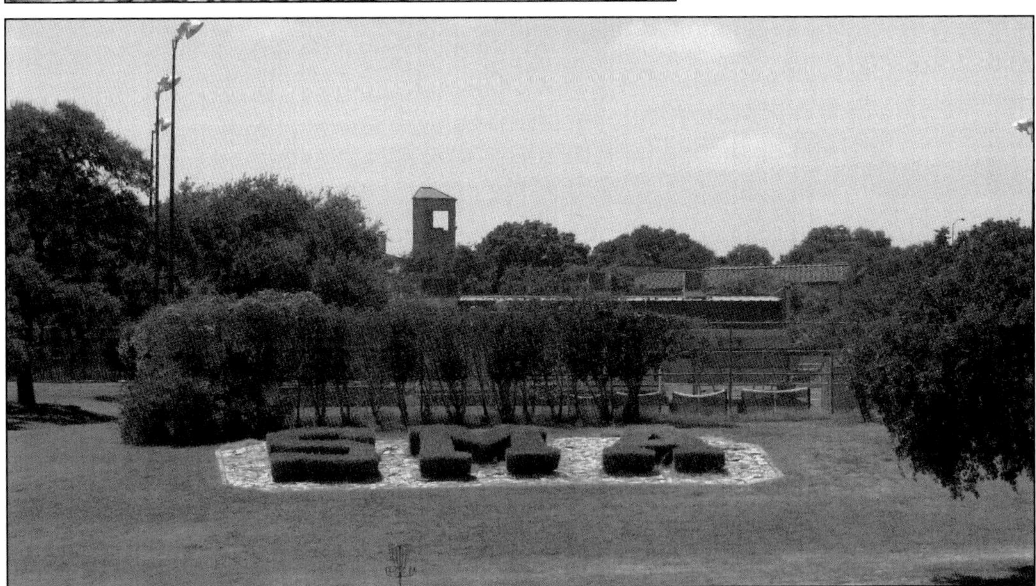

Modern Campus of San Marcos Baptist Academy. In 1979, the San Marcos Baptist Academy sold its campus to Texas State University with an agreement that allowed the academy to continue in its old facilities until a new campus was planned and constructed. The new facility, shown here, is located on a 200-acre site in the Hill Country on the far west margins of San Marcos. Classes on the new campus began in January 1982.

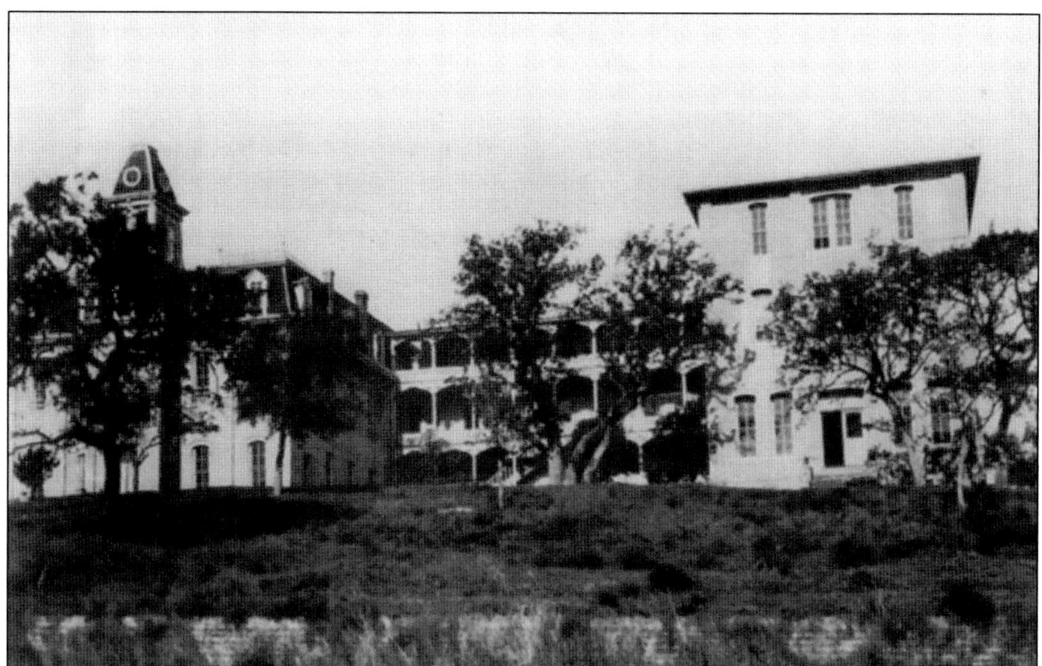

Coronal Institute, Corner of Moore and Hutchinson Streets, c. 1900. The Coronal Institute was established in San Marcos in 1868 by educator O.N. Hollingsworth. It was a coeducational private school affiliated with the Methodist Church. It also offered military training to boys. The building shown here, on the corner of Moore and Hutchinson Streets, was built in the 1890s after the original building burned in 1890. (SMPL.)

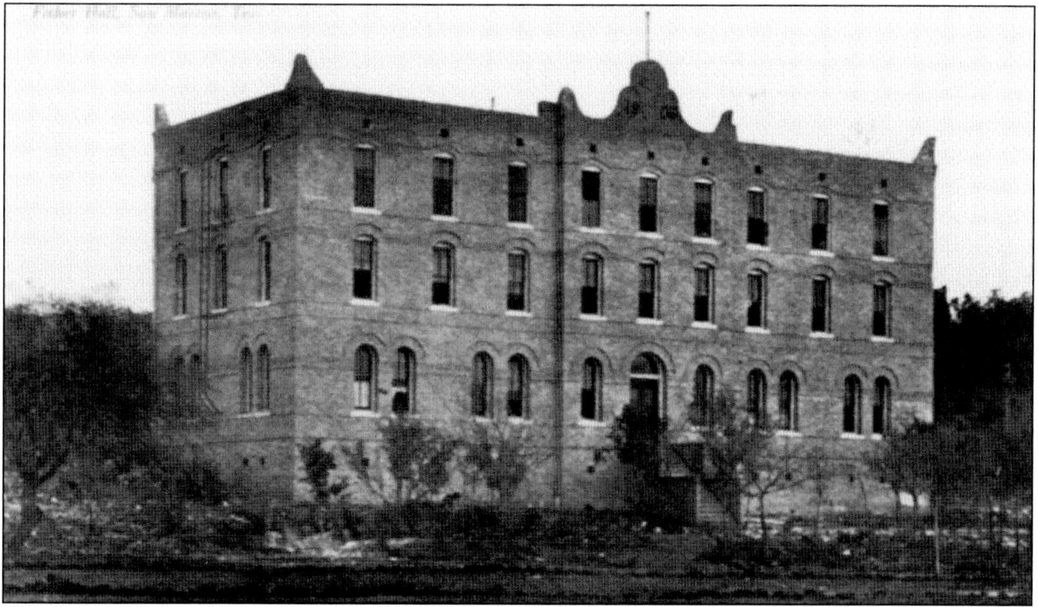

Fisher Hall, Coronal Institute Boy's Dormitory. Fisher Hall was built in 1906 as part of the Coronal Institute. It was constructed on a nine-acre lot at 1132 Belvin Street as a boys' dormitory. The Coronal Institute was closed in 1918, and the main buildings were torn down. Fisher Hall, however, survived. (SMPL.)

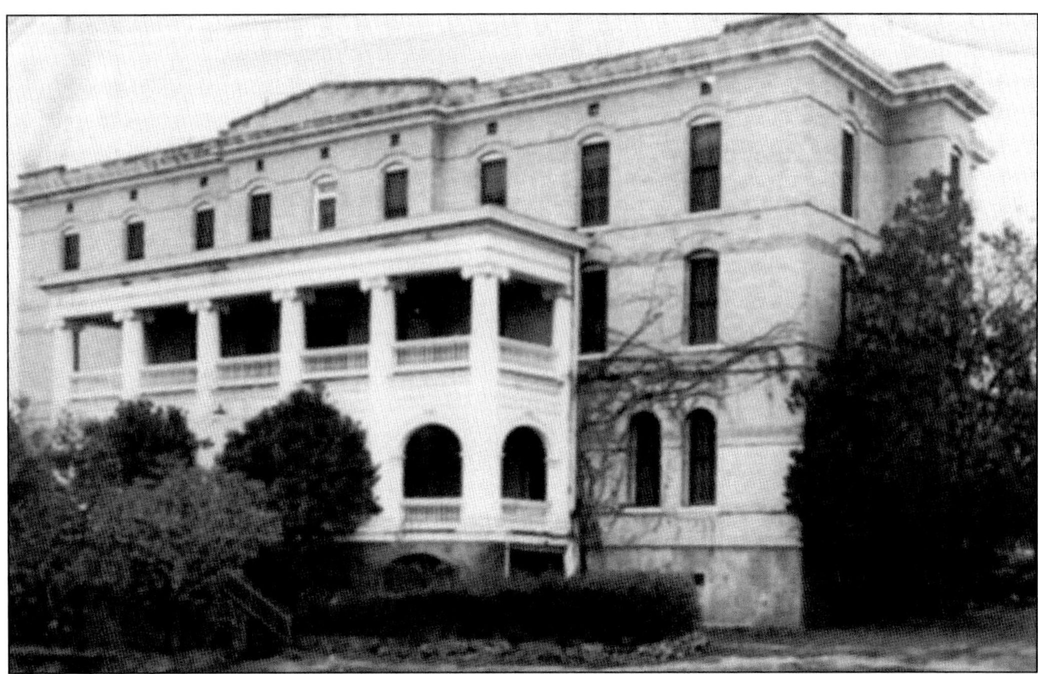

Fisher Hall Becomes Memorial Hospital, 1923. After the closing of the Coronal Institute, Fisher Hall on Belvin Street was sold and in 1923 became the Hays County Soldiers, Sailors and Marines Memorial Hospital, as shown here. It served in this capacity until 1963, when it was purchased by the American Legion and leased to the San Marcos Baptist Academy as a boys' dormitory. (SMPL.)

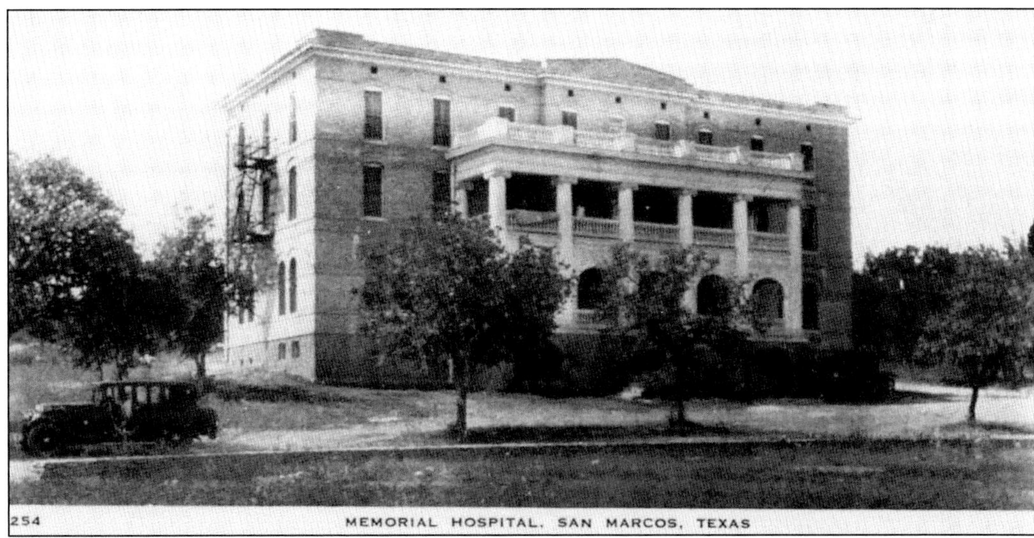

Memorial Hospital on Belvin Street, Late 1920s. Memorial Hospital is pictured here in the late 1920s. In 1969, the former hospital and dorm was sold to the Pi Kappa Alpha fraternity. The fraternity use of the building was controversial because of its location on residential Belvin Street. In 1997, it was sold and abandoned, and the building succumbed to an arson fire and was subsequently razed in 2007. (SMPL.)

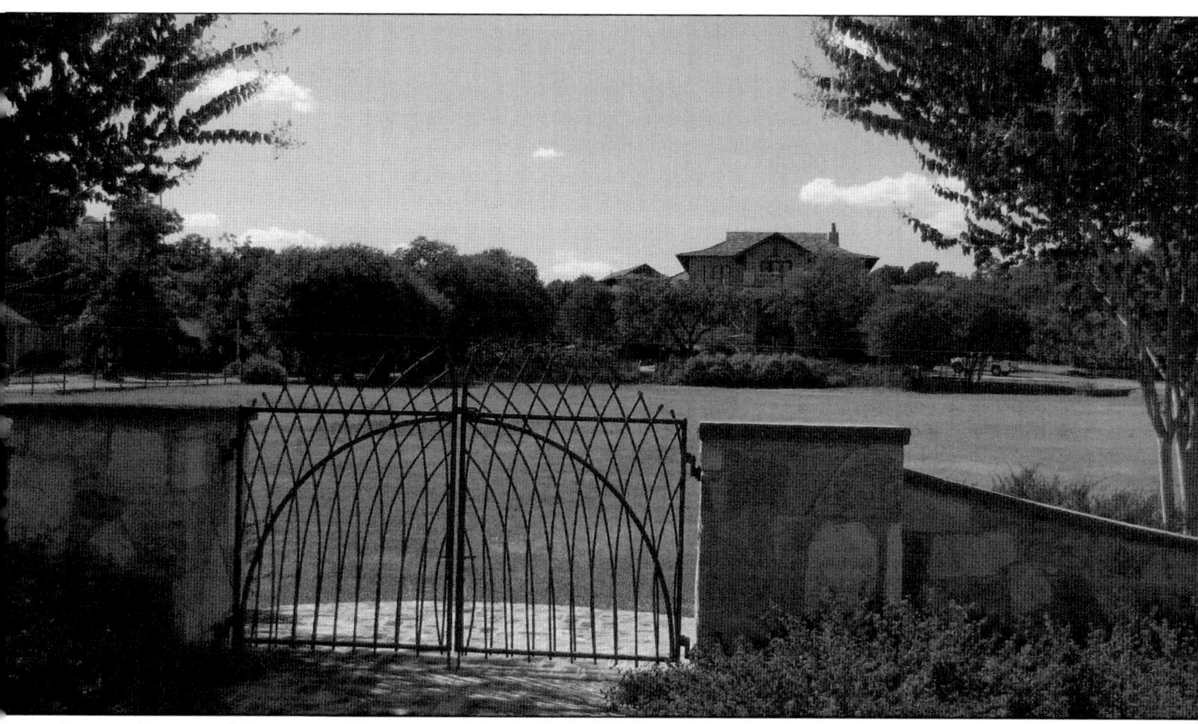

SITE OF FORMER MEMORIAL HOSPITAL. The former Memorial Hospital and eventual fraternity house was located on this site on Belvin Street. The arson fire in 1997 made the building structurally unsound and required its removal. An attractive lawn occupies the site today.

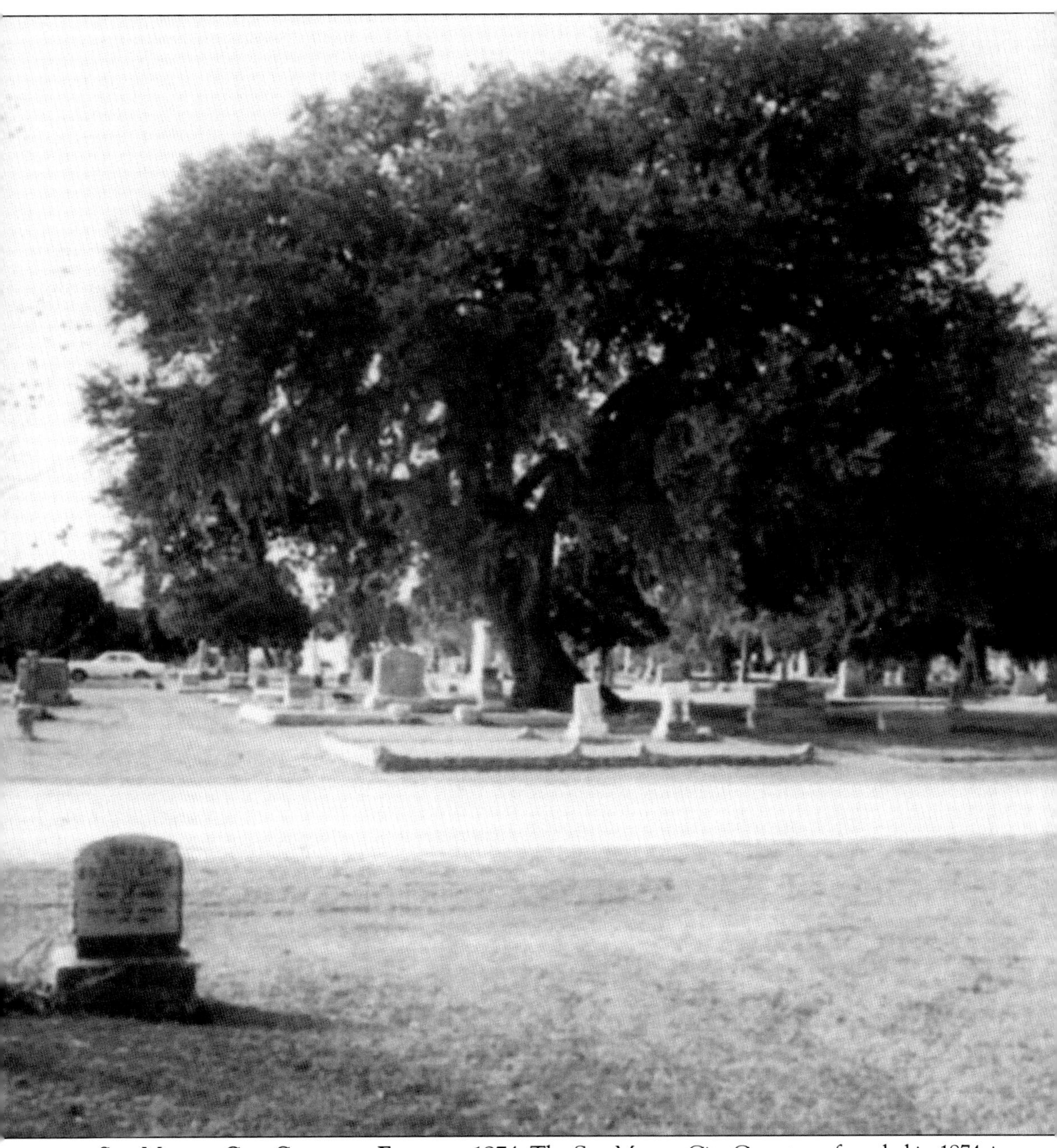

San Marcos City Cemetery, Founded 1874. The San Marcos City Cemetery, founded in 1874, is located on 45 acres at 1001 Old Ranch Road 12. It is the burial ground for many of Hays County's pioneers, and contains the graves of military veterans dating back to the War of 1812. (SMPL.)

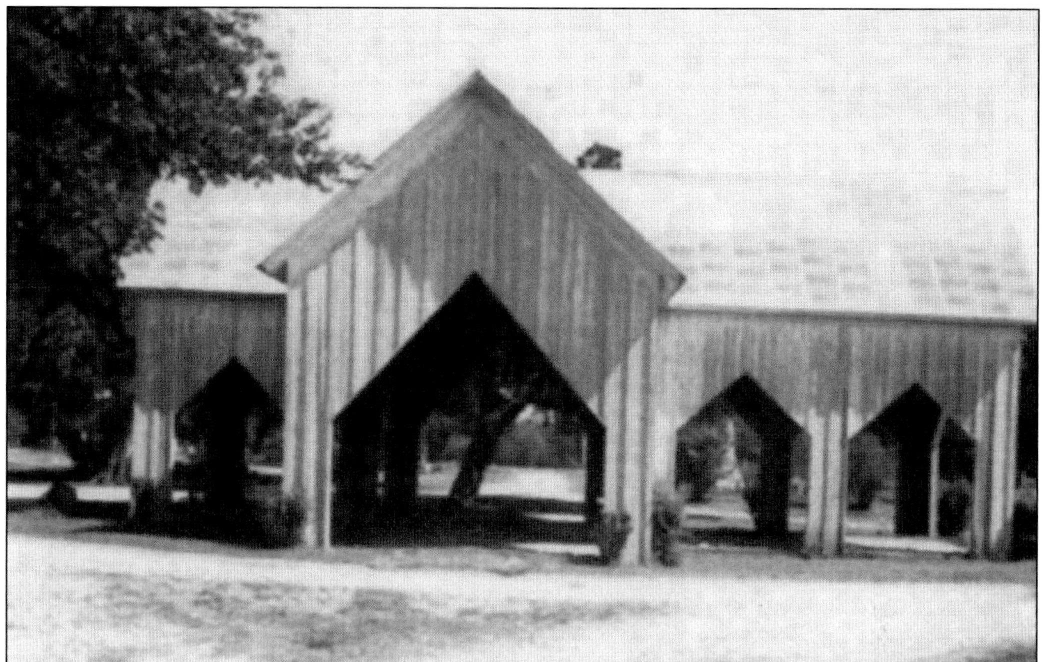

San Marcos City Cemetery Chapel. The San Marcos Cemetery Chapel was designed in 1886 by Ed Northcraft, and within a month, a contract to build the chapel was awarded to Ralph Smith, who was to build the chapel for $450 within five months. The chapel's style is referred to as Carpenter Gothic architecture. (SMPL.)

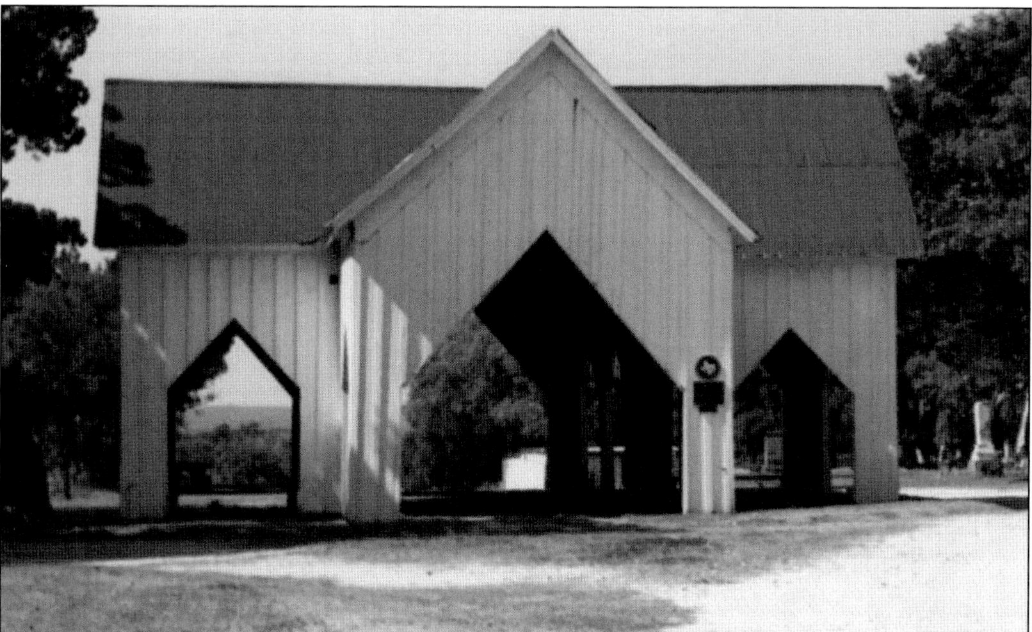

A Historic Landmark, San Marcos Cemetery Chapel. The San Marcos Cemetery Chapel was sold to the city, along with the cemetery, in May 1924. In 1973, the chapel was named a Recorded Texas Historic Landmark. The chapel was also listed in the National Register of Historic Places in 1983. (SMPL.)

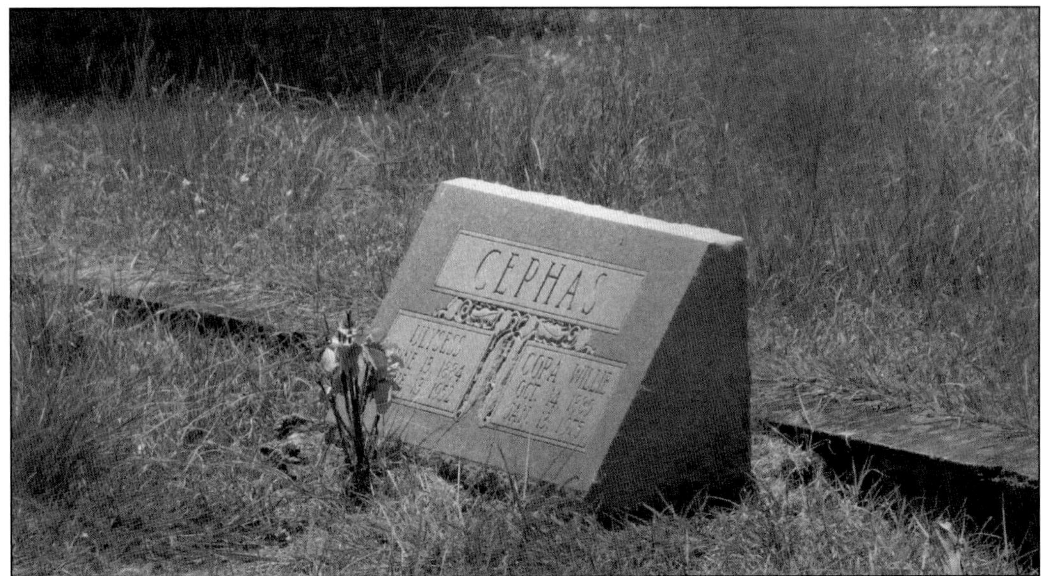

Historic San Marcos–Blanco Cemetery. The San Marcos–Blanco Cemetery, established in 1893, is an African American cemetery and is still in use. It has also been used as a pauper's cemetery. It is located on the north end of town on Post Road. Shown here is the grave of Ulysses Cephas and his wife, Cora Willie Cephas.

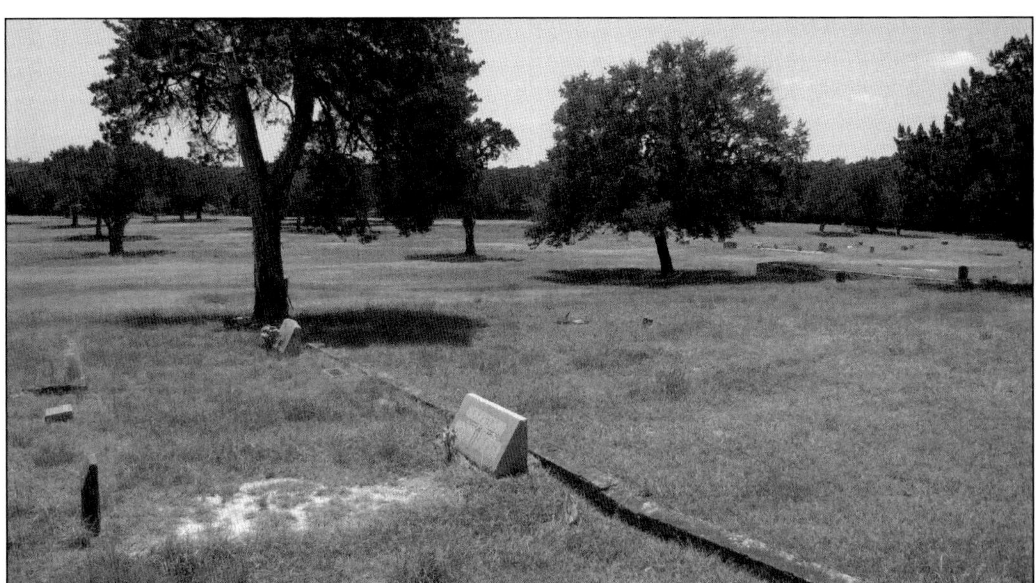

San Marcos–Blanco Cemetery Today. The historical African American cemetery continues to be used in the 21st century. The pastoral setting is very peaceful. Some graves' headstones and markers are well tended, whereas others have fallen into various states of disrepair.

Seven

Modern Destinations

Town Growth and the Outlet Mall

San Marcos has grown dramatically since the 1960s, and in 2013–2015 was the fastest-growing small city in the United States according to the census bureau. Numerous attractions around the city make tourism one of its primary economic activities. Education also continues as a primary economic activity via Texas State University and the Gary Job Corps Center.

The San Marcos outlet malls, located on the east side of the intersection of Interstate 35 and Centerpoint Road, is the largest outlet shopping center in the United States. The outlet malls are comprised of two separate units, the Premium Outlets north of Centerpoint Road and the Tanger Factory Outlet Center to the south. Together, the adjacent malls have over 350 stores and more than one million square feet of shopping. The outlet malls are a major tourist attraction, bringing in shoppers from across Texas and also from Mexico. In 2006, ABC's *The View* named the San Marcos outlets the third-best place to shop in the world, trailing only New York City and Dubai.

Dick's Classic Garage, part of the Central Texas Museum of Automotive History, opened on the southern end of San Marcos on Stagecoach Trail in 2009. It is dedicated to the preservation and display of the history of the automobile, showcasing vehicles and memorabilia from the 1900s though the 1950s.

Wonder World Park, in south-central San Marcos, is a theme park centered around Wonder Cave, located on the Balcones Fault escarpment. The park also features a 110-foot-high observation tower with a commanding view of San Marcos as well as a wildlife petting park and a train ride.

The Gary Job Corps Center, opened on March 4, 1965, is an ongoing educational facility initiated by then-president Lyndon Johnson as part of his War on Poverty. The center occupies the former Gary Army Air Field on the northeast edge of San Marcos. Today, the Gary Job Corps Center is the largest in the United States, with over 1,600 students on facilities covering 775 acres.

Other major employers in San Marcos include the Central Texas Medical Center, the San Marcos Aquatic Resources Center (the former fish hatchery), and the San Marcos Consolidated Independent School District.

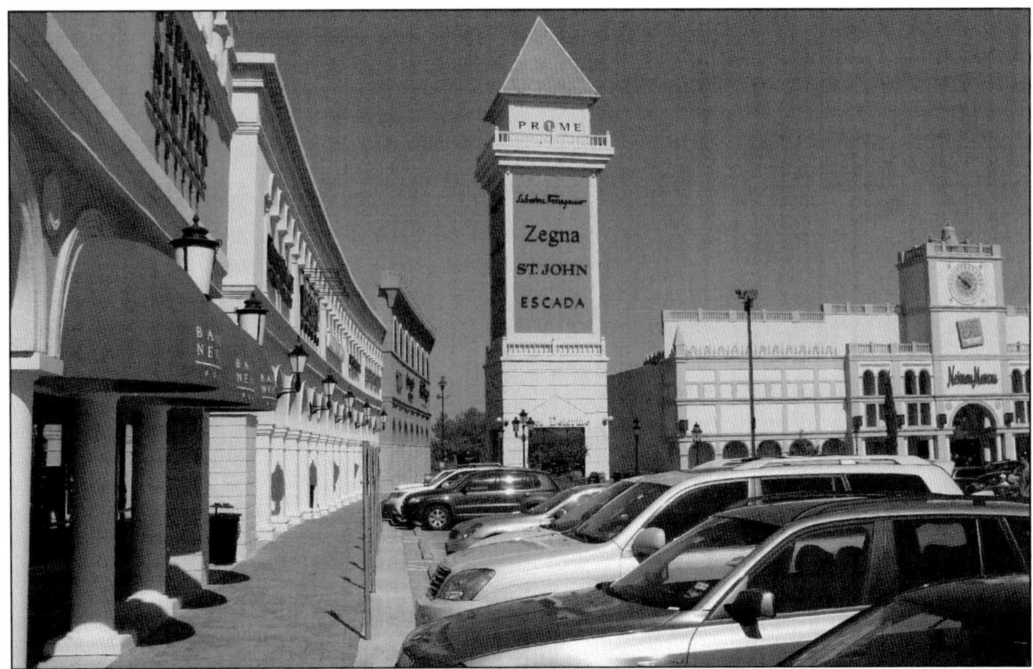

Premium Outlets at the San Marcos Outlet Malls. The Premium Outlets comprises the northern half of the San Marcos outlet malls, north of Centerpoint Road. The structures are designed to look somewhat like famous European landmarks. Here the tower evokes the tower that dominates St. Mark's Square in Venice, Italy, appropriate for a town (San Marcos) whose name is Spanish for St. Mark. (Zereshk.)

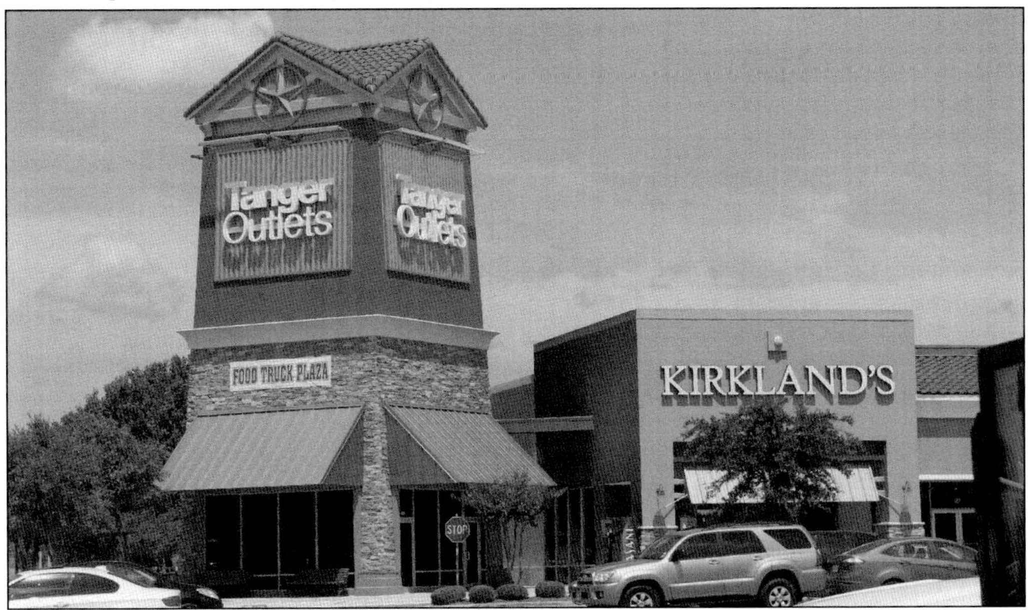

Tanger Outlet Center at the San Marcos Outlet Malls. The Tanger Outlet Center is located across Centerpoint Road from the Premium Outlets to the north. This half of the San Marcos outlet malls has a more Texas feel to the architecture, with the state Lone Star symbol prominently displayed. Over 125 separate establishments call the Tanger Outlet Center home. (Billy Hathorn.)

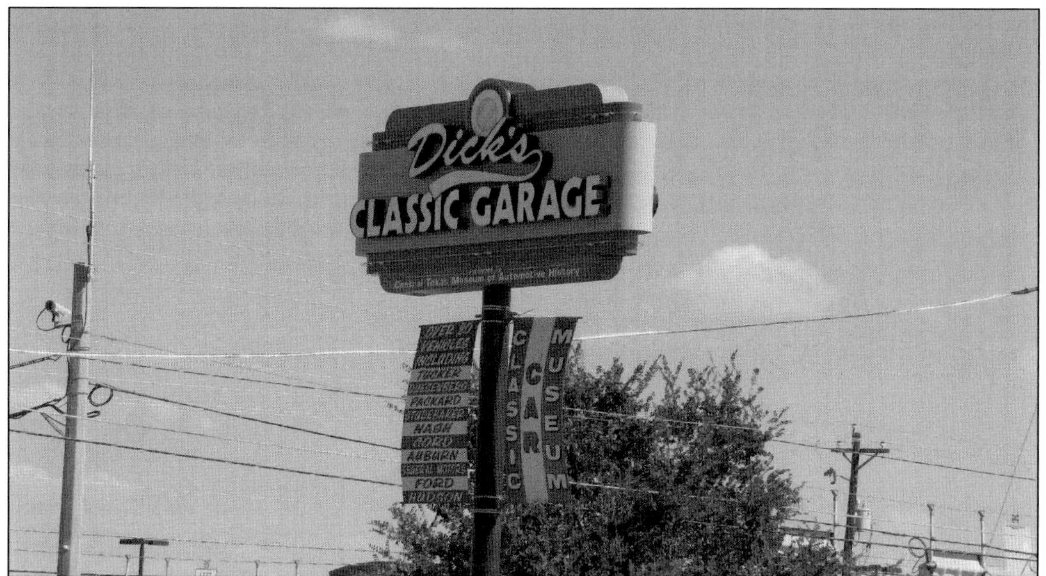

Dick's Classic Garage, a Museum of Automotive History. Dick's Classic Garage, founded by Dick Burdick, opened in San Marcos in 2009. The garage is a museum that showcases American vehicles and memorabilia from the 1930s through the 1950s, with some older displays from the early 20th century. One of the featured displays is a 1948 Tucker sedan with only four-tenths of a mile on the odometer, the lowest mileage Tucker in existence.

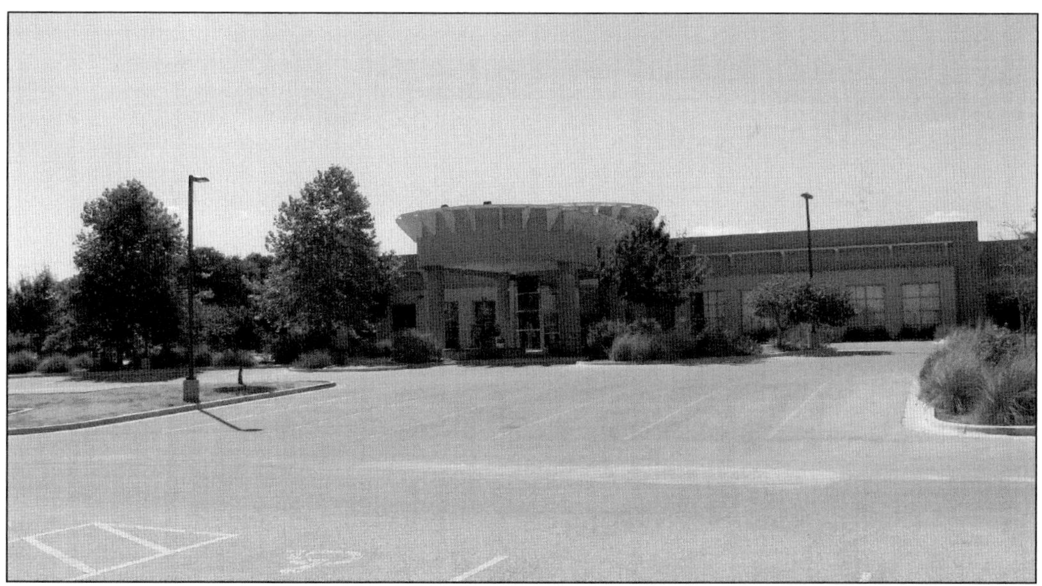

The Front Portico of Dick's Classic Garage. The exterior of Dick's Classic Garage includes this impressive portico covering the entrance to the museum. The primary purpose of the museum is to show today's guests and future generations the evolution of the automobile and how it has impacted society and the effect society has had on the automobile. The garage also houses a 2,500-square-foot conference center, available for renting, that is fully equipped with modern audio-visual equipment.

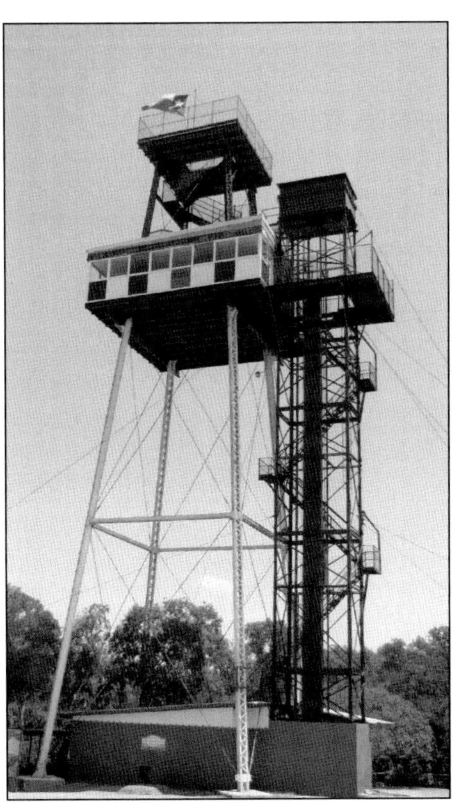

Tejas Observation Tower at Wonder World Park. The 110-foot-high Tejas Observation Tower, shown here, rises high above the surrounding Wonder World Park in south-central San Marcos. Located on and directly above the Balcones Escarpment, an ancient fault, the park offers family fun below, on, and above the surface. Views from the top of the observation tower illustrate the striking contrast between the Texas Hill Country west of the Balcones Escarpment and the Blackland Prairie of the Gulf Coastal Plain to the east.

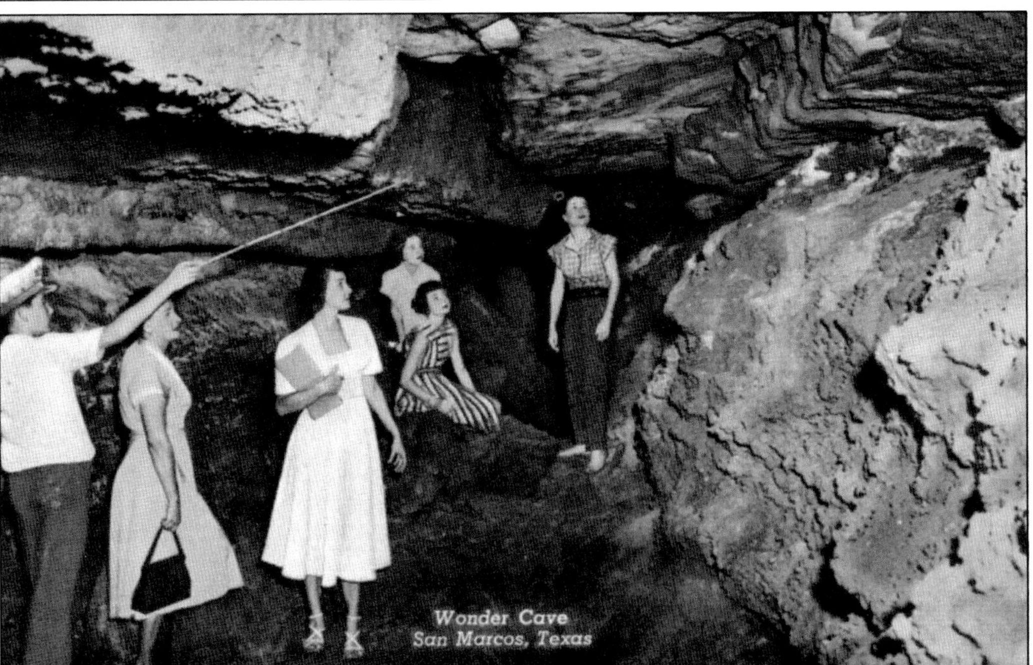

Wonder Cave at Wonder World Park. A 1950s-era tour group is shown the Balcones Fault in Wonder Cave. Wonder Cave was the first commercially owned cave in the state to give guided tours, beginning around 1900. (TxSt.)

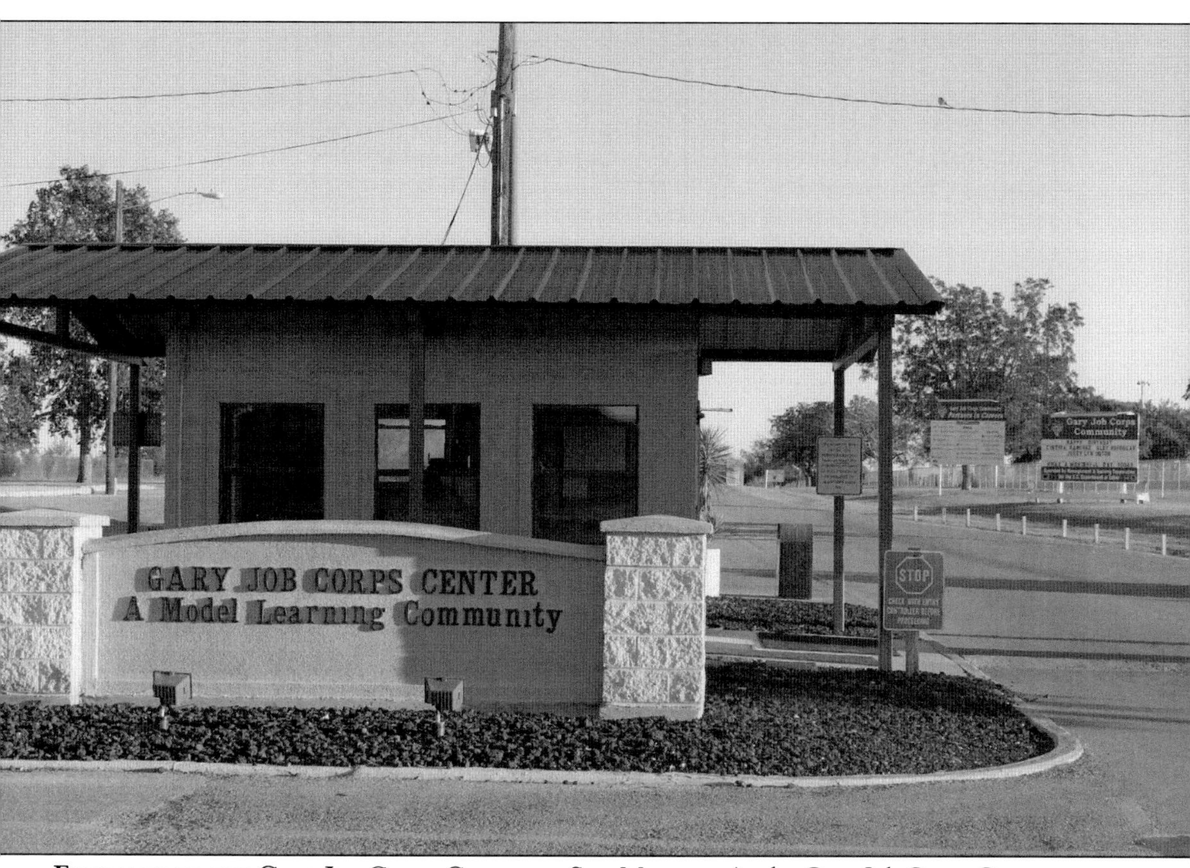

Entrance to the Gary Job Corps Center in San Marcos. At the Gary Job Corps Center on the northeast edge of San Marcos, young people aged 16 through 24 can gain career skills and academic training to help in improving the quality of their lives. The mission of the center is carried out here on a 775-acre campus offering 18 career technical training opportunities in areas such as health occupations, business technology, construction, manufacturing, and correctional- and security-officer training. (Billy Hathorn.)

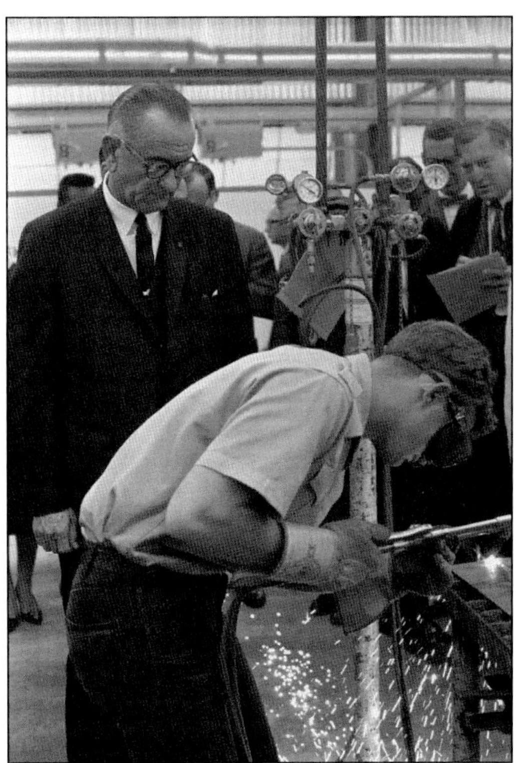

President Johnson Visits the Gary Job Corps Center. Initiated by Pres. Lyndon Johnson in a speech to his alma mater, Southwest Texas State College, in November 1964, the job corps opened at the Gary Job Corps Center on March 4, 1965. President Johnson is shown here visiting the center on November 8, 1965. (LBJPL.)

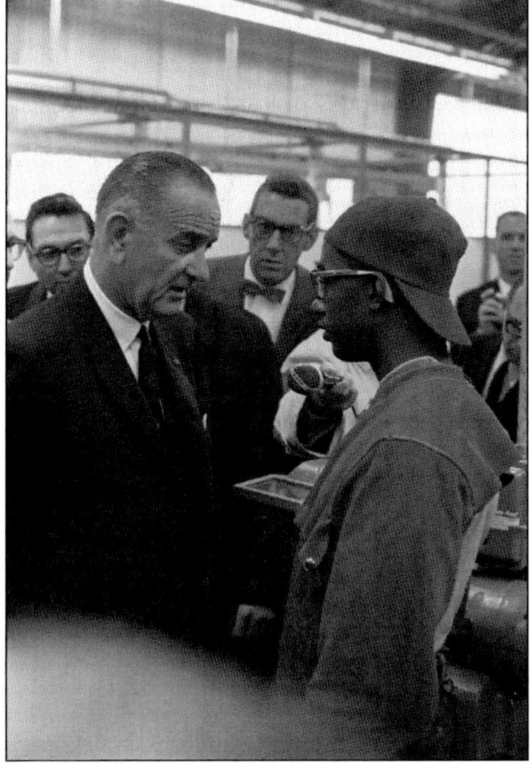

President Johnson and Job Corps Student. President Johnson is shown here continuing his visit to the Gary Job Corps Center on November 8, 1965. At first, only male students were accepted at the Gary Job Corps Center, but today up to 1,600 male and female students attend the center. The 775-acre campus hosts a cafeteria, dormitories, post office, student bank, and wellness center as well as athletic fields and recreational facilities. (LBJPL.)

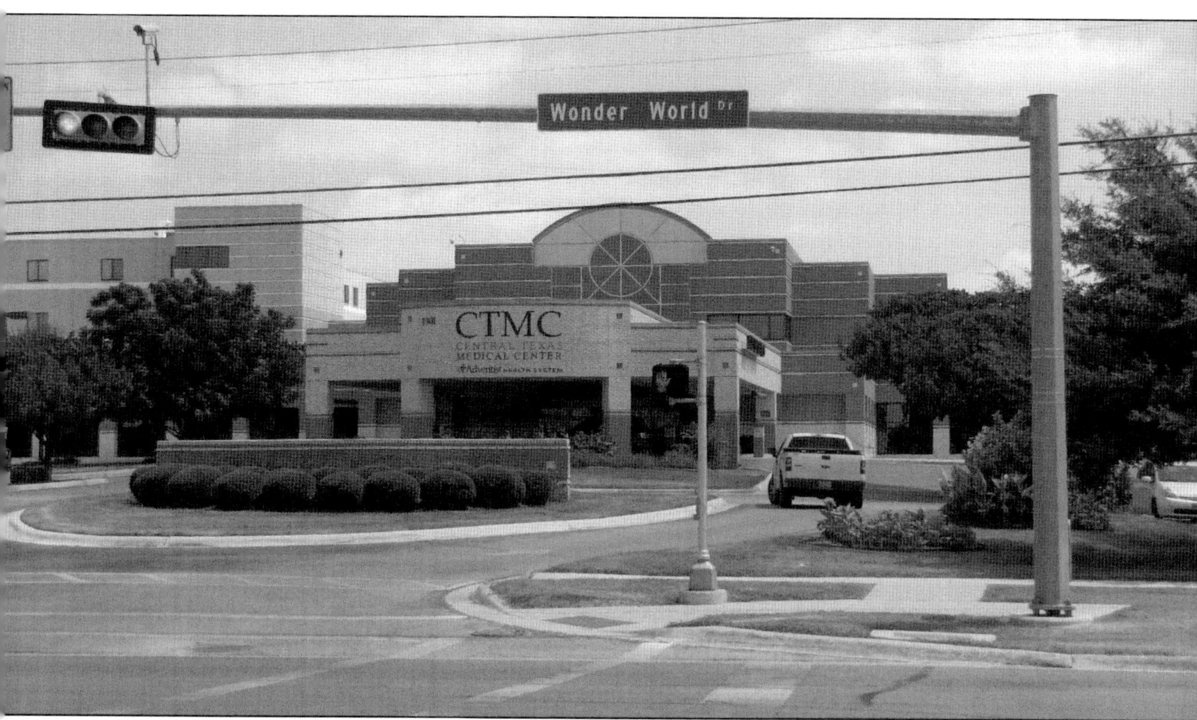

THE CENTRAL TEXAS MEDICAL CENTER. The Central Texas Medical Center (CTMC) in San Marcos is a modern full-service hospital and medical facility. The center traces its roots to 1923, when the Hays County Soldiers, Sailors and Marines Memorial Hospital was established on Belvin Street in the former Fisher Hall of the Coronal Institute (see chapter six). CTMC today is a 178-bed hospital with a staff of over 700 employees working with more than 200 active and consulting doctors.

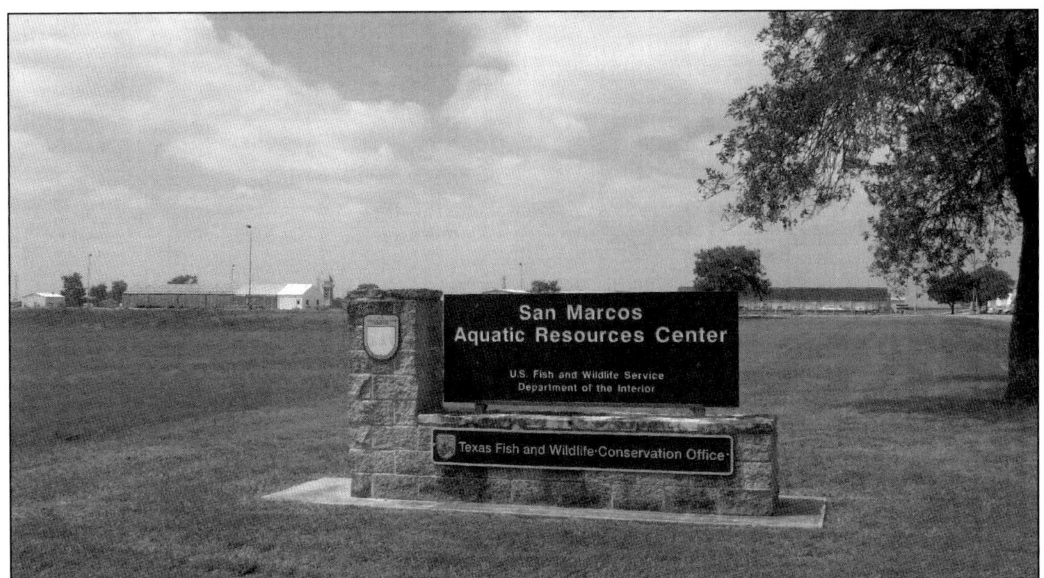

Modern Fish Hatchery Site. The original San Marcos fish hatchery, adjacent to the campus of the normal school, was donated to what is now Texas State University in the 1960s in exchange for 116 acres of land south of San Marcos. The new San Marcos National Fish Hatchery and Cultural Development Center was dedicated in 1976. The name was subsequently changed to San Marcos National Fish Hatchery and Technology Center in 1983. The name was changed in 2012 to the San Marcos Aquatic Resources Center.

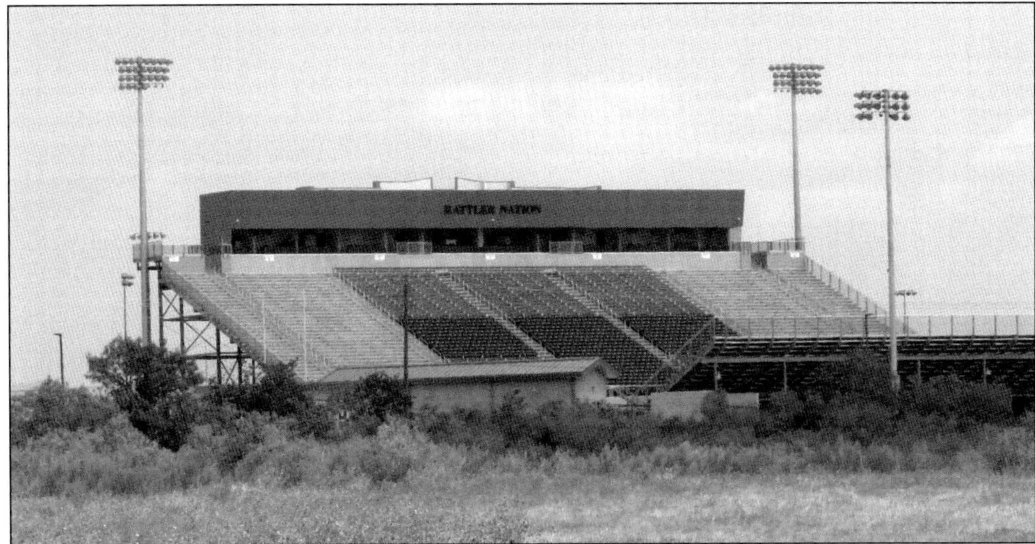

Rattler Stadium at San Marcos High School. The San Marcos Consolidated Independent School District serves San Marcos with six elementary schools, two middle schools, and one high school. San Marcos High School is the home of the Rattlers athletics teams. The new Rattlers Stadium, opened in the fall of 2014, provided the Rattlers with their own stadium for the first time; previously, all Rattlers home games had been played at Bobcat Stadium on the Texas State University campus.

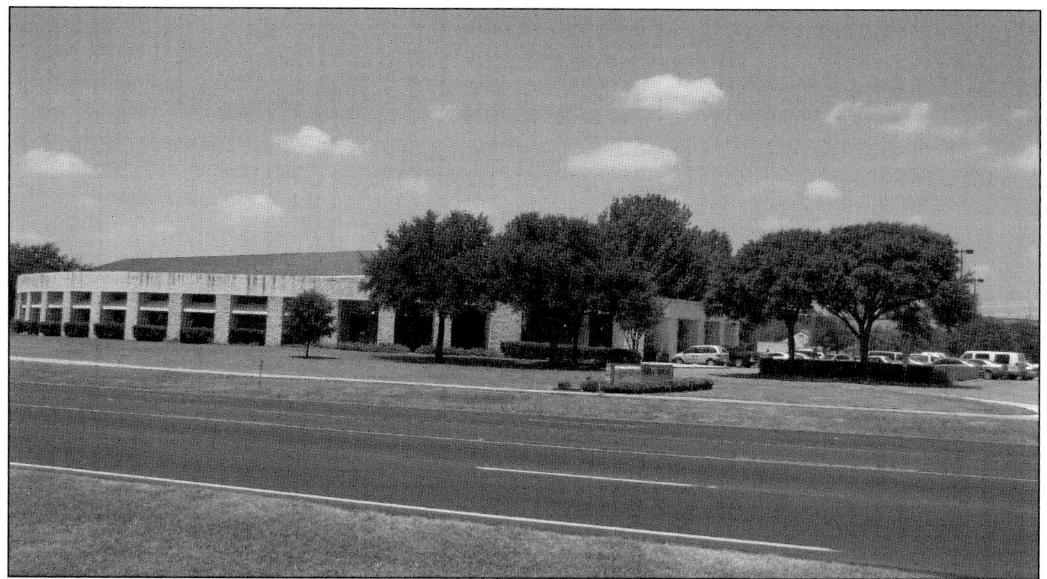

Modern San Marcos Public Library Facility. The San Marcos Public Library offers numerous programs for the public as well as access to its large collections of books, microfilms, and other historical documents. It is located on East Hopkins Street.

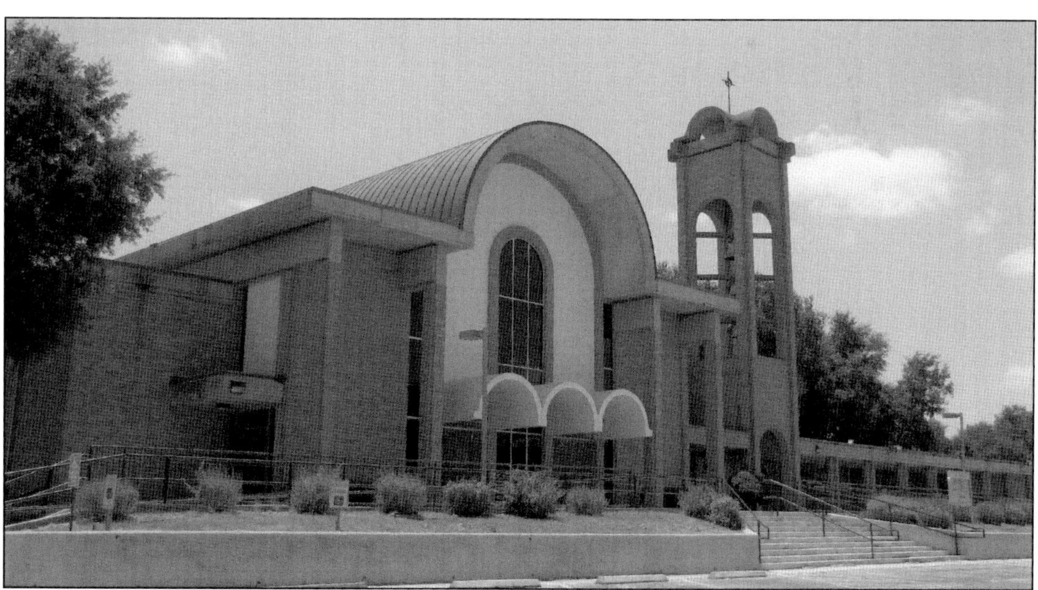

Modern St. John's Catholic Church on East Hopkins Street. The modern St. John's Catholic Church on East Hopkins Street was opened on Easter Sunday 1970. The facility is adjacent to city hall and across the street from the San Marcos Public Library.

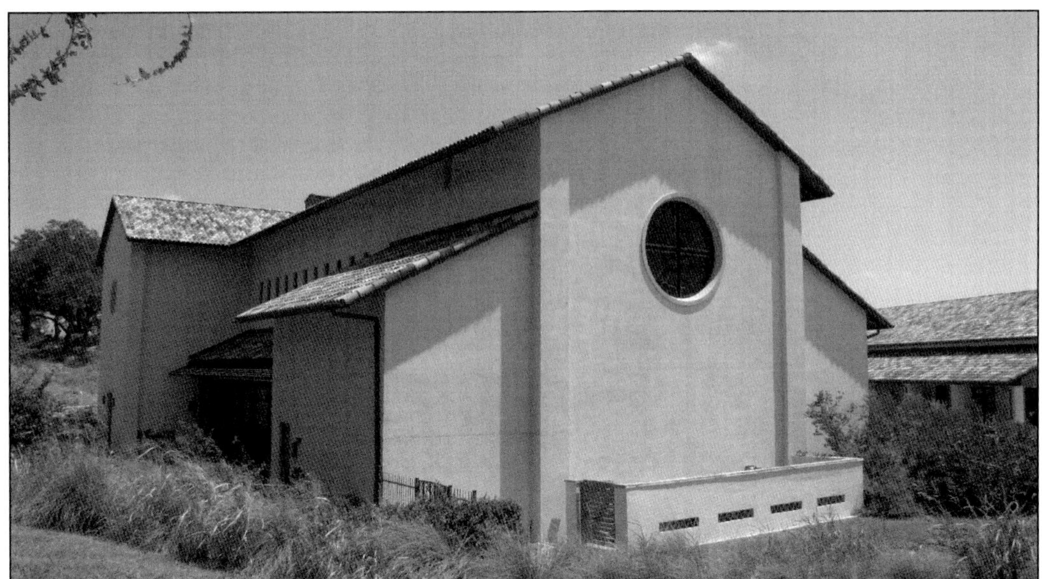

PRESENT-DAY ST. MARK'S EPISCOPAL CHURCH. The modern St. Mark's Church traces its roots to 1999, when the parish voted to start looking for a new location. The parish was outgrowing the building it shared with the Christ Chapel student ministry adjacent to the Texas State University campus. The parish purchased a 20-acre tract from the San Marcos Baptist Academy, and on February 14, 2010, the present-day church was dedicated at 3039 Ranch Road 12.

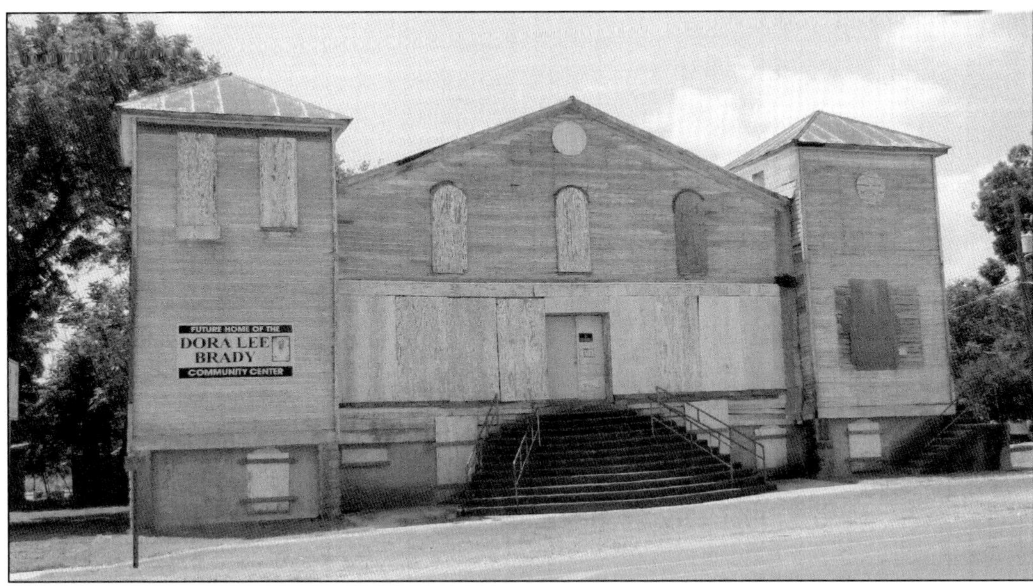

CURRENT STATUS OF OLD FIRST BAPTIST CHURCH. The Old First Baptist Church NBC, located in the Dunbar District on Martin Luther King Drive, was a vital component of the early 20th century African American community of San Marcos. Today, efforts are underway to save the historic building and convert it into a community center for the neighborhood.

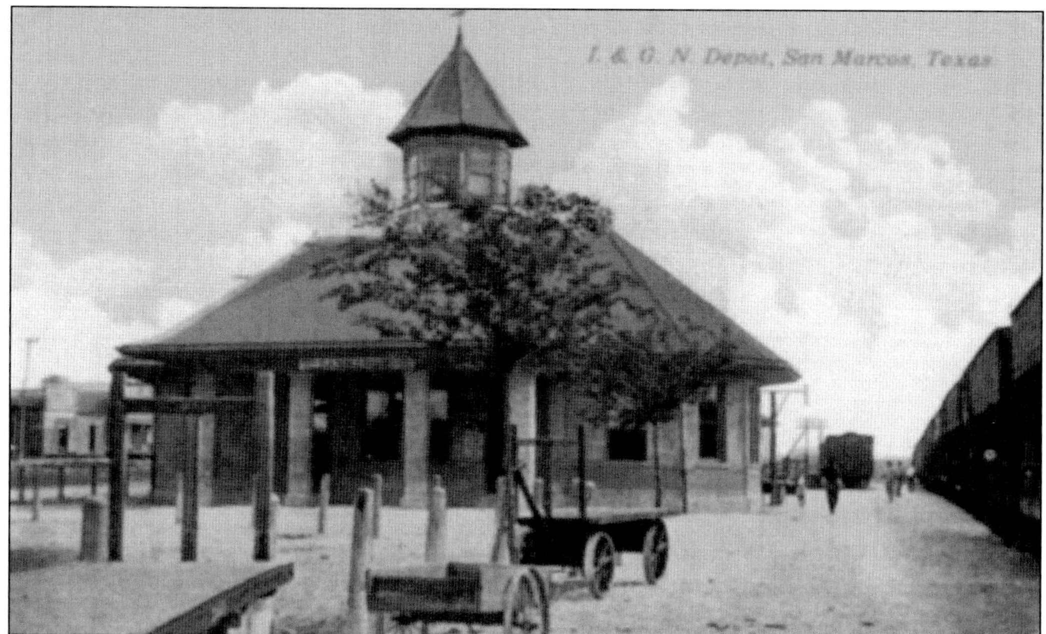

Early View of San Marcos Train Station. The International–Great Northern Railroad arrived in San Marcos in 1881. The depot shown here is probably the second one at the site, the first one having been built only of wood. The Missouri Pacific bought the International–Great Northern Railroad in 1924. (Texas Transportation Museum.)

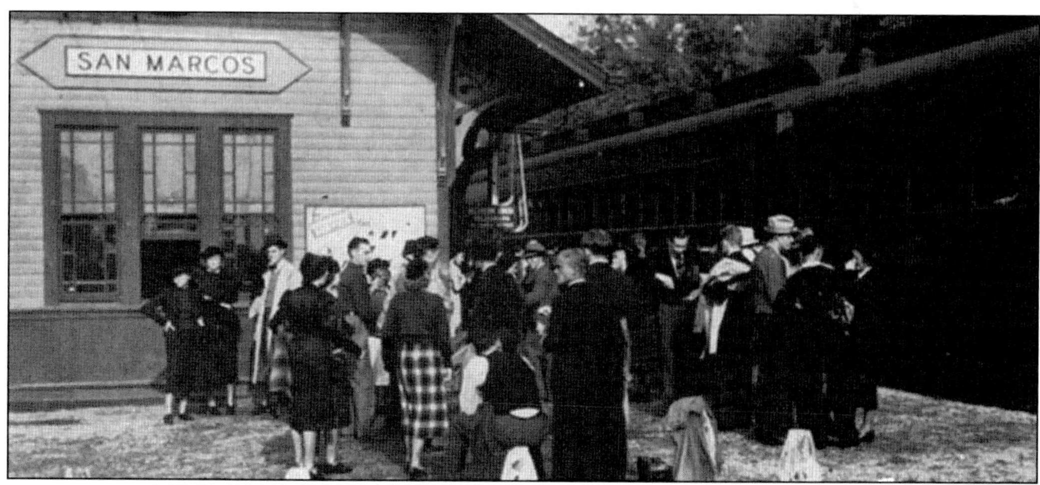

Missouri Pacific Train Station. In this undated view from the 1940s or 1950s, a group of people are gathered around a passenger train at the main San Marcos station. As late as 1967, two passenger trains a day traveled in each direction. The depot remained in use until the Missouri Pacific completely abandoned passenger service in 1970. (TxSt.)

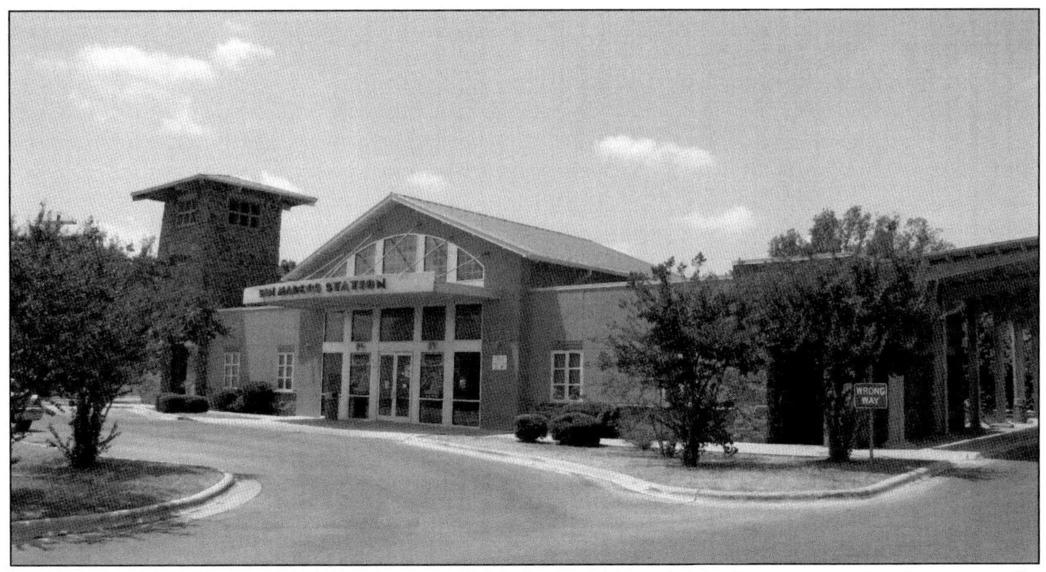

Modern View of San Marcos Train Station. Today, Amtrak services the dramatically remodeled San Marcos Train Station twice a day, one train coming from Fort Worth on its way to San Antonio and another going in the opposite direction. The train station now also serves as the bus station for San Marcos.

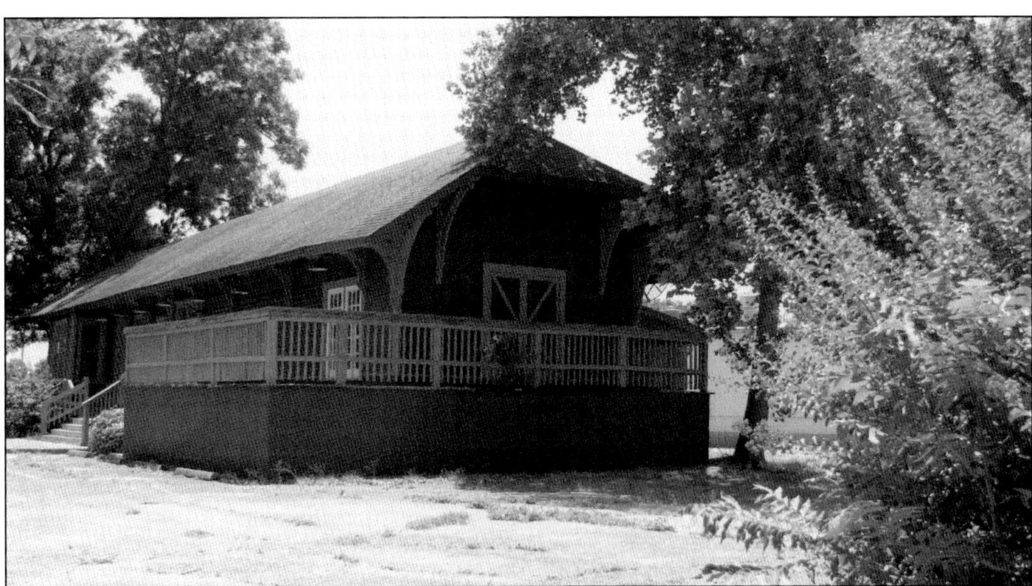

Katy Station. The Missouri, Kansas, and Texas Railroad was nicknamed the "Katy." It built its own line from San Marcos to San Antonio in 1900. When the Katy abandoned passenger business in 1964, the station depot became surplus and was abandoned. The station was eventually moved a few blocks and restored by a local entrepreneur. At present, after having been used as a restaurant during the 2000s, the building is currently unused.

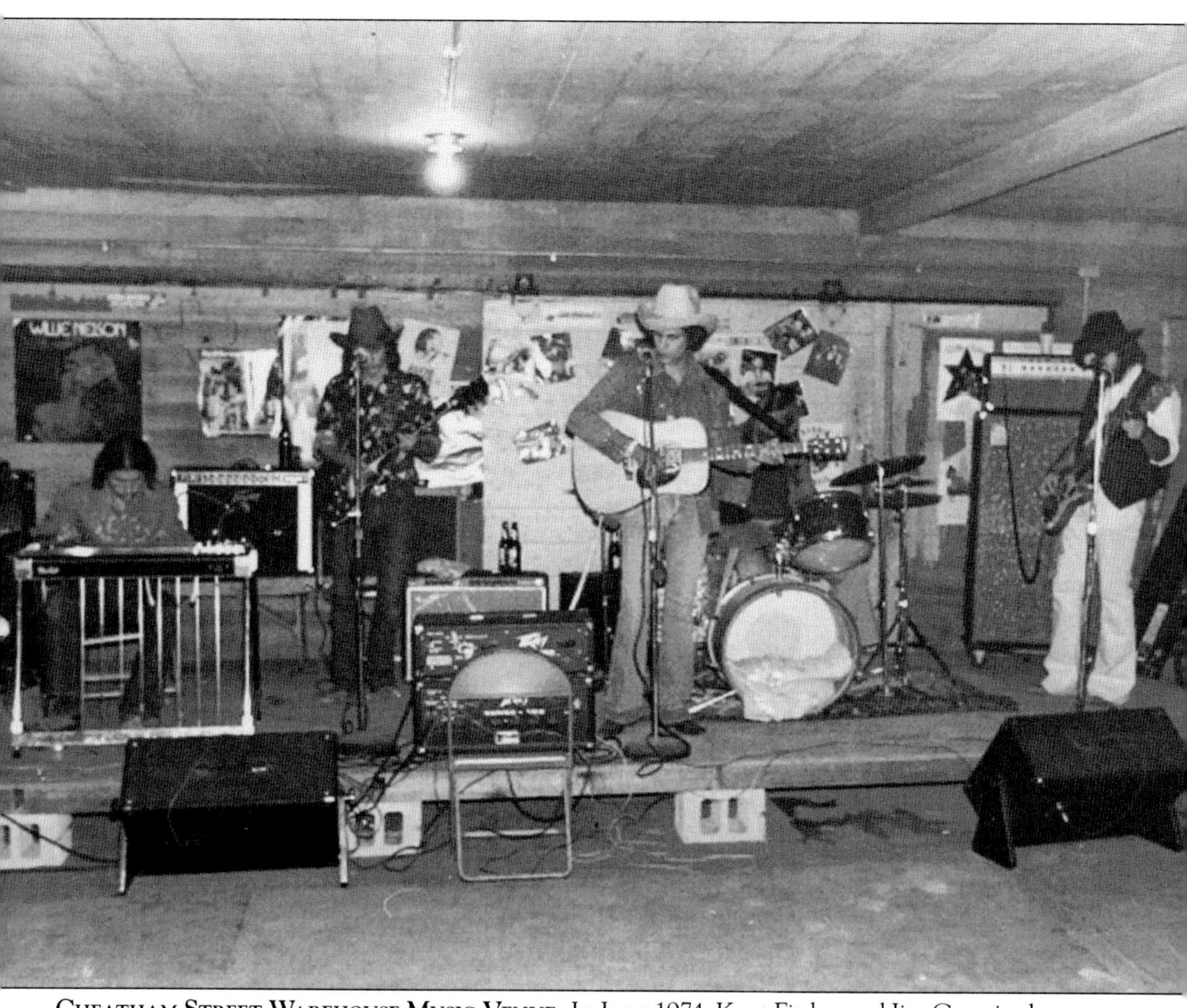

Cheatham Street Warehouse Music Venue. In June 1974, Kent Finlay and Jim Cunningham took out a lease on an old warehouse on Cheatham Street along the railroad tracks in San Marcos. They converted it into one of San Marcos's most vibrant music venues, a honkytonk that has hosted music legends such as George Strait (shown here with his Ace in the Hole band in 1975) and Stevie Ray Vaughn. (TxSt, Cheatham Street Warehouse.)

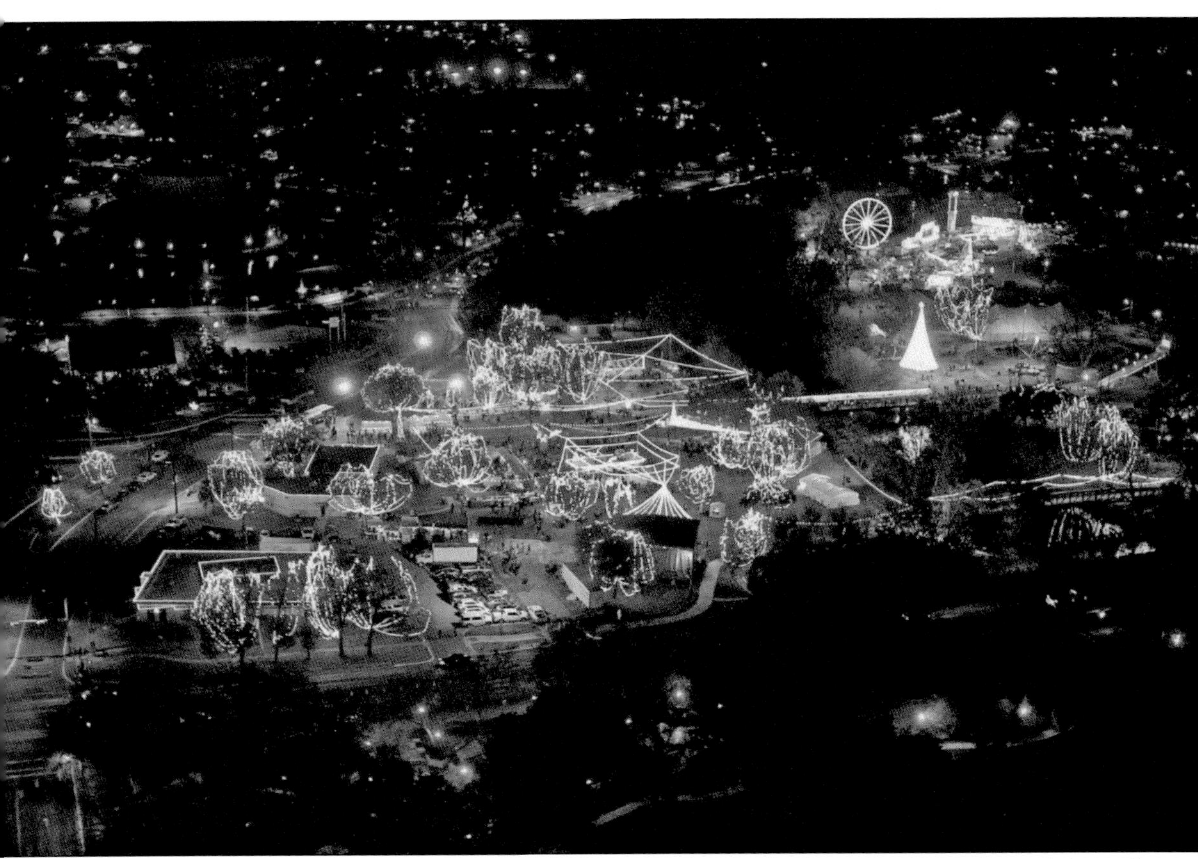

Sights and Sounds of Christmas. The Sights and Sounds of Christmas is an annual festival held over four days along the San Marcos River adjacent to the Texas State University campus, just east of downtown. It features a carnival, skating rink, a Bethlehem display, food court, live performances, arts and crafts, and of course, photographs with Santa and Mrs. Claus. (TxSt.)

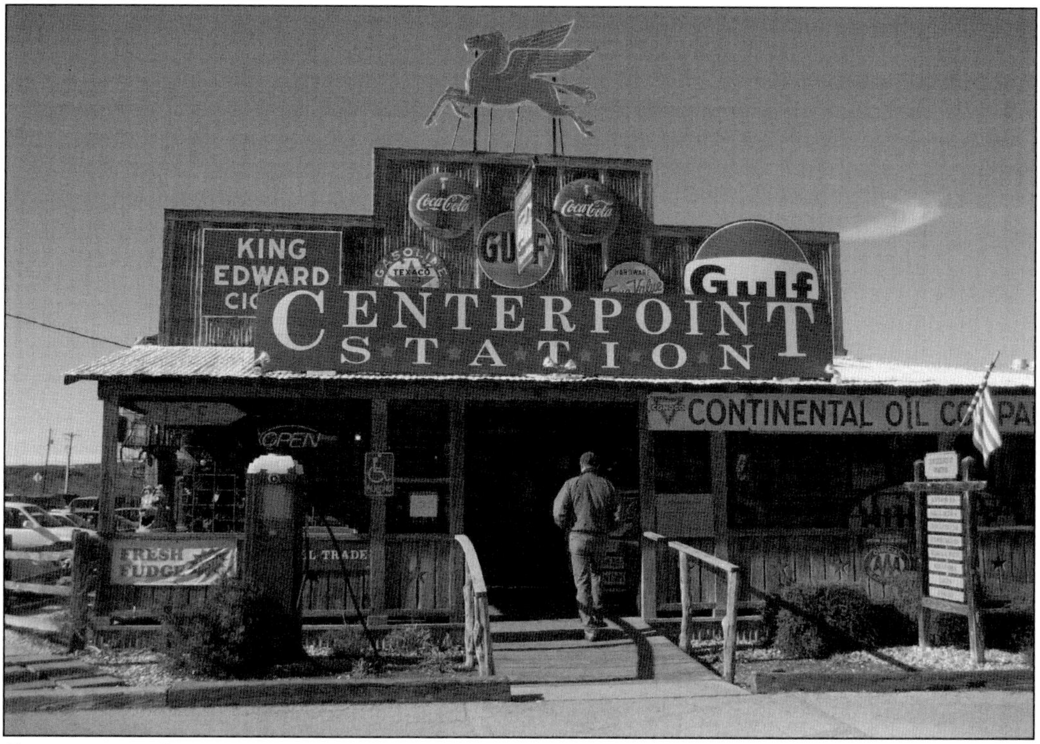

Centerpoint Station Near the Outlet Malls. Centerpoint Station, across Interstate 35 from the San Marcos outlet malls, was described by local author Rodney Van Oudekerke as a "rustic combination of restaurant, gift shop, and antique store." Many shoppers from the outlet malls also find their way to this unique slice of San Marcos. (Travis Witt.)

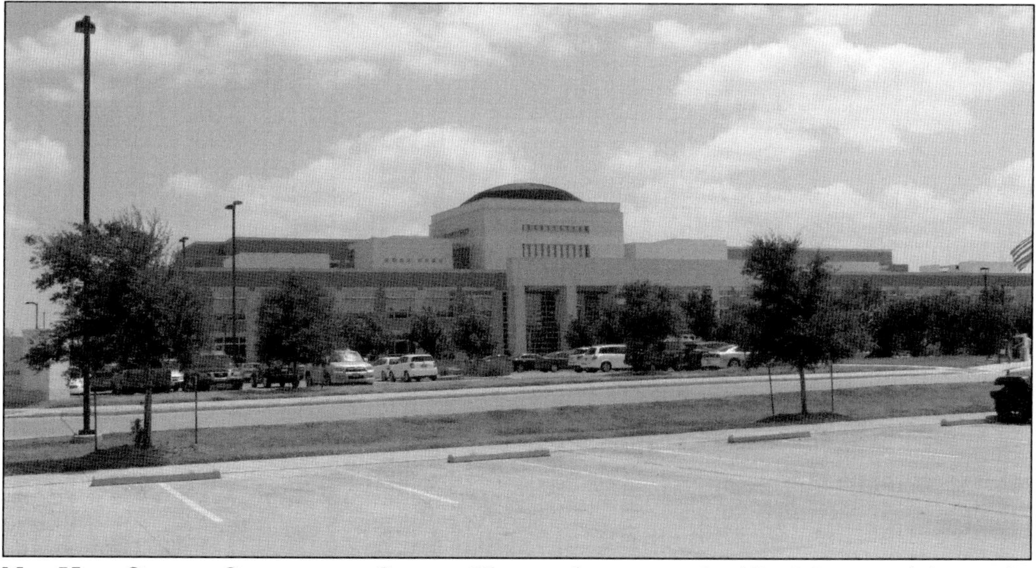

New Hays County Government Center. The population growth of San Marcos and the nearby communities of Kyle and Buda led to a need for more space than the historic downtown courthouse offered. The new government center is located at 712 South Stagecoach Trail, north of Wonder World Drive. The San Marcos Municipal Court of Record is located in the new center.

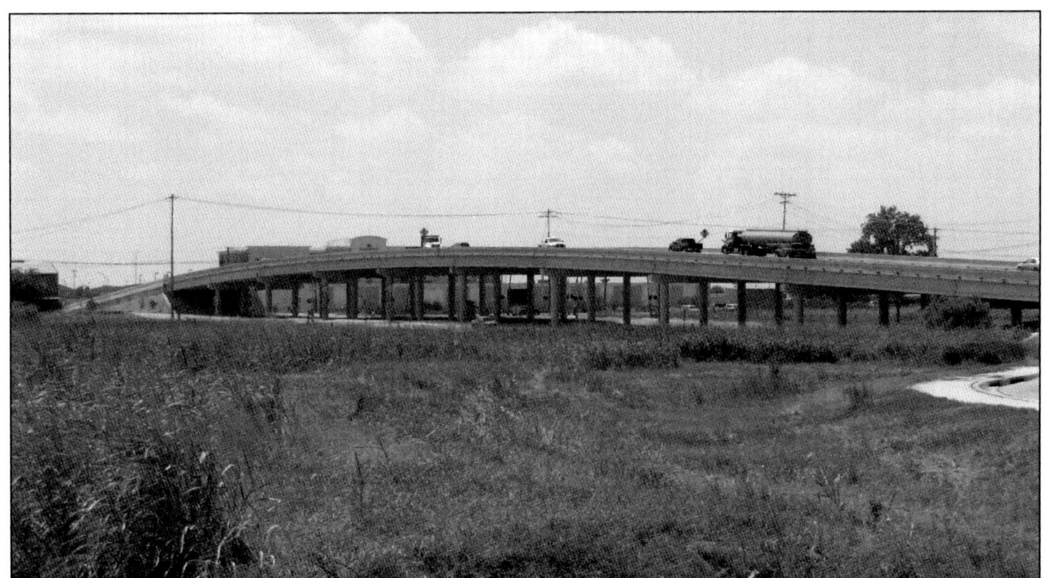

San Marcos's First Railroad Overpass. San Marcos has 26 rail crossings, and until 2006, none of them had an overpass for automobile traffic. Most of the population of San Marcos resides west of the Union Pacific tracks that run through town, but the hospital and Interstate 35 are east of the tracks, making for inconvenience and potentially deadly delays in accessing the hospital. In December 2006, the Wonder World Drive overpass shown here provided the first rail-crossing-free access to the east side of San Marcos.

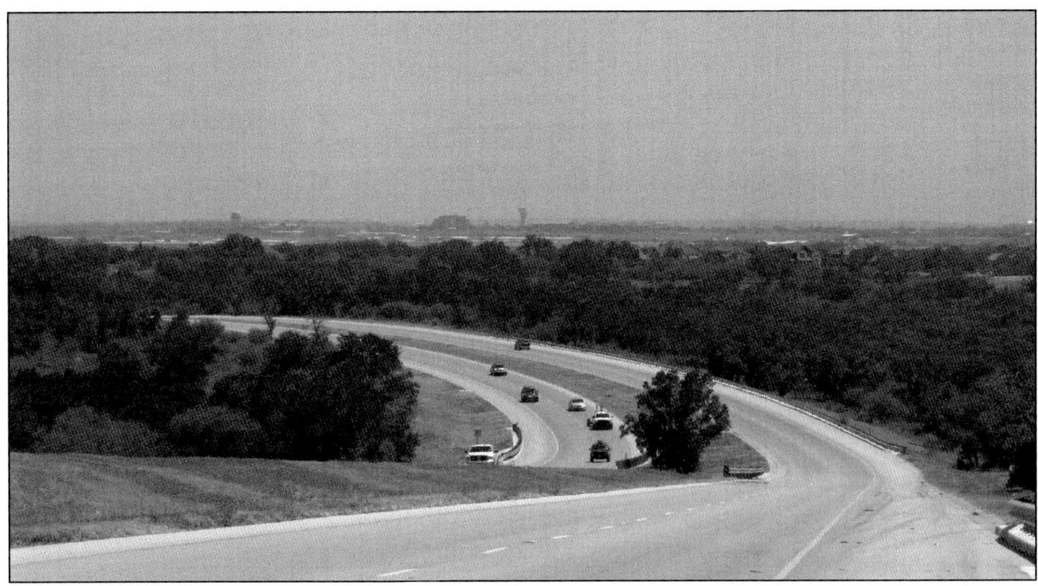

Ranch Road 12 Bypass. In July 2010, the new $26-million Wonder World Drive expansion west of Hunter Road opened. The new four-lane road eases congestion by connecting the Hill Country with Interstate 35 without having to pass through downtown San Marcos. It also provides better access for emergency vehicles to the Wonder World Drive overpass and the Central Texas Medical Center down the road.

Bibliography

Bussemey, Michelle. *Analysis of Landscape Change of the Rio Vista Dam in San Marcos, Texas.* San Marcos, TX: Department of Geography, Texas State University, 2007.

Kimmel, Jim. *The San Marcos: A River's Story.* College Station, TX: Texas A&M University Press, 2006.

San Marcos Daily Record and the *Free Press. Celebrate San Marcos 150!* San Marcos, TX: *San Marcos Daily Record,* 2001.

Stovall, Francis M. *Clear Springs and Limestone Ledges: A History of San Marcos and Hays County for the Texas Sesquicentennial.* Austin, TX: Hays County Historical Commission, 1986.

Van Oudekerke, Rodney. *Historic San Marcos: An Illustrated History.* San Antonio, TX: Historical Publishing Network, 2011.

Weber, Doni. *Aquarena Springs.* Charleston, SC: Arcadia Publishing, 2009.